Praise for *Ten Hours Until Dawn*

"With a steady hand, Michael Tougias draws us into the vortex of this historic winter storm of 1978, and a high seas rescue attempt gone wildly awry. The dynamics of this adventure alone would make it well worth the journey. But as a writer, Tougias's true gift is his ability to plumb the depths of human emotion, to take us ever deeper into the hearts of those who survived the ordeal—and even into the lives of those who do not. He re-creates not only the super-human efforts between the imperiled crewmen and their would-be rescuers, but the gut-wrenching experience of their loved ones waiting helplessly ashore. In this, he clearly succeeds. We come away feeling that we know these people, that we understand what it must have been like for them and our hearts go out to them."

—Spike Walker, bestselling author of
Coming Back Alive and *Working on the Edge*

"I was a college senior in Providence, Rhode Island, during the Blizzard of '78—a meteorological holocaust of snow and wind that I'll never forget. To learn twenty-six years later that there were men brave enough to attempt a rescue at sea during that storm still has me awestruck with wonder. Michael Tougias's *Ten Hours Until Dawn* tells their story—an incredible tale of heroism and sacrifice."

—Nathaniel Philbrick, author of the *New York Times* bestseller
and National Book Award winner *In the Heart of the Sea*

"What a story! Tougias's research and writing make the reader feel as if he is onboard the *Can Do* during the Blizzard of '78. *Ten Hours Until Dawn* is a gripping book about a fascinating event of courage and tragedy that few people, including those of us who were deeply involved in fighting that storm, know enough about."

—Michael Dukakis

"Arguably the best story of peril at sea since Sebastian Junger's *Perfect Storm*. A superb narrative!"   —*Booklist*

"Tougias delivers a well-researched, vividly written tale of brave men overwhelmed by the awesome forces of nature. An absorbing account . . ."   —*Publishers Weekly*

TEN
HOURS
UNTIL DAWN

ALSO WRITTEN OR COWRITTEN
BY MICHAEL J. TOUGIAS

TEN
HOURS
UNTIL DAWN

THE TRUE STORY OF HEROISM
AND TRAGEDY ABOARD THE *CAN DO*

Michael J. Tougias

St. Martin's Griffin
New York

To the men on board the *Can Do*: Frank E. Quirk II, Charles Bucko, Kenneth Fuller, Jr., Norman David Curley, and Donald Wilkinson. And the men and women of the U.S. Coast Guard who put their lives on the line helping others.

TEN HOURS UNTIL DAWN. Copyright © 2005 by Michael J. Tougias.
All rights reserved. Printed in the United States of America. For information, address St. Martin's Press, 175 Fifth Avenue, New York, N.Y. 10010.

www.stmartins.com

Map by James Sinclair
Title page and part opener photograph by Kathryn Parise
Book design by Kathryn Parise

ISBN-13:978-0-312-33436-9

30 29 28 27 26

I believe that man will not merely endure: he will prevail. He is immortal, not because he alone among creatures has an inexhaustible voice, but because he has a soul, a spirit capable of compassion and sacrifice and endurance.

—WILLIAM FAULKNER

Contents

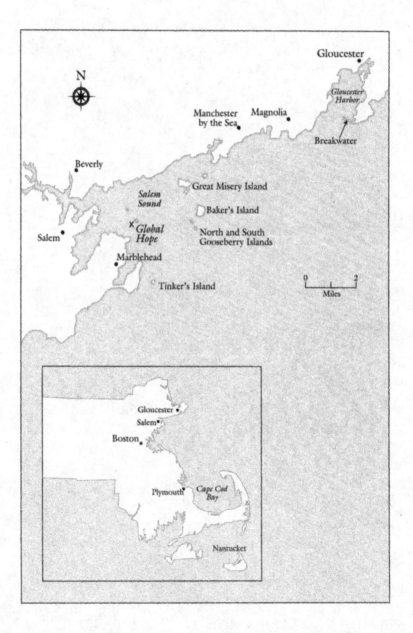

| PROLOGUE |

Samuel de Champlain discovered Gloucester Harbor in 1606 and
named it Le Beauport, the beautiful port. For weary seamen it is
just that. A mile wide and almost two miles long, the harbor is
sheltered by land on three sides and is one of the best on the
northeast coast. From Champlain's discovery up to 1905 a long
and dangerous shoal, Dogbar Shoal, extended almost halfway
across the harbor's opening to the ocean. Although the harbor
offered safety, some storms were so powerful their fury reached
inside the harbor by sending tremendous seas through the opening and over the shoal. In 1839 a great gale slammed into the
port, crashing at least twenty schooners along the western shore
and dismantling thirty more at anchor, resulting in an unknown
loss of life. Witnesses said that intermittently above the tumult
they heard the cries of perishing sailors pleading for help. Some
were drowned and dashed upon the harbor's surrounding ledges
while others were swept up and over Dogbar Shoal and sent tumbling out to sea. In 1898 another gale breached the harbor, resulting in the loss of at least twenty lives within the confines of

the harbor. Author Joseph Garland, in *Down to the Sea,* likened the mariners' deaths to "drowning in a bathtub." Because of these events, construction of a breakwater began at the turn of the century, when granite blocks and rocks were positioned atop the shoal. The resulting Dogbar Breakwater was completed in 1905 and it, along with the adjacent granite mass known as Eastern Point, made the harbor considerably safer, protecting it from the full fury of northeast winds.

In 1978 Gloucester Harbor was still the beautiful port, and because it was large and protected by the breakwater it was an active one. Tankers, freighters, fishing vessels, and pleasure boats were constantly entering or exiting its calm waters. Because of their great size, the tankers and freighters had to be guided through the harbor by local pilots who had intimate knowledge of its depths and hazards. The pilots were brought out to ships aboard a forty-nine-foot pilot boat called the *Can Do,* captained by Frank E. Quirk II. Quirk would pull the *Can Do* alongside a huge ship and the pilot then climbed a dangling rope ladder to board the vessel. Once the pilot was onboard he would take over the controls, maneuvering the vessel to port. Frank sometimes led the way in the *Can Do,* communicating with the pilot by radio to ensure a safe entry. Often the *Can Do* would be involved in the final docking, nudging the ship into the proper position.

Although the *Can Do*'s dock slip was in Gloucester's South Channel off Rogers Street near the Coast Guard station, Frank also serviced Salem Harbor, just fifteen miles to the south. It was here, on February 1, that Quirk helped guide in a huge 685-foot Greek-registered oil tanker, named the *Global Hope.* The job was a routine one for Quirk, and he thought the next time he'd hear from the tanker would be when it was ready to leave and a pilot was needed.

Instead, fate, the actions of the tanker's captain, and a blizzard of incredible fury conspired to set in motion events that spiraled out of control.

PART I

| 1 |

THE GATHERING
STORM

Frank Quirk, Jr., often spent the night aboard the *Can Do,* and on the morning of February 6, 1978, he awoke on his vessel wondering when it would snow. The prior evening's weather forecast called for snowfall to begin in the early-morning hours, yet there wasn't a flake in the sky, just low leaden clouds and a bitter cold breeze. He could have caught a little more sleep, because no piloting jobs were scheduled, but that wasn't his nature. The forty-nine-year-old former navy Seabee (construction battalion), with a wife and three children, was disciplined and full of energy. Although Frank's crew-cut style hair was mostly gray, he kept in tip-top shape and was quite strong, with a stocky build. He was well liked, with an easygoing manner and a ready smile.

Frank had been plying these waters for over twenty years and had a healthy respect for the sea, but he also knew the location of most every peril and felt comfortable navigating his boat in all kinds of weather, even on the darkest nights. He considered himself quite fortunate: his work allowed him to be his own boss and, instead of being trapped in an office, he could be on the ocean nearly every day. Frank loved the sea, both the freedom it affords as well as its challenges and ever-changing nature. He felt the same about the *Can Do*, which he had dubbed with the Seabees' motto.

Among Gloucester's fishing and boating community Frank was well known. He had received two Mariner's Medals for heroism at sea and countless times aided boaters in distress. Sometimes he just brought fuel to a skipper who had run out of gas, or dived overboard to retrieve a pair of eyeglasses dropped by a careless boater. One recreational boater recalls radioing for assistance when the engine on his runabout conked out on a beautiful Saturday afternoon. Frank was relaxing on the *Can Do*, several miles away. When no boaters close to the runabout came on the radio, Quirk went on the air, offering a tow from Gloucester to the boat's home port in Marblehead, several miles away. The tow and return trip consumed six or seven hours of Quirk's day off, but he refused to accept any payment. He usually just said, "It was nothing at all," or if the boat had fishermen aboard, "Just throw me a fish next time you see me." His kids said Frank brought home a lot of fish and lobsters.

On that Monday morning, Quirk was listening to the marine radio in the *Can Do*'s wheelhouse. Surrounded by small rectangular glass windows, he had a good view of Gloucester's inner harbor, where all manner of boats were docked, from battered and rusting fishing trawlers to sleek modern pleasure yachts. The National Weather Service was announcing an updated weather forecast, saying the snow was still coming and would be accompanied by high winds. Meteorologists explained that the snowfall could be significant and some even used the term *blizzard*, but few gave any inkling that New Englanders were about to be pounded by a blizzard of incredible proportions. New England's "storm of the century" was on the way, heading directly up the eastern seaboard toward Massachusetts.

The storm was a deceptive one at this early stage. It was located off the Maryland coast, and during the morning hours the mid-Atlantic states as well as New Jersey and New York were receiving significant snowfall accompanied by strong winds. This region, however, was absorbing just a glancing blow compared to what was in store for Massachusetts and Rhode Island, because with each passing hour the storm intensified. The storm was strengthening so rapidly, meteorologists later would refer to it as a "bombo-genesis" or simply a bomb. As it moved north, winds would go from "strong" to hurricane-force, clocked at a ferocious 92 miles per hour when they reached Massachusetts. Winds of this magnitude caught everyone off guard, and no meteorologist predicted the other surprise the storm had in store—that it would stall south of Nantucket Island, allowing it to concentrate its full strength just to the north, along coastal Massachusetts. Before the storm finally headed out to sea its raging winds coupled with three feet of snow would claim ninety-nine lives.

After a quick breakfast, Frank did a little engine maintenance down in the underbelly of the *Can Do,* followed by some paperwork. About the time his work was finished, the wind began kicking up a considerable chop in the harbor. A few flakes of dry snow began falling as Frank left the *Can Do* and walked to his car, pulling the collar of his jacket more snugly around his neck in the cold breeze. His coat was a gift from the Gloucester Coast Guard Station, an olive green officer's jacket, which Frank wore with pride. He hopped in his car and drove southwest on Rogers Street and Western Avenue, along the waterfront, passing the Coast Guard station and the Fisherman's Memorial, where the names of hundreds of men lost at sea are etched in granite blocks. At the western end of Gloucester Harbor he crossed the drawbridge that spans the narrow canal connecting the harbor to the Annisquam River. Then he turned right on Essex Avenue and pulled into the parking lot of the Cape Ann Marina, where a large American flag snapped overhead. Frank was greeted by his friend and marina vice president Louis Linquata, who was not surprised to see him. Frank always wanted to be near his boat during foul weather and make himself available just in case the Coast Guard needed his services.

Linquata and Frank were joined by maintenance supervisor Gard Estes, and the three men fanned out to the marina's many docks to secure boats and equipment. A few people lived on their boats year-round, and as Gard tightened lines he made sure no one intended to remain aboard a boat during the storm. The breeze died down briefly, and in the eerie calm Gard noticed he was being followed by three seagulls, walking on the dock just three feet behind him. When he stopped they stopped, but as soon as he resumed walking they stayed right at his heels. Usually the gulls gave Gard a wide berth, yet that day they followed him everywhere, as did two ducks in the water, and he wondered if the birds knew something about the coming snow that he didn't.

When the men's work was done at 1:00 p.m. they went inside for lunch and a beer. The marina's restaurant and lounge were only a few years old, and its furnishings still looked new. One of Gard's friends had recently added his own personal touch, bringing in a six-foot-long Styrofoam bluefin tuna and hung it on the back wall "to add a little more character." The tuna was so well crafted that most customers thought it was a mounted specimen caught off Georges Bank. On one side of the restaurant a polished wooden bar with a blue Formica top ran from end to end, and adjacent to that was a wall of large glass sliding doors that opened to a deck above the river. The other two walls were finished with rough pine, stained a light gray, giving the restaurant a rustic feel. In the back corner, a large metal cone-shaped fireplace radiated heat, emitting a pleasant scent of wood smoke. The restaurant and bar had become a cozy meeting place for

Frank's wide circle of friends from Gloucester, including cops, carpenters, and fishermen.

Sitting down to a bowl of steaming chowder at the bar, Frank looked out the sliders and noticed how the wind had picked back up and was angrily stirring the black waters of the Annisquam River. The snow was still relatively light, but it was now being driven horizontally each time a particularly strong gust swept up the river from the ocean. During lunch the three men discussed the latest weather reports and learned that the snow was piling up in Providence, Rhode Island, ninety miles away, and that peak gusts of wind at Boston's Logan Airport had hit 45 miles per hour. At this point it was still possible that the storm might swing out to sea and spare Gloucester, but their eyes told them otherwise; outside the sky was getting darker and it looked more like dusk than midday.

Over the course of the afternoon the men were joined by other friends: commercial fisherman Kenneth Fuller, thirty-four, of Rockport; Norman David Curley, thirty-five, a Gloucester electrician; and thirty-six-year-old Don Wilkinson of Rockport, who managed the Captain's Bounty Motor Lodge. The men were relaxed, eating chowder and sipping beer while shooting the breeze, glad for an early end to the workday because of the approaching storm. Being the only customers in the restaurant, they could be as noisy as they liked, and because they were all such good friends they started teasing one another. Some of the men were standing around the bar, others sitting and smoking cigarettes. Frank enjoyed himself as much as his friends, but he also had one ear glued to the radio, monitoring the news about the storm.

At midafternoon the group was joined by Bill Lee, an oil barge captain who filled commercial vessels with fuel. Lee knew all the men, as their paths frequently crossed either on the waterfront or in the harbor. He and Frank had a lot in common, as they were both navy Seabees and they saw each other almost every day while they were working. Sometimes Frank would be in the *Can Do* waiting to off-load a pilot and Lee would be right next to him in his barge waiting to fuel the ship. Lee considered Frank an excellent mariner and very competent.

Lee socialized with the other men at the marina and recalled how nobody called Curley by his real first name of Norman, because he went by his middle name, David. "He was a quiet guy," said Lee, "but he could be very funny. And he could take a joke, too: we always gave him the business about his bald head. He was at home on boats, because he had a twenty-four-foot cabin cruiser that he loved. He was always there to do a favor. Don Wilkinson was always talking about his two children and wife. His big thing was football, and I remember he went to the Superbowl every year. Don also raced powerboats. He was the bookworm of the group as well, and very bright. At one time he ran the marina and later became its business manager."

Lee recalls Kenny Fuller as a street-smart guy who was constantly coming up with new ideas to make money. He was a real free spirit who was always up for fun but willing to pitch in if work needed to get done. As a commercial fisherman who owned his own boat, he would go far offshore fishing for tuna in the summer and fall and often ended the season by navigating his vessel from Gloucester to Florida.

When Lee joined the group at the marina that afternoon he told Frank that while he was out fueling boats he had heard that the *Global Hope* was dragging anchor down in Salem. The northeast winds had pushed the ship a few hundred feet to the southwest, despite its having its anchor set. "I realized," says Lee, "that was one of the ships Frank had brought in and figured he'd want to know. By this time it was snowing pretty good and the winds were getting stronger each hour."

The first people to notice that the ship had shifted position were concerned residents along the Beverly waterfront. They

called local police who in turn notified Warren Andrews, the operator of the Salem Control (Radio) Station, which monitored all
shipping in busy Salem Channel. Andrews had lost his sight at a
young age but was a superb radio control operator, able to juggle
all the incoming radio traffic and coordinate the activity. He always wore dark glasses and kept his graying hair combed straight
back. His radio control room was off an L-shaped addition to his
house, and Andrews knew exactly where each piece of communication equipment was located and was able to glide from one
radio to another on a wheeled swivel chair. Warren grew up in
Salem, and he could remember all the features of Salem Harbor
from when he had his sight. Frank's son Frank III recalls several
visits to Warren with his dad: "Warren was amazing. He could
move from one radio to the next in that control room in an instant. I marveled at his skill without the ability to see. I once said
to my dad, 'Are you sure he's blind?'" Others compared Warren to
an old lighthouse keeper, because he was always there.

Andrews made tape recordings of most of his daily radio activity, as a way to check facts at a later date if someone had a question
Andrews couldn't answer off the top of his head. That afternoon
was no exception, and the tape chronicles how Warren notified the
nearest Coast Guard station (in Gloucester) when the first calls
came in regarding the *Global Hope*.

Coast Guard Station Gloucester immediately made contact
with the captain of the *Global Hope*, asking if the captain had noticed a position change in his vessel since he last anchored. The
captain had a strong accent and sometimes he struggled for the
right word in English.

Station Gloucester repeated the question: *"We need to verify if
you have dragged anchor. Over."*

The *Global Hope* responded: *"No, nothing."*

*"Roger that. We received a report that you did drag anchor. Are
you in distress now? Is there any reason you would be in distress?"*

"No, up to now, up to now, nothing, ship stay in this position. We are in same position, same position as anchored."

"Keep us informed, skipper, if you drag anchor any more."

"OK, thank you."

From this exchange it seems the Coast Guard doubted the captain's ability to judge whether the *Global Hope* had dragged anchor or not. Their qualms were well founded.

✻

After Bill Lee left the group to finish a final fueling job, Frank, Curley, Wilkinson, and Fuller paid their bill and headed down to the *Can Do* docked in the South Channel. Once on the boat Frank called Warren Andrews for the latest news on the *Global Hope*, then radioed Station Gloucester, informing them that he was dockside and standing by on channels 16 and 12. The Coast Guard men and woman at Station Gloucester all knew Frank and were aware that he could be counted on should they need his services. Several times he had assisted on rescues and also conducted dives for the Coast Guard, often helping draggers free their nets from submerged debris.

The group of men sat around a table in the *Can Do*'s wheelhouse, directly behind the captain's chair and wheel. Visitors to the *Can Do*'s wheelhouse, surrounded with thick aluminum, compared it to a tank with windows. Everything about the boat was solid, prompting one mariner to call it a "fortress," while another described it as a "surface submarine." The *Can Do* was bobbing next to the dock, but the hissing of the wind was muffled by the thick superstructure and the men could carry on conversations as normal. They monitored the radio and realized the storm was going to be a bad one, with wind gusts approaching hurricane-force. On board the *Can Do*, the men were quite comfortable. The forty-nine-foot boat originally had been the pleasure yacht of a wealthy family from Rhode Island. Frank had bought the boat because it was built to take a beating with a three-eighths-inch Cor-Ten steel hull and a quarter-inch aluminum pilothouse. Frank modified the boat for his piloting, such as adding a rubber bumper at the tip of the bow and installing fat racing tires on the sides for protection when the *Can Do* was brought alongside tankers and freighters. In addition, he had installed an array of electronics for communication and guidance: two FM radios, two CB radios, a ship-to-shore AM radio, loran (long-range electronic navigation device) for land coordinates, top-quality radar, and huge searchlights.

The *Can Do* also had all the luxuries of home. A spiral staircase with a stainless-steel railing and mahogany steps led from the pilothouse forward to the "mates' quarters," which had two bunks, mahogany drawers beneath each bunk, a retractable television, a sink, and a toilet. From these quarters there was access to a storage compartment in the bow where anchorage material was stowed. In the aft section were the captain's quarters and the galley. Four people could sleep in the captain's quarters, which featured a walk-in closet, carpeted floor, mahogany woodwork throughout, large eighteen-by-eight-inch portholes that opened, and a toilet, sink, and shower. A full-size refrigerator, sink, counters, gas range, and stove made up the galley. Amidships, between the captain's and mates' quarters, was the engine room with the power pack radar, compressor for the air horn, battery system, oil burner for the forced hot-water heating system and domestic water, a one-cylinder diesel generator, and the main engine, a Cummings 220-horsepower that turned a large single propeller. A hatch located just steps from where the captain stood in the pilothouse opened to a ladder leading to the engine room.

When Frank piloted the boat, he literally had everything at his fingertips: steering wheel, stainless-steel compass, chrome navigational controls, access to all the radios, drawers for the charts and logbooks, controls for the searchlights, and a long wooden handle suspended from a chain for the whistle. Just aft the captain's controls was the large mahogany table with cushioned benches where the men now sat, shooting the breeze and, like many others in Massachusetts, wondering if this blizzard would be as bad as the one that had struck just three weeks earlier. That storm set a record for snowfall but caused little damage, and seaside communities weathered that blizzard in stride.

About four-thirty Bill Lee finished his last fueling job, anchored his barge, and then checked on his pleasure boat in a slip within a stone's throw of the *Can Do* before rejoining his friends. The men were relaxing, listening to the marine radio for more information about the *Global Hope*. There were no further transmissions between the Coast Guard and the ship, however, and they assumed the tanker was holding position and in good shape. They still had no idea just how quickly the storm was turning into a monster. "We knew it was shitty out there," said Lee, "but nobody had any idea how bad it was beyond the breakwater. Frank was talking about maybe going down to Salem so he could have his boat on hand in the morning, knowing a pilot or shipping agent would want to be brought to the *Global Hope*."

About 5:00 p.m. Lee figured his wife might wonder where he was and headed home. Just after he left, the men still onboard heard a frantic, crackling distress cry on the radio.

"*Coast Guard, Coast Guard, this is* Global Hope!"

"*This is Coast Guard Station Gloucester.*"

"*We are in dangerous place! The water is coming inside into engine.*"

"*Did you say you are taking on water?*"

"*Water in engine room, engine room! Hull is broken!*"

"*Did you say the hull is broken and you are taking on water in the engine room?*"

"*Yes, that's correct.*"

"*We will dispatch a boat with a pump at this time; stand by.*"

Station Gloucester immediately contacted Boston Search

and Rescue, which dispatched the ninety-five-foot cutter *Cape George* and instructed a much larger cutter, the 210-foot *Decisive*, to leave its anchorage outside Provincetown, Cape Cod, and speed to Salem. Boston, however, is about twenty-five nautical miles from Salem, and Provincetown is fifty. With sixty-knot winds blowing they might not get to the crippled tanker in time.

Station Gloucester next radioed Warren Andrews at Salem Control, hoping against the odds that there would be a boat in Salem that could aid the *Global Hope*. Warren said there were no boats available at this time of year.

This was what Station Gloucester feared. With Salem fifteen nautical miles from Gloucester and the storm building by the minute, Station Gloucester was faced with a terrible choice. The only boats at their disposal were two relatively small patrol boats, one a forty-one-footer and the other a forty-four-footer. On the one hand, to send them into the storm, which by then had whipped the ocean's surface into ten-foot seas, was dangerous. On the other hand, there were thirty-two men aboard the *Global Hope* who were in jeopardy.

Frank had been monitoring the nervous exchanges on the radio and broke in:

"There's nothing we can do at this end, either, at this time, but we will be standing by still dockside at Gloucester. I want you to be aware that as far as I know the ship is about six hundred and eighty feet long and she is light, very light, [most of the cargo off-loaded] *and the last I got she is about eleven foot forward and twenty foot aft* [below waterline], *and whether they ballast* [add seawater to designated ballast tanks] *it down after that or not I don't know. And it is going to be one great big problem if they do have a problem due to conditions here."*

Station Gloucester responded: *"Roger that; I think I'm going to get a boat under way, and give him* [the *Global Hope* captain] *a call to see how bad he is taking on water."*

Frank urged caution: *"I would think twice, you know, your discretion, but I would think twice about sending a boat up there tonight. You may get up there, but I don't think you're going to get back to Gloucester the way this is making up here now. If we can be of any help—I don't have any pumps onboard, but if we can be of any help we'll be standing by here."*

Frank then made a call to Charlie Bucko, twenty-nine, who had recently left the Coast Guard to take a job repairing boats at the Gloucester Marine Railway. Bucko and Frank were the best of friends, and because of Bucko's Coast Guard training and rescue missions he had plenty of experience in stormy seas. When Frank called him, Bucko was living with his fiancée, Sharon Watts, on Eastern Point Road in Gloucester not far from the *Can Do*. "We had just finished dinner," says Sharon, "when Frank called. He said there was a tanker in trouble in Salem and he wanted Charlie onboard in case they needed to go down and help. Charlie said he'd be right over. By this time it was snowing really hard and I could hear the winds howling outside. He knew I was concerned, and he said 'Don't worry; it was just as bad during the *Chester Poling* [another ship that needed rescuing] and I made it back, so I'll make it back from this.' Then he gave me a big hug and said, 'I love you.'"

Bill Lee was also a friend of Charlie's and recalled that when Charlie was a coxswain in the Coast Guard the younger men looked up to him because he was confident, outspoken, and had been decorated for bravery twice while fighting in the Vietnam War. But he also had a soft side, like the time he found an injured seagull. The seagull had a broken wing and Charlie felt sorry for it. Somehow he was able to get his hands around the injured gull and brought it back to Station Gloucester. Then he built a little pen for it out back, and every day Charlie would tend to the gull, feeding it fish and making sure it was OK.

When Bucko reached the *Can Do,* the situation with the

Global Hope had become more confused because communication with the tanker had suddenly ceased, presumably from water shorting out its power. Station Gloucester had no way of knowing if the ship was sinking, breaking apart, or not in any immediate danger. It was ink black outside, with blinding snow, and no one down in Salem could see the *Global Hope*.

Station Gloucester made the difficult decision to send both patrol boats down to Salem, probably thinking with two boats together one could help the other if they encountered trouble on the way.

2

THE COAST GUARD
RESPONDS

The two patrol boats that Station Gloucester dispatched to the *Global Hope* were usually sufficient for rescue operations along Boston's north shore. The forty-one-footer, *41353*, was a utility boat whose primary duties were boarding, firefighting, law enforcement, and search and rescue in seas up to seven or eight feet. Its sleeker, lighter design made it considerably faster than the forty-four but not nearly as tough. The forty-four, *44317*, was a motor lifeboat also used for patrols and search and rescue, but it sacrificed speed for seaworthiness in heavy weather. First built in the 1960s, the vessel had eight watertight compartments, twin-diesel engines, a heavy steel hull, and a cement-weighted keel. If the twenty-ton forty-four rolled over, she could right herself. The righting process, however, could take up to thirty seconds—which would have seemed like an eternity to anyone onboard. Although her wheelhouse was sturdy steel, with thick glass wind-shields, its upper sides and rear were covered only by canvas curtains with plastic windows. In bad seas, water could enter the wheel-house, but because it was not totally enclosed the water could drain off just as quickly as it entered. Prior to the Blizzard of '78 only one of these twenty-ton crafts had ever been wrecked, and there were no fatalities among the "forty-four" crews.

Although forty-fours are almost unsinkable, today the Coast Guard is gradually replacing them with a real tank of a boat, the forty-seven-foot motor lifeboat. This craft has the advantage of being able to recover from a roll in eight seconds. It is made almost entirely of aluminum and is completely watertight, with an enclosed cockpit that looks more like that of a fighter jet than a boat. Electronics are everywhere, and the usual large, round steering wheel has been replaced by a lever or "joystick," giving the impression that the coxswain is sitting down to play a massive video game. Seamen have reported little trouble cutting through twenty-foot seas in these babies. An additional advantage is that the new forty-seven-footer is faster than the forty-four.

The cutter classification is reserved for Coast Guard vessels sixty-five feet in length or greater with adequate accommodations for the crew to live onboard. While Station Gloucester did not and does not have a cutter of its own, cutters often dock in Gloucester for two-week periods between patrols. Unfortunately, during the Blizzard of '78 the region's ninety-five-footer cutters, the *Cape George* and *Cape Cross,* were berthed in Boston and the larger *Decisive* was even farther away, at Provincetown, Cape Cod, Massachusetts.

Every Coast Guard man or woman seems to have his or her own special preference for the type of vessel to be assigned to. However, one common theme expressed has more to do with the length of time at sea rather than the vessel itself. "I couldn't stand those cutters," says a thirty-year veteran of the Coast Guard. "If you were out in sloppy weather and you were seasick, it was pure hell, because the cutters stayed out so long. I'd be puking for five days straight not caring if they threw me overboard. At least with the forty-fours you know there's an end in sight. Once the mission was accomplished we went back to port since there are no sleeping accommodations onboard. I don't even like to hear the term *ninety-five-footer*. I was on one for a short while, and I vowed never again."

Some rookies in the Coast Guard think that the larger the boat, the safer you are, but this is not necessarily the case, since the cutters stay out in nastier weather. An example of what can happen to a large cutter in harm's way was the *LV 73*, a 123-foot, 693-ton vessel that was stationed at Vineyard Sound, Massachusetts, in 1944. The ship sank off the Martha's Vineyard coast during the Hurricane of 1944 with the loss of all twelve hands onboard. One hundred and twenty-three feet isn't much compared to the brute force of hurricane-whipped seas.

While Coast Guard vessels are not indestructible, they are always shipshape and well maintained. The floundering *Global Hope*, however, was reported to be neither. The tanker had begun its final voyage in the Bahamas with a cargo of fuel oil heading north to Salem, where it would off-load the oil at the New England Power Company terminal. The ship arrived without incident, and Frank Quirk was called to deliver the pilot to the vessel, who then guided the tanker through Salem's narrow shipping channel. Once in port the *Global Hope* proceeded to unload its fuel. Most of the oil had been off-loaded when a worker noticed water had mixed with the fuel, possibly from a broken water line or heating coil used to keep the fuel at an optimal temperature for discharge. When the water was discovered the tanker was ordered to move away from the terminal and drop anchor outside the harbor. Some accounts also reported the ship had inadequate fire protection—yet another reason to move it away from the terminal. The Salem harbormaster referred to the tanker as "an old ship, built about twenty-eight years ago and not in very good shape."

Approximately two hundred thousand gallons of oil was still onboard, and the plan was to let the fuel solidify so that the water could then be pumped off. Once the water was removed the tanker could then return to the terminal and finish off-loading the fuel. The Blizzard, however, would scratch that plan.

❁

With a potential disaster in the making, Chief Warrant Officer Edmund "Mike" Paradis, the commanding officer of Station Gloucester, now felt compelled to take charge of the radio and direct the operation personally. At some stations the commanding officer is close to his men, socializing a bit and getting to know the crew personally. Paradis, however, kept a strict chain of command and was described by the men he led as "aloof" and "by the book." He was in his late forties, tall and fit, with hair that had gone prematurely white. Usually he had a glowing pipe in his mouth, occasionally sending up a puff of smoke from a stern and unsmiling mouth. In the mess hall he had his own section partitioned off from the rest of the men and his table was the only one with linen. You joined him by invitation only. Men who served under him describe him as all business, a real no-nonsense kind of guy whom no one wanted to cross. He treated the station like an underway ship and almost never dealt directly with the younger Coasties who did not report directly to him. Despite his distant, reserved nature, he was proud of his crew and they in turn respected his competence.

Paradis and Frank knew and respected each other, often discussing the latest Coast Guard news. Although their personalities were quite different, they had a common bond by virtue of being older than all the other servicemen, and they had both seen a lot more of the ocean's moods than the others. Station Gloucester was just a couple wharves away from the *Can Do*'s slip, and Frank swung by the station for coffee almost as frequently as off-duty

Coasties dropped in on Frank. The station, a nondescript three-story brick building, is right on the waterfront, with a helicopter pad and a pier for the patrol boats. Inside is a radio room, equipment room, a cafeteria that seats about thirty, and sleeping quarters. Men stationed there say they can wake up and not even look out the window to know when the seas are rough because the water in the toilet bowls sloshes around. On this day in 1978 the toilet bowl water was really hopping.

When word first reached Paradis that the *Global Hope* was taking on water his primary concern was for the welfare of the crew. However, it's probable he was also thinking about her cargo of oil, especially in light of the *Argo Merchant* disaster, which had occurred just a year earlier. The *Argo Merchant* was a 29,870-ton Liberian-registered oil tanker, approximately the same length as the *Global Hope*. It, too, ran hard aground and took on water in the engine room, although the *Argo Merchant* did not meet its demise by dragging anchor but instead through the poor navigation of its captain, who led the ship directly into a treacherous patch of shoals south of Nantucket Island, Massachusetts. The crew was rescued by the Coast Guard and every effort was made to free the tanker from the shoal, but the incessant pounding of seas caused the hull to break apart, sending more than seven and a half million gallons of oil spreading over the ocean.

Paradis knew the *Global Hope* had off-loaded some of its cargo, but the ship was only a mile or two from shore, and an oil spill here would have been a calamity, sending the black goo over pristine beaches and important fishing grounds, fouling not only the coast and the marine environment but the local economy as well. If his men could make it to the tanker and stabilize the situation by getting pumps onboard, perhaps the tanker could hold together until the larger cutters arrived.

Paradis had approved the dispatching of the forty-one- and forty-four-footers, and now as the boats set off he took over the radio, sitting down before a broad array of communications equipment. A window looked out upon the harbor. Although Paradis could see nothing in the black void, he heard the wind howling, and when a particularly strong gust pummeled the building he hoped the window would stay intact. In the interior of the room, next to the entry door, a large glass window separated the room from a main hallway, and curious Coasties stole glances at the chief, concerned about their station mates now out in the blizzard. Their concern was well-founded, because as the forty-one and forty-four reached the opening of Gloucester Harbor they were slammed by raging seas and a screeching wind coming out of the northeast. The skipper of the forty-one thought the boat might flip, and near the breakwater, by Round Rock Shoal, he radioed Paradis that they were heading back in. *"Taking quite a beating,"* the skipper shouted over the howling wind, *"seven-footers out here, breaking, too. We are taking them solid right over the bow."*

Now it would be up to the forty-four and her crew of four: seamen Robert Krom and Roger Mathurin, engineer Tom Desrosiers, and skipper/coxswain Bob McIlvride. All four men were young, from nineteen to twenty-three, and this was the first time these four had been teamed on a mission. As soon as the forty-four exited Gloucester Harbor they had problems with their radar, fathometer, and FM radio, probably due to icing and the size of the seas. At that time there was no loran on the forty-four, so right off the bat they were at a disadvantage and used the spotty radar along with dead reckoning and the compass to navigate. None of the four men, however, thought of aborting the mission, because they thought they could make it.

McIlvride was tall and thin, with blond hair and a "baby face" that made him look like he was sixteen rather than twenty-one. He was described by crew members as extremely bright yet low-key and unassuming—the perfect kind of coxswain you would want in a situation like the Blizzard. As the forty-four left the safety of Gloucester Harbor, even the soft-spoken McIlvride had tension in his voice as he shouted to be heard over the canvas curtains cracking in the wind. He had been on search and rescue missions before, but never in seas like this, and he gripped the wheel until his knuckles were white. He also got soaked with icy spray as a particularly strong gust blew away a section of the canvas curtain. The windshield was covered in ice and snow, and McIlvride had to rely on his crew to help him search for buoys in the blackness. All four of the men were standing in the pilothouse, hanging on as best they could, taking turns watching the faltering radar and peering through blinding snow for buoys. The binnacle light on the compass went out, and they had to shine flashlights on the needle to get a directional fix. Heading southwest toward Salem, they were in following seas, each wave catapulting the boat ahead.

Desrosiers, the boat's engineer, explained that the seas were so large—approximately fifteen to twenty feet—that when they were in the troughs of the waves they couldn't see a thing. Then, each time they crested a wave the men would anxiously search for the flashing lights of buoys in near whiteout conditions. One enormous channel buoy nearly killed the men just a few minutes into their mission. They never saw it until the buoy rode up a wave and was directly *above* the boat. Desrosiers shouted, "Turn! Turn!" Bob McIlvride turned first to port, then quickly to starboard, to clear the stern, and the buoy just missed smashing the forty-four before it crashed back into the sea. Had it hit the boat it might have caused it to capsize and if it hit a crewman it would have crushed the man like a bug. As the buoy receded to stern McIlvride said, "Well, I guess we found that one."

"I was glad Bob was piloting the boat," Desrosiers recalled. "Even though he was as young as the rest of us, he had a mind like a vise and knew exactly where those aids [buoys] were supposed to be from all his time studying charts." Seaman Bob Krom has similar praise for the coxswain: "I had a lot of confidence in McIlvride; the tone of his voice showed he was in control of himself. Sea conditions were so bad, though, I must admit I wondered if we were going to make it. It's pitch-black and we could only see the breaking waves at the last second; then a wall of white water would crash on the stern. I was thinking, how on earth does this boat stay afloat? If we rolled, the only thing we could do was take a quick bite of air and hold on. . . ."

McIlvride couldn't see a thing out the windshield, as it was iced and covered with snow: "The front windshield was in three panels. The middle panel, right in front of the wheel, was fixed in place, but the ones on either side could be opened. I had the crew open those two and keep a sharp lookout for the buoys. Because we were going with the seas and the wind was at our back, we didn't take much water through these openings—all the water was coming over the stern and the sides.

"I never thought about turning back, and my objective was to find the light at Baker's Island. The only safe way to enter Salem Sound is through the gap between Baker's and Misery Island—if you go north or south of those islands it's all shoals. So I figured if we could just find Baker's and keep it on our port side we'd at least get into Salem Sound. I was way too busy to be afraid. It was probably tougher for the other guys because they had time to think—and to pray. I kept thinking about the tanker and wondering what the heck we were supposed to do once we found it. It would have been impossible to take men off and they would be crazy to jump at night. But when we left nobody had any idea how bad it was and no way of knowing if the tanker was breaking apart and men were in the water."

McIlvride had a somewhat unusual boyhood. His father was a minister who was assigned to Thailand, and that's where Bob spent seven years of his boyhood. When he was in the states he spent summers on his uncle's thirty-foot Chris-Craft, and that's how Bob learned boat handling and deepened his attachment to water. After graduating from high school he attended Penn State and was a member of the sailing team. During his second year the team was participating in meets in Chesapeake Bay and McIlvride watched the Coast Guard boats cruising the bay. As he observed the men on the boats it dawned on him that that was what he wanted to do with his life. He considered that very moment the first time he really took control of his life, and he made the decision to leave school and join. McIlvride had always dreamed of being in the Coast Guard but never really acted on it until then. At home he had a Coast Guard poster on the door of his bedroom that said: *It's not just a job, it's an adventure.* The picture on the poster was of a patrol boat crashing through a huge wave. The boat on the poster was a forty-four.

Once McIlvride joined he made it his objective to become a coxswain of a forty-four. He found boot camp was a grueling ordeal, but once he realized he could survive it, he felt his self-confidence grow. Friends and relatives who saw him after boot camp ended told him he'd changed, and he had. He felt like an entirely new person, with a newfound confidence that made him feel he could do anything he put his mind to and gave him the perception of being almost invincible. Out of a boot camp group of about seventy young men, McIlvride graduated number two. With the high ranking came the opportunity to pick his "billet," his first duty station. Out of anywhere in the country, McIlvride chose Group Boston, because they had search and rescue operations on small boats, including the forty-four. Friends said he was crazy, asking why he didn't pick Hawaii, Florida, or California, but McIlvride knew he made the right choice.

On the one hand, McIlvride was a typical young Coasty, gung ho and ready to tackle any mission, but he also had an unconventional streak. He was friendly with his fellow servicemen at Gloucester, but he also spent a fair amount of time alone, rarely joining in the off duty drinking and partying. In fact, he used some of his free time to learn and practice Transcendental Meditation, often sitting in the upper stairwell landing of the three-story station to find solitude and meditate.

While at Station Gloucester he did whatever he could to reach his goal of becoming a coxswain on a forty-four. Whenever he had radio watch, which was usually very slow, he spent much of the time studying the charts in the communications room, particularly the chart that covered an area from Marblehead to the north side of Rockport. McIlvride studied that chart so diligently he had it memorized, which was a blessing the night of the Blizzard—there was no way charts could be read on the open bridge.

He reached his goal of the coxswain designation in January of 1978, just one month before the Blizzard struck.

※

Despite the pounding the four men were taking, they battled their way south and at 6:45 p.m. radioed that they were one-third of the way to Baker's Island, which is located at the mouth of Salem Sound. They had no idea if the *Global Hope* was still afloat or if the tanker's crewmen were dead or alive. But a few minutes later Warren Andrews radioed that he was getting reports from people who had been hearing a ship's whistle continually blowing short blasts, indicating distress. The men on the forty-four assumed that the whistle was from the tanker, and they wondered if they would find the ship in pieces, with men in the water.

Back in Gloucester Harbor, Frank was growing more concerned about the forty-four as he monitored the radio and heard their mounting problems. He knew each of the young men on the forty-four, and it's likely that because they were about the same age as his oldest son, he was as worried as a father would be. They might have been Coast Guard trained, but the combined maritime experience of the four was still less than his own days at sea. By this time he and the four men aboard the *Can Do* had discussed the risks involved in going out into a storm that showed no signs of weakening. Charlie Bucko, being a former Coast Guard coxswain, had committed himself to staying onboard with Frank, but Frank tried to dissuade the others from making the trip to Salem Sound.

Fifteen-year-old Mark Gelinas, a friend of Frank's younger son, Brian, had trudged down to the *Can Do* that evening: "I wanted to go out with the men, but of course Frank said 'no way.' Frank also told Wilkinson, Fuller, and Curley not to go. He said it was going to be awful out there and that once they got to Salem he wasn't going to come back that night, and he wasn't sure when he and Bucko would be back."

Each man wanted to help, knowing they would be needed if they had to pluck men from the forty-four or the tanker out of heavy seas, and they elected to accompany Frank and Charlie. Maybe the group dynamics made it hard for one person to leave when all the others were prepared to go. No one wanted to appear afraid. On the other hand, the men had so much experience at sea that they never would have taken the conditions lightly, and they knew the risks involved. They knew that once the *Can Do* was beyond the breakwater they would be on their own, in an unpredictable situation, where the unforeseen could mean disaster. If they got into trouble, there were no other Coast Guard boats in Gloucester that could help them.

Somehow Charlie managed to run to a phone and call Sharon before they headed out. He simply said, "We'll be heading out soon. I love you." On the surface this might seem an odd thing to do, because just thirty minutes earlier he had said good-bye to Sharon and told her he loved her. But Charlie may have had a premonition about the mission. He had spent the last twelve months working on a manuscript that he hoped would be published, and the story was eerily similar to what was taking shape that night. In Charlie's book five men head out to sea during a nighttime blizzard to rescue friends whose boat is in jeopardy of sinking. Sharon had read the manuscript and says, "Charlie wrote it out in longhand in a spiral notebook and it was ninety percent finished. He had titled it *The Boat Job,* and you would think Charlie could see into the future—that's how similar it was to the night the *Can Do* went out."

Whether Charlie had a premonition or just a sense of foreboding, the phone call to Sharon showed his concern. It's possible that he had no qualms when Frank first called and talked about going to the tanker, but when the situation changed and the forty-four was in trouble Charlie knew the seas must be huge. Yet despite any misgivings, it would be virtually impossible for him not to try to aid his fellow Coasties. He had not only the Coast Guard mentality of helping those in need but also the marine mind-set of leaving no man behind. Going out to help was part of who Charlie was, and taking action was instinctive.

※

Frank radioed Paradis for an update and let him know his intentions. *"What's the status of the forty-four? How are they making out?"*

"She's about one-third of the way down there. We had to turn the forty-one back."

"Let's wait a few more minutes. In about another fifteen minutes I may give it a shot. We'll give it a try to get over there."

"What do you have for crew?"

"I've got Bucko here and a couple of hands."

"Pat wants you to give him a shout if you want another man. He would be glad to go with you."

In this exchange it's clear that Frank was willing to "give it a try," implying that if the conditions proved too much for the *Can Do* he would turn back. The men aboard figured there was no harm in seeing what it was like outside the harbor, believing they had the option of turning back. Both literally and figuratively, they wanted to test the waters and see how the *Can Do* responded—after all, Frank's boat was forty-nine feet, a bit larger than the forty-four. To sit in the harbor and do nothing while four young Coast Guard men were out there alone in increasing danger was unacceptable to all five men.

While Frank grew restive and prepared to head into the Blizzard, the ninety-five-foot Coast Guard cutter *Cape George* left port in Boston and began the journey to the *Global Hope*. The cutter's home port was Falmouth, Massachusetts, but on that day the ship was moored in Boston after a patrol. Aboard the cutter was Executive Petty Officer Myron Verville, who recalled that the seas grew with each passing mile as the *Cape George* made its way to the tanker. The cutter's fathometer (depth gauge) went out near Logan Airport, and when it approached Governors Island the seas were six feet, with winds at forty-five knots. Verville knew things were going to be bad, because these heavy seas were still in the shelter of Boston Harbor. Once the cutter got past Governors Island and headed to port (northeast) toward Salem they were pounded by chaotic seas greater than twenty feet. Verville had never seen salt water freeze so fast, and the entire boat was covered and weighted down with ice, significantly slowing its progress. The ice on the boat weighed an estimated forty tons, and Verville was worried about all that extra weight. The ice not only affected their speed but also was a real danger to the vessel's stability, especially the ice that built up well above the waterline.

Normally the *Cape George* could make a run from Boston to Salem in under two hours, but because they were going into the teeth of the wind and slowed by the weight of ice, each mile gained was taking four times longer than normal. The forty-four, however, was racing with the seas, like a toy boat propelled down a raging river. At 7:00 p.m. they reached Baker's Island in Salem Sound with frayed nerves as the storm exploded into its full fury.

"With the searchlights on," says Roger Mathurin, "all we could see was snow coming down almost horizontally and enormous seas. Let me give you an idea of how bad it was. The top of our radar antenna extended exactly thirteen feet, three inches, above the waterline. When we were down in the troughs I could look up, and see a wall of water that was about fifteen feet *above* the top of the antenna. When we were down in those troughs it was eerily quiet. The wind didn't reach down there, but as soon as we rode up the next wave there was incredible shrieking from the wind. I've been in the Coast Guard twenty-five years and I've never seen seas that were anything like those."

Just before reaching Baker's Island, the forty-four was clobbered by an enormous wave, which put the vessel on its side, its antenna masts in the water. For a harrowing split second it seemed the boat would keep rolling and capsize. Then it quickly came back up and McIlvride regained control. Although the forty-four was designed to right itself from a roll, the crew would have been swept off — none of the crew had strapped themselves in, because they needed to be able to move quickly and be searching for navigation aids. Even after the near capsizing there was no way they could locate the crude harnesses and get them on in the wildly pitching boat.

Paradis told McIlvride to be very careful approaching the tanker, because it had a black hull and white superstructure and was probably not showing any lights whatsoever. McIlvride asked for a more accurate position for the *Global Hope*. Paradis didn't know for sure — the tanker could be in a thousand pieces for all he knew. Warren Andrews wasn't sure about the tanker's status, either, but assumed if the whistle blasts he had heard earlier were in fact from the *Global Hope* it had probably run hard aground somewhere near Misery Island. (The tanker was actually much closer to Salem, hard aground on Coney Island Ledge.)

McIlvride was coaxing the boat onward like a jockey on a Thoroughbred running full-speed on a slippery track. One false step and down they go. *Just a little more,* he thought, *just a little farther.* But his mount was slowly succumbing to the brutal pounding. He and his crew struggled with a radar system that had completely shut down. They could have been four feet from slamming into the *Global Hope* and not even know it. Even if the crew could locate the tanker there was little they could do. The storm was strengthening rather than weakening, and with seas of twenty feet the forty-four could not possibly be brought alongside the tanker to rescue any crewmen. Searchlights could not cut through the whiteout conditions, and the seas were so violent that turning the boat might cause it to roll. Without radar the forty-four could be in as much trouble as the *Global Hope* . . . or worse. The storm had also taken its toll on other equipment; the fathometer was broken. Not only did the crew not know what was in front of the boat; they also didn't know what was below them—they could be in 50 feet of water or 5 feet. (The forty-four drew 3.5 feet of water.) This was particularly troublesome because there were shoals and shallow ledges all around them and the next wave might hurl the boat into a foaming mess of water swirling around submerged rocks. If that happened they would have their propeller flattened, their hull split, or if the hit was sudden enough, the boat would lurch to a stop and the next wave would push it broadside, leaving it vulnerable to capsizing.

Navigation around Baker's Island does not allow much room for error. To the south are Pope Head Shoal, North Gooseberry Island, South Gooseberry Island, and the ominous-sounding Dry Breakers. Aptly named Misery Shoals and Misery Island are to the north, where more than one mariner has met his end. Between Misery Island and Baker's Island is a thousand-yard passage. Then it's four miles through Salem Sound to the ports of Salem and Beverly, but scattered through the region are more islands and submerged obstructions such as House Ledge, Hardy Rocks, Rising States Ledge, Bowditch Ledge, Eagle Island, and Great Haste Ledge, likely named for the careless mariners who were run aground. Nautical charts of Salem Sound show depth contour lines in crazy, haphazard patterns where it might be twenty feet on one side of the boat and four feet on the other. Navigating through Salem Sound blind, without radar or visibility, would be like trying to run Class V rapids at night in a kayak.

When Paradis realized the radar and fathometer on the forty-four were out for good and his men didn't know exactly where they were, his concern tripled. He understood that the topography of the ocean's floor around Baker's Island resembles the craggy spine of a ridge with a mix of level areas, swales, and sharply rising peaks. It was the peaks he was most worried about, because they are the submerged granite humps that, along with the sandy shoals, litter outer Salem Sound. Those ledges could grab a boat and crumple a steel hull as if it were made of aluminum foil.

Paradis knew he had to get the men onboard the forty-four to safety and barked into the microphone, *"The moment you can identify a floating aid* [buoy], *any known aid, and you can work your way into Beverly, do so immediately."*

"Roger. That sure is what we're going to do. We've just been trying to run a course, but with these seas we're trying to stay as close to range as possible."

For emphasis Paradis added: *"You can forget about the vessel* [Global Hope] *at this time and proceed to Beverly."*

Proceeding to Beverly, however, was easier said than done. Even though the forty-four had made it to Baker's Island and was just four miles from the docks at Beverly, the crew was disoriented without functioning radar, wondering if the next wave would thrust them into rocks. The men half-expected to hear the sickening grinding noise of their hull on a shoal or, even worse, the crash of their bow into ledge.

Paradis radioed Frank to resume their discussion. There was uncertainty in the comments of both men, who seemed to be groping to make the right decision:

Paradis: *"If I can get that boat [44317] back to safe water, that's what I'm going to do. Do you figure on going up there?"*

Frank: *"Well, we'll take a shot at it. I don't know. And if I do get up there I kinda know the area a little bit, for what it's worth. I don't know; it's going to be one hell of a mess from here."*

Paradis: *"Roger. At this time, we don't know for sure whether anybody is in fact in jeopardy. We know there is a probability the ship is dragging her anchor. We have other Coast Guard facilities coming on the scene, a two-ten and a ninety-five. I don't see any reason for jeopardizing a small boat crew that doesn't have the facilities at their disposal."*

Frank: *"Roger on that. Well, with your OK, I'd like to take a look outside the harbor and see about heading up that way or whether I stay here."*

Paradis: *"Roger. Proceed outside, Frank, and give it a look. I appreciate it."*

Frank: *"OK, we'll give it a look. The way it looks, we might be right back."*

3

FRANK QUIRK AND
CHARLIE BUCKO

Normally, the Coast Guard does not have such frequent communication with a pilot boat captain, but Frank's many years of cooperation and assistance put him in a unique class. Quirk seemed to know how to make himself and the *Can Do* available to Station Gloucester without interfering or stepping on any toes. When dangerous situations occurred and Quirk was in the vicinity, he simply let the Coast Guard know he was standing by should they need him, often saying, "This is the *Can Do;* let me know if there's anything we can do to help." Sometimes the Coast Guard took him up on his offer, and other times, when they had adequate vessels and personnel available, they didn't. And on rare occasions, there was no time for a discussion and immediate action was called for. One such incident involved a ten-year-old boy, Michael Almeida, who was drowning in Gloucester Harbor on an August afternoon in 1974.

Frank, wife Audrey, and younger son Brian were aboard the

Can Do in the process of towing the refrigerator ship *Reefer Merchant* into Gloucester. It was late in the day, about 5:30 p.m., when Brian shouted, "Someone's in the water!" Frank looked over to where Brian was pointing and saw a body floating about twenty feet from the end of the state pier. He immediately contacted the captain of the *Reefer Merchant* and said to proceed on his own and next radioed the Coast Guard. Gunning the engine, Frank steered the *Can Do* toward the body and then handed over control of the boat to Audrey. Just a few feet away from the scene Frank lost sight of the body but then noticed a pair of fingertips barely breaking the water's surface. He also noticed a second person struggling in the water next to the pier. Grabbing a life ring, Frank ran to the stern of the *Can Do* and dived in.

Gloucester Harbor was quite murky, with all manner of foreign matter—including fish entrails from the nearby processing plant—suspended in the waters of the busy port. Swimming through the cloudy gray-green sea, Frank reached the submerged body and made a grab for the hair on its head, but because of the oil and grease in the harbor he could not sustain a grip. He took a big gulp of air and dived below, grabbing the victim around the chest and then kicking for the pier, now aware that the body was that of a young boy (ten-year-old Michael Almeida) who showed no signs of life.

A thirty-foot Coast Guard patrol boat roared toward the pier, and two seamen onboard jumped over the side and helped Frank haul the boy the remaining feet to the pier. The skipper of the boat, Fiora Metall, maneuvered the boat to the dock and then assisted the men in the water. Together they raised the boy to the top of the pier, where Metall immediately began giving mouth-to-mouth resuscitation.

Meanwhile the person who was struggling in the water, Fred Delourchry, made it back to the pier with the help of the seamen and collapsed. Delourchry had been sitting on the pier reading a book when the young boy passed him on a bicycle, riding to the end of the pier. "I looked up," said Delourchry in a police affidavit, "and noticed that he was no longer there. I jumped, looked around and saw him in the water. At that point the bicycle that he was riding was dragging him down. I dove into the water and saw the bicycle was attached to his pant leg. He was five feet underwater about 10 feet to the side of the pier. I shook the bicycle loose and as I came up from under water I struck my head on a camel [a floating pole at water level] that was adjacent to the pier. I was either unconscious or semi-conscious." Delourchry said there was a gap in his memory, because the next thing he knew he was on his back talking with Audrey Quirk on the pier.

Young Almeida was rushed to a local hospital, but his condition was so critical he was immediately moved to Boston's Children Hospital. Besides having his lungs filled with water from his ten to fifteen minutes under the surface, his condition was exacerbated by bacteria ingested from the pollution. Fortunately, after a lengthy stay in the hospital he made a full recovery. Frank Quirk and Fred Delourchry both received Gloucester's Mariner's Medal for helping to save the boy's life. One of nice things that came out of the accident was the close friendship that developed between the two rescuers. Almost every weekend in good weather, Fred would drive up from his Wellesley home and hang out on the *Can Do*. And Michael Almeida's parents didn't forget, either: they sent Michael's school picture to Frank for several years with a big thank-you note.

Warren Andrews says the rescue was typical Frank—"but there were other times, maybe less dramatic, that Frank also saved people from death or injury, and no one but Audrey and I knew about it." Warren points out that while Frank would do whatever he could to help those in need, including lending money to down-and-out fishermen, there was a tougher, no-nonsense side to him as well: "He once took two German officers from the hospital ship SS *Poseidon* to a local Gloucester restaurant for dinner. Two fishermen were there and they became abusive to the German officers. Frank went over and asked them to cool it. One of the fishermen gave Frank a shove. Before you could bat an eyelash that guy was on the floor clutching his stomach and the other was on his knees 'cause Frank had him in a hammerlock. It was all done so smoothly and quickly, most of the customers in the restaurant never even knew about the fight."

❈

In many respects Frank and Charlie Bucko were quite similar. Charlie also went out of his way to help others—and other creatures like the seagull—but he could be tough as nails, too. A former U.S. Marine, decorated in Vietnam with two Purple Hearts for combat wounds, Bucko had seen the crap life can throw at you—from the horrors of war to thirty-foot seas. He was big and burly but handsome, with blue eyes, a perfect smile, and long dark brown hair. Known as a first-rate boatswain's mate and an excellent boat handler, he was seen by other Coasties as a true leader.

A seaman at Station Gloucester recalls how all the young Coasties looked up to Charlie because he was in his late twenties and had been around. Charlie was the kind of guy they wanted to emulate, and they were quick to follow his orders and welcomed his suggestions.

Although Bucko left the Coast Guard on good terms in 1977 and had been cited for bravery, his career in the service had started out rocky. Executive Petty Officer Brad Willey recalls that Bucko once punched out a commanding officer at another Coast Guard station prior to his assignment at Gloucester. "They put him in the brig," says Willey, "and then they transferred him to me down at Point Allerton. You can imagine the reputation he had. One morning reveille was going and Charlie didn't show up. I found him still asleep in his bed. I took his mattress and flipped it, and he smacked into the floor. He jumped up and glared at me but then smiled and said, 'You've got a lot of balls.' Somehow that cemented a respect. He was a bright guy, and could do just about anything he set his mind to. When I got transferred up to Gloucester one of the first things I did was to ask for Charlie Bucko to be assigned there. He had matured so much and was a first-class guy."

Bucko had a zest for life as well. Another coxswain at Gloucester Station recalls that one afternoon he taught Bucko how to ride his motorcycle. "Well," says the coxswain, "the next day he shows up at the station in leather riding pants, biker's boots, and leather vest. He was hooked and ready to bike across America."

Doug Parsons, a friend and coworker of Bucko's at the Marine Railway Company, says Charlie was a riot to be around and could fit in anywhere. When Charlie was first hired at the Marine Railway all the workers had fun picking on the "new guy." One hot August day a flatbed truck pulled up to the shop with 450 bags of grit used in sandblasting and each bag weighed one hundred pounds. Doug Parsons explained that there were no forklifts but rather a long line of workers to pass the bags down the line from the truck to inside the shop. They positioned Charlie right in the middle of the line and then went as fast as they could: "There was no way he could keep up and we were razzing him about that. It was like boot camp all over again. But Charlie knew how to handle it. He always had a big smile."

Parsons remembers having discussions with Charlie about what they would do if caught in a desperate situation in bad seas. Charlie said he would tell his crew that if they ever got in real trouble "never leave the boat; the boat is your only chance."

Parsons recalls that on the evening of the Blizzard, Bucko's fiancée, Sharon, called and said, "Charlie wanted you to know he might be going out on the *Can Do* to help a tanker in trouble." Parsons's first response was to say, "That son of a bitch, why didn't he come and get me." Later he wondered why Charlie had her make the call in the first place. "Looking back now, I think the reason he asked Sharon to call me was because he wanted someone besides her to know what was going on. He probably made it sound like no big deal to Sharon, but he knew I'd know it was going to be dangerous. Maybe it was his way of asking me to be there for Sharon if something should happen."

Both Parsons and members of Bucko's family say that Charlie had never been more happy and contented than in 1978. A lot had to do with Sharon. They met in January of 1977, when Sharon was a teller at the Gloucester National Bank and Charlie was opening an account. Charlie asked Sharon out, and she said yes, attracted by Charlie's ear-to-ear smile. When Sharon brought Charlie home to have dinner with her family she tried to play a little trick on him involving her twin sister. They had plans to go out after dinner, so Sharon went upstairs to change. Her twin sneaked upstairs as well and changed her clothes, then came back down and told Charlie she was ready to go, taking him by the arm and leading him outside. But Charlie immediately recognized the deception and said, "Where's Sharon?" Sharon's sister went back upstairs and proclaimed, "He's a keeper."

It didn't take long for Sharon and Charlie to fall in love, and they were engaged in less than a year. The wedding was planned for May 14, 1978. Charlie was still in the Coast Guard when the couple first met, and leaving was a difficult decision. But he told Sharon that after a dangerous experience with a rescue involving an oil tanker called the *Chester Poling* he should get out of the Coast Guard or he'd make her a widow.

"Charlie had only been in Gloucester a couple years," recalled Sharon, "but he really liked the town, and we dreamed of building our own home. In fact, the day before the Blizzard, he sketched a floor plan of the house he wanted to have built. We were hoping it would be close to the ocean, because he loved the sea and said he always wanted to be near it. Even on vacations we had to be by the sea. His favorite time was right after a big storm, when he could watch the surf. In that sense he and Frank Quirk were two kindred spirits. They were the best of friends and really watched out for each other. Charlie had been out with Frank on the *Can Do* several times. When conditions were bad Charlie would go to help out on piloting jobs. He was getting a good feel for what the *Can Do* could do in really bad seas."

Few people who knew Charlie Bucko and Frank Quirk were surprised to learn they decided to head out into the storm.

❊

Paradis had shifted his focus from a search and rescue mission of the *Global Hope* to a search for his own forty-four-foot patrol boat. He knew the boat was somewhere in the vicinity of Salem Sound, but the Sound does not offer the protection of Gloucester Harbor and the men onboard could drown just as easily one mile from shore as they could ten miles out. The potential for the patrol boat to lose engine power (as a result of their screws hitting a rock and stalling the engine) and capsize was actually greater in ledge-strewn Salem Sound than it had been earlier on the open ocean. And although the forty-four was a rugged boat, it had vulnerabilities, especially if an obstruction turned it broadside or its engine quit in heavy seas. Even if the crew had strapped themselves in with surf belts, it still would not have ensured their survival, as evidenced in a more recent tragedy, which also involved a forty-four-footer attempting a night rescue, in a February storm.

The incident occurred at a dangerous ledge-strewn river mouth in La Push, Washington, when four young crewmen at the Quillayute River Coast Guard Station were roused from their sleep by the shrill sound of the search and rescue alarm. A Mayday had come in from a small sailboat that was being pushed by roiling waves into the rocky coastline. The crewmen scrambled on board their forty-four, and as they were getting under way all four men put on surf belts. These belts are nylon waist harnesses with three-foot-long straps that hook onto the boat to keep the men onboard if the boat rolls.

Ben Wingo, a nineteen-year-old seaman apprentice on that forty-four-footer, said conditions were especially treacherous at the river's mouth, where its current collides with oncoming breakers. In an interview with the *Seattle Times,* Wingo later described each wave as being so large that the boat was lifted for three long seconds before being slammed down into the trough. The crew had to bend their knees before each fall, because they feared they would shatter upon impact. As they crossed the sandbar that separates the river from the sea, Wingo shouted, "Rock! Starboard! Ten feet!" Almost simultaneously another crew member screamed, "Wave!" and a twenty-five-foot swell slammed the boat into the rock and the boat rolled 180 degrees. Wingo said it felt like he was in a vacuum, with immense forces tugging him one way and then the other.

The keel, weighted with concrete, was now on the surface of the ocean, and all it needed was another wave to tilt it and the vessel would roll back over, righting itself. The forty-four did exactly that, and when it came up all four men were still strapped onboard, bloody and bruised but alive. As they were struggling to orient themselves, the coxswain barely had time to radio that they had rolled when a second wave flipped the boat again. When the boat righted itself, two of the crewmen, including the coxswain, were gone. The seas had ripped their surf belts from the boat's metal clamps and flung the men out into the murderous waves. Wingo said the wheelhouse was gone and the coxswain's seat had been sheared in half.

What was left of the boat was deposited on a rock ledge, a few feet up from the seas, with Wingo and Petty Officer Matthew

Schlimme still onboard. By this time Wingo had had enough and in a panic screamed, "We've got to get out of here!" and started to remove his surf belt. Schlimme, however, knew another wave was coming and felt the surf belts would keep them from drowning, and he shouted, "We stay with the boat; put your belt back on and pass me the radio mike!

Wingo, who did as instructed even though he could see the radio was useless, said, "Schlimme was just trying to distract me and calm me down. And it worked." Even though Wingo's panic subsided, the seas did not, and a second later a wave, like a giant hand, grabbed the boat, yanking it off the rocks and into the seas, where it rolled yet again. This time when the boat came back up, Wingo was alone—Schlimme's harness had also been ripped from the boat clamps. Wingo felt the boat spin around and saw how its still-functioning searchlight illuminated the shore. Now he knew which way safety was, and as the next wave sent the boat careening toward the rocky coast Wingo unfastened his belt and jumped overboard. He swam ashore and started to claw up a cliff, using every ounce of power to get away from the sea, which he felt was still not done with him and might pluck him from the rocks. Finally, fifty feet above the water, he collapsed, shivering uncontrollably.

At dawn Wingo was rescued and the bodies of the other crew members were found—all three had died from blunt injuries to the head rather than drowning. The coxswain on the forty-four was singled out for taking needless risks and not alerting the station commanders to the true severity of the storm. The investigation report cited him for failing to "assess the rough bar conditions correctly and/or exercising inappropriate judgment by crossing the bar." Wingo, however, had a different view: "He was screwed no matter what. What if he hadn't gone and those people [on the sailboat] had died? He would have hung for that, too."

As a result of the tragedy the Coast Guard made several

changes, including speeding the replacement of the forty-four with the safer forty-seven-foot vessel. Equally important, the old surf-belt hooks were replaced with self-locking models and new safety procedures became mandatory, emphasizing that surf belts and helmets must always be worn in heavy seas.

※

Concern for the forty-four was growing by the minute. Warren Andrews was restless in his radio room, running his fingers through his wavy black hair, fidgeting in his seat with a helpless feeling. He wondered what more he could do when the idea came to him to have spotters looking for the forty-four along the shore. Andrews picked up the phone and began calling members of the Northeast Surf Patrol, asking them to take handheld marine radios and drive to various points along Salem Harbor's north side. It was a long shot, but Warren hoped that maybe one of these volunteers would spot the blue light on the forty-four and could then radio him with their position, so Andrews could guide the patrol boat into safe waters.

On board the forty-four the crewmen, although quite young, were keeping their cool. Most of them had already experienced tough missions and dangerous seas. In fact, Bob Krom, the youngest of the group at nineteen, had been injured just a few months earlier on a rescue. Although he looked like he could be a defensive end in the NFL, the six-foot, seven-inch Krom found that he was no match for angry seas and pounding boats. He had been part of a crew on the forty-four that went out in a storm to rescue a man who was having a seizure on a slow-moving charter boat. When the forty-four reached the charter boat they pulled up alongside and Krom went to help transfer the ill passenger onto the Coast Guard boat. Just as Krom grabbed the man the two boats crashed together. Krom felt a searing pain in his right foot and looked down to see that the end of his boot had been sliced away, taking the tips of several toes off in the process. Krom recalled he and his crew first got the man with the seizure on board the forty-four, then Krom hobbled below. He wouldn't let the others take his boot off because he knew the injury was severe and he didn't want to see just how bad it was. He kept his foot elevated while the forty-four raced back to Gloucester. Krom ended up in the hospital, and although he lost part of four of his toes, his big toe was intact and his balance was not affected.

While the Blizzard of '78 was worse than anything the crew of the forty-four had ever seen, their training and prior missions helped keep them focused and working as a team while crowded together in the pilothouse. McIlvride was at the wheel, Tom Desrosiers, the engineer, was to his left for quick access to the engine room if needed, and seamen Roger Mathurin and Bob Krom were to McIlveride's right, taking turns shining a flashlight on the compass, struggling with the malfunctioning radar, and peering out into the driving snow hoping to see a buoy. As each wave broke over the stern, water rushed up in the cockpit, frequently reaching the thighs of the men. Being soaking wet in twenty-degree temperatures should have chilled the men to the bone, but they barely noticed the cold—too much was happening. Their muscles involuntarily coiled and tensed, ready to spring into action should the boat suddenly flounder. Adrenaline, at least in the short term, shut out the discomforts of being wet in a gale with windchills below zero.

Heading west-southwest, they were in extreme following seas—a situation that can cause pitchpoling, where the stern of the boat is lifted up and over the bow, causing the boat to flip. As each wave catches the boat the stern tries to overtake the bow and the vessel begins to sideslip. Each time this happens the propeller loses its effectiveness and the vessel is momentarily out of control.

The forty-four is a relatively slow boat and McIlvride needed full power almost all the time, especially since the waves were moving faster than the boat. The water on the back side of a wave moves backward, and he didn't have enough boat speed to climb the waves so the boat would slide down in the trough, then pick up speed as the next swell came. On the front of the swell the water in a wave moves forward at a rapid pace, and McIlvride required full power to keep the wave from overtaking the boat too quickly. Simultaneously he had to try to limit the broaching so the boat didn't turn sideways to oncoming waves. He also needed the speed to give him as much steering capacity as possible, because the effectiveness of rudders depends directly on how fast water flows past them. "We were going at full speed," says McIlvride, "with each passing wave surging us forward at an accelerated pace, and usually knocking us off course. I had to fight to keep the boat from broaching on the face of the wave, and we'd get thrown off course as the wave passed. So on the back of the wave I'd look at the compass and get us back on course for a few seconds until the next wave came."

Even if McIlvride had wanted to change engine speeds, it would have been a difficult maneuver in high seas on the twin-engine screw forty-four, because both engines had to be running at the same speed. It takes a few seconds to adjust the speed while looking at the tachometers to ensure they are synchronized, and it's almost impossible while you're being battered about like a Ping-Pong ball.

Roger Mathurin recalls that they did see the light on Baker's Island and as they entered Salem Sound were probably somewhere near the tanker. He knew there was no way they were going to get any men off the tanker in thirty-foot seas and their primary goal was to keep trying to grope their way farther into Salem Sound. Without their fathometer they were at a distinct disadvantage, because they had no idea of the depth of water they were in. And as each minute passed, spray continued to freeze on the forty-four, increasing its weight and reducing stability.

Mathurin and the others were expending incredible energy just to stay upright in the crowded pilothouse, because the boat was not only pitching up and down but also sliding from side to side. "One of our pumps we were carrying to the tanker," says Krom, "came loose below. I went down to secure it, but there was such unbelievable motion I was knocked to the deck. As I struggled with the pump the big compartment heater was blowing directly on me. Between that and the boat's broaching and falling, I got sick and puked in the engine room. Even though it was freezing up above and we were constantly getting wet, anything was better than being down below. I went back up and continued to search for a buoy. We could barely hear each other shout because of howling wind and the snapping of the tattered plastic and canvas covering."

While the men on the forty-four did their best to operate "blind" and avoid the ledges, the *Can Do* was on its way to look for them. As the pilot boat plowed out of Gloucester Harbor, Frank, Bucko, and the others prepared for the unknown.

"We're under way, Warren," radioed Frank. *"Just going up by the Coast Guard station here. Will see what it looks like outside. I don't know if we're going to get clobbered. If we can poke along that way we might take a look around."*

"Roger, Frank. It is a beauty. We have very heavy snow, zero visibility, and the winds estimated here at sixty to seventy. I just hope my radio tower stands up."

"Yeah, I don't even want to see it. If you get a chance I would appreciate it if you call my base [wife] and advise her that I won't be in touch for a while."

4

ROGUE WAVES AND
DEAD ENGINES

While the forty-four struggled in Salem Sound, the *Can Do* cleared the breakwater of Gloucester Harbor. Although Paradis had already asked Frank what men were aboard the pilot boat, he did so again, stress edging into his voice: *"Frank, what do you have for crew?"*

In the heaving boat, Frank picked up the radio transmitter and snapped, *"Yeah, just stand by here."*

Although Frank didn't say any more for a few minutes, from the tone of his voice it was clear the boat required his full attention. The *Can Do* was now beyond the safety of Gloucester Harbor and Frank, like McIlvride, was putting every ounce of energy and concentration into controlling the boat. Like a bucking horse that had been spooked, the *Can Do* seemed to have a mind of its own. Cresting seas hurled the pilot boat down enormous steep-faced waves so that the vessel literally surfed, going much faster than the skipper had intended. Frank worked the throttle and the

rudder as best he could to avoid going too fast down the mountainous seas, worried his bow might bury in a trough. And when
he felt the stern yawing, he corrected the sideslip immediately,
before it was too late. As much as he could, he controlled the pilot boat's power so that she rode the backs of waves without
actually going over.

A few minutes later Paradis radioed the forty-four that the
Can Do was heading down to assist them. "Although we never
asked for help, we were relieved to hear the *Can Do* might be
coming out," says Tom Desrosiers, "because we were still without radar and didn't know exactly where we were. Since Frank
Quirk was a pilot boat captain we knew that he had to know the
area like the back of his hand. In the meantime we tried to avoid
the ledges and maybe find a buoy to tie up to."

Just minutes later, at 8:30, the greatest fears of the forty-
four crew were realized when they heard a bang as the boat
struck an obstruction. Both engines immediately stalled from
the sudden hit.

Having the engines quit was the darkest moment for the
crew of the forty-four. "We hit some rocks pretty good," says
Desrosiers, "and that's when the engine quit. After running all
that way from Gloucester we had a certain comfort from the
sound of those engines, and when they went dead it was a deafening, eerie silence." Mathurin agrees, adding, "When the engines quit I thought maybe we would have to go down below
and try to ride out the storm. And I was praying we wouldn't
have to do that."

In the darkness, McIlvride, wet and weary, radioed Paradis
that the engines were dead. The commanding officer shouted
out, *"Drop your hook* [anchor]," and McIlvride answered, *"Roger."*
Paradis was worried sick the boat would be hit broadside by a
wave or maybe take a breaking wave over the stern. He knew
these disasters could be avoided by setting anchor, because the

anchor would be dropped from the bow and when it took hold the forty-four would swing around with its bow into the waves. Although McIlvride answered, "Roger," he had no intention of following this order. There was no way he was going to send one of the crew out on the bow to drop the anchor and secure it. The boat was pitching like a roller coaster, and if one of the men fell off he would die almost instantly. The skipper figured if the engines wouldn't restart there might still be time to drop the anchor—but he wasn't about to tell Paradis that. The rest of the crew, of course, agreed with the decision, and they didn't waste a moment worrying about lying to Paradis. Their focus was on the engines.

Paradis's concern reached a new level and it showed in his impatience. After waiting a few agonizing seconds, he came back on the radio: *"Have you restarted your engines?"*

"We're working on it."

"Let me know immediately."

When the engines died, Desrosiers, the engineer, flung open the hatch and ran below. He looked through the porthole into the engine room, and when he didn't see any water coming in he went in. Everything looked in order, even the propeller shaft, so Desrosiers figured he'd simply press the electric-start engine button and see what happened. The engines started and that was the most beautiful sound the engineer had ever heard in his young life.

McIlvride quickly notified Paradis: *"Engines restarted at this time. We're going to try to circle into the wind and waves."*

"If you see any aid at all make a real attempt to tie up to it or stay as near to it as possible. Commencing now, I want you men to give me a radio check every ten minutes."

"We are looking for an aid but nothing in sight. We're still proceeding in slow."

Although the engines were working, the radar and depth finder were not, and should the forty-four slam into a ledge again her engines might not restart. Paradis tried another suggestion for getting the radar back on track: *"Try tuning it down; there may be too much tune-up with the snow."*

"There's no result playing with the tuner. We tried, but there's just no picture at all."

The worrying went on for Paradis, and he contacted Frank to give him an update and to let him know his help was still needed: *"Frank, whatever he hit, he's clear of it. He's maneuvering. Totally disoriented at this time. He doesn't have compass or radar. If it's at all possible I'd appreciate it if you would head over that way."*

"OK, we'll give it the best shot we've got, Mike, and believe me, you need a compass and radar out here tonight. You wouldn't believe it. Well, maybe you would. Once we get a point of kickoff we're going to stand off for Salem and keep you posted."

❉

Additional assistance was on the way as the ninety-five-foot cutter *Cape George* slowly headed north from Boston and the 210-foot cutter *Decisive* was dispatched from its anchorage just off Provincetown, Massachusetts. However, both ships had their own troubles and they were heading into the seas and wind, which made for a snail-like pace. Bob Donovan was a twenty-year-old seaman at the wheel of the *Cape George,* working alongside Myron Verville and Skipper Glen Snyder. Now that the *Cape George* was outside Boston Harbor, Donovan knew there was no turning back, and he gripped the wheel like a vise. The wheel was four feet in diameter and power assisted, but it was still difficult to control. But the worst part for Donovan was that he couldn't see the towering waves, just feel them. The cutter would be lifted almost straight up, then slammed back down, and Donovan used the wheel as much for support to keep on his feet as for steerage. His arms had quickly become black-and-blue from banging into the edge of the wheel and the front console as he struggled to keep his footing. Donovan felt like he was in the air as much as on the deck as the cutter pitched violently on its northward journey. Around him crewmates would be standing one minute, then hurled to the deck the next. Wind gusts had now hit 100 miles per hour, and some of the waves were thirty feet.

While Donovan manned the wheel, Verville read the charts and gave advice to Skipper Snyder, who then checked the compass course and the loran C before making the final decisions on their course and speed. While they were physically taking a pounding, Donovan thought that Tom Murrin, one of the engineers, had the toughest assignment of all. Donovan later recalled that Murrin "was in the engine control booth, alone, for the entire trip. It was no bigger than a telephone booth and extremely hot. I don't know how he managed. When he got out he was a little wild from going through that experience. It was like being locked in a cage and placed inside a clothes dryer—and expected to do your job. I'm now a commercial fisherman, and have been for some time, and I've never seen conditions like that night—not even close."

Vern DePietro, also on the *Cape George,* had only been in the Coast Guard for six months, and he took his cues from the more seasoned men. Despite the cold temperatures on the bridge, he was sweating beneath his coat. "Even though I was the new guy," says DiPietro, "I knew we were in serious shit just by the way some of the more experienced guys were acting. They were deadly serious, saying very little, and you could see the stress in their eyes. There were about twelve guys onboard and I was one of the men up on the bridge acting as a lookout, but of course I couldn't see anything and our radar wasn't worth a damn because there was so much clutter from snow. Half the time I was puking my guts out. One way to alleviate seasickness is to get fresh air and watch the seas and the horizon, but that night it would be suicide to go out—the only time we could see the ocean was when it was literally on top of us. One thing I do remember was hearing Frank Quirk on the radio having a discussion with Gloucester and then making the decision to go out."

Conditions were a little better on the larger cutter, the *Decisive,* but not much. Damage Controlman Jim Quinn was part of the engineering group aboard the 210-foot cutter, and he remembers that even before the *Decisive* got under way it encountered difficulties. He and the mates were heaving in the port anchor when they noticed it was fouled with steel cables just as it broke the water's surface. Quinn strapped a harness on, grabbed a cutting torch, and then leaned over the side of the ship to try to free the anchor. The seas were building and Quinn had to time each swell perfectly as he bent over the rail and began cutting. It took a while, but eventually he freed the anchor. The *Decisive* then got under way, but because the cutter was going into the seas Quinn estimates it was only able to make five nautical miles per hour as the seas pounded the bow.

Quinn then joined three men down in the engine room. He was the designated "throttleman," whose duties included taking readings of the various gauges on the engines, generators, and other machinery and making adjustments accordingly to keep the equipment on line. The engineer of the watch and the throttleman spent a good portion of their watch in the control booth located aft in the engine room. They were mostly seated as the cutter pounded through the waves; both men held on to the safety handrails to maintain their positions and to prevent any accidental contact with the various control switches. An "oiler" attempted to maintain his roving status in the engine room and other engineering spaces the best he could. "At the end of your watch you were physically worn out," says Quinn. "It took at least twice as much energy as normal just trying to keep your balance."

The *Decisive* had a high superstructure, and on this trip the hull was riding higher than normal because the cutter had been out on patrol the prior week, expending a good portion of its fuel. Although at 210 feet it dwarfed the *Can Do* and the forty-four-footer, the men on board the *Decisive* still didn't feel safe, because of the extreme seas. "If one thing goes wrong we knew we could be in serious trouble," says Quinn. "It was a fine line between making it and not making it. One of my worries was that we were taking green seas [not just the tops of waves] over the stern and our exhaust vents were horizontal, so water could have gone into the engines. If we lost power, I'm sure we would have capsized. I remember looking out the mess deck windows that are normally about eight feet above the water, and it was like looking into an aquarium. One rogue wave hit us and it sent everything and everybody over and down on the deck."

A rogue wave is one that is not in step with the other waves and is usually much larger, often catching the crew by surprise. They can come out of calm seas or heavy seas but always pose a danger because of their unexpected nature. In 1995 during rough seas, the *Queen Elizabeth II,* 963 feet long, with a weight of 70,327 gross tons, took a rogue wave directly over her bow while cruising the North Atlantic. The crewmen in the wheelhouse said they saw the wave approach out of the darkness and it felt as if time slowed as they watched it advance, astonished that the crest of the wave was level with their line of vision on the bridge, which was ninety-five feet above the sea surface. The sea cascaded over the forward deck and the bridge, temporarily blinding the men in the wheelhouse, bending steel railings, and denting deck plating. The wave was so powerful it even caved in the Grand Lounge windows, located aft of the wheelhouse. (Canadian weather buoys confirmed the rogue wave's massive size, measuring it at exactly ninety-eight feet.)

Often rogue waves form when conditions are just rough but not extreme, with winds at twenty-five knots and waves in the five-to-seven-foot range. Charter fishing boats sometimes challenge these conditions because customers are prebooked and waiting to go. Usually the boats encounter nothing more than a bumpy ride, with some passengers becoming seasick and wishing they had stayed home. However, every now and again an outing goes from merely uncomfortable to deadly, because mixed within the six-foot waves is a wave double that size. Such was the case on *Joan La Rie III,* a forty-seven-foot charter fishing vessel out of Point Pleasant, New Jersey. The vessel was under way around 6:00 a.m. and reached the fishing grounds, known as "the slough," located about nine miles east of Manasquan Inlet, New Jersey, before 8:00 a.m. Many of the passengers didn't even bother to fish, because they were ill from the rolling motion, and they lay in the cabin throughout the morning. Others caught bluefish, but fishing rods were lost when the boat took heavy rolls of thirty degrees or more.

At 10:45 the captain weighed anchor and began the trip back to port. The Coast Guard Marine Casualty Report says: "At about 1100 while headed in a westerly direction the vessel was hit on the starboard side by an unusually large wave estimated to be about 12 feet high, rolled over to port and capsized. The vessel initially heeled 55–60 degrees and momentarily stayed at that angle of heel." While passengers screamed in terror, water flooded the cockpit, cabin, and engine room and the vessel continued its roll to ninety degrees on the port side and then stayed there. The boat's starboard propeller was now in the air, still turning. The wave hit so suddenly no distress call was transmitted, and the boat was not equipped with an emergency position-indicating radio beacon (EPIRB).

For those onboard it was sheer hell. Inside the cabin the people on the starboard side were thrown onto those on the port side with gear crashing down on them. The only opening was through a narrow door that led to the cockpit, and passengers rushed to get out before water completely filled the cabin. A few passengers—sensing they would not have time to exit the door—kicked out the starboard side windows and climbed to the bow. One woman, Carol Gorman, grabbed life jackets from the storage bin and threw them toward the cabin door in an effort to save those exiting. None of the passengers were wearing life jackets when the accident occurred.

As the engine space filled with water the stern slipped beneath the surface, and the bow was all that remained above the swells. The Coast Guard report described the desperate struggle for survival: "Some passengers were clinging to the bow, others to the anchor line, and others were floating on top of debris. Others were clinging to PFDs and each other." The captain was swept overboard with a passenger and together they drifted seventy-five feet from the vessel. The captain told the passenger their only chance of survival was to swim back toward the boat and get the life floats. Together they immediately started swimming, but without a life jacket the captain tired and drowned en route.

The bow of the boat stayed above the waterline for forty-five minutes before it sank. Chances of survival for those who were still alive were bleak, but they were blessed with incredible luck. When the boat first capsized, a freighter from Brazil was approximately ten miles away and an officer on deck actually saw the *Joan La Rie III* go down the trough of the rogue wave and not come up. The officer immediately had a Mayday radioed to the Coast Guard, and the freighter changed course and headed toward the stricken vessel. The Coast Guard dispatched its nearest forty-one- and forty-four-footers from Station Manasquan, and two helicopters departed from Air Station Brooklyn.

The freighter reached the victims first, but it was two hours after the boat first capsized. Using its small rescue launch, a crew of five Brazilians set out for the people bobbing in the waves. Six people were plucked from the water, and a seventh, too heavy to be lifted, was lashed to the side of the rescue boat. When the rescue boat returned to the freighter the passengers were too weak to climb the ship's ladder, and the seas made the off-loading extremely dangerous. Fortunately, the helicopters arrived, and using a bullhorn, a crew member in the chopper instructed the small rescue boat to pull away from the tanker. The pilot and crew of the helicopter hovered over the launch and using their rescue basket removed the hypothermic passengers one at a time. As this was happening the forty-four-foot Coast Guard patrol boat arrived on the scene and crewmen rescued the remaining people still alive in the water. Of the two crew and twenty passengers who originally set out on the *Joan La Rie III*, eight died.

Mariners who have encountered rogue waves sometimes call them holes in the seas because of the deep trough that precedes the steep forward face of the wave. The reason that a single wave is larger than all others is not entirely clear. In the case of the *Joan La Rie III*, the Coast Guard theorized that the rogue wave was formed when three or more smaller waves coalesced and formed an unusually large one. The report stated "these waves may only last for 5 to 30 seconds and may stretch 500 yards from one end of the crest to the other. It will hit unexpectedly because of its sudden generation, short life and dissipation." Other rogue waves might originate when currents or random eddies meet steady wind-produced incoming wave swells head-on and the interaction reduces the spacing between waves, creating a single giant wave and often even changing its direction. Proponents of this theory cite the frequency of rogue waves off the southeastern coast of South Africa, where the fast south-flowing Agulhas Current has the potential to sporadically alter the configuration of storm waves surging up from Antarctica. Every year one or two supertankers suffer severe structural damage in this region, and smaller ships are often broken in two. Off the New England coast the northeast-flowing Gulf Stream may account for monster waves when it interrupts storm-produced waves moving in the opposite direction. Originating in the warm waters in the eastern part of the Gulf of Mexico, the Gulf Stream is about fifty miles wide and three thousand feet deep. Its rate of flow in the south is as fast as seventy miles a day, slowing to thirty miles a day off the New England coast, and captains of freighters and tankers coming up the eastern seaboard ride its current to save time and fuel.

Topography of the ocean's floor may also play a role in the formation of rogue waves, particularly when swells from a distant storm move over an area of reduced water depth. Another possible cause for rogue wave creation is several different wave trains of differing speeds and directions meeting at the same time, briefly forming an extreme wave. Scientists are also analyzing the release of natural gas from the ocean's floor and its effects on waves. Some experts simply say that there is no single wave height occurring over a specific time period but rather a wide spectrum ranging from small to large, with forecasters focusing on "significant waves"—the average of the highest waves. The probability of encountering such a wave is about one in ten. However, there is a one-in-a-thousand chance of encountering a wave nearly double the significant wave.

One thing for certain is that on a storm-ravaged sea like the night of February 6, 1978, the waves were not uniform, and extremely large waves of thirty to thirty-five feet prowled the sea, using the cover of darkness to surprise the men who dared to be out. There was no time for humans to react, but instead they must trust in the seaworthiness of their boats that were already at their limits.

❋

The *Decisive* recovered from the rogue wave and continued on its north-northwest course. However, the waves were continuing to grow as the storm exploded in intensity during the early-evening hours. A look at the *Decisive*'s log reveals that at 6:00 p.m. the swells were only five feet, but they jumped to eighteen feet at 8:00 p.m. With each passing minute the waves had a chance to grow larger because of the three components that determine wave size: the speed of the wind, the amount of time the wind blows, and the fetch, the distance of open water over which the wind is blowing. Just as troubling, visibility dropped from half a mile to zero during that same time period.

The *Can Do* was out on the open ocean just as the seas were beginning to show their full fury. In the pilothouse Charlie Bucko was standing next to Frank at the wheel. Each time the boat rode up and out of a trough they anxiously glanced at the radar screen for the brief view of what was ahead. As the *Can Do* crested the next wave and was propelled downward, green water temporarily engulfed the boat, making the men feel entombed. While fear might grip other experienced mariners in this situation, Charlie and Frank kept their cool. Together, they had been through an eerily similar rescue effort just a year before.

5

RESCUE OF THE
CHESTER POLING

The rescue Frank and Bucko had participated in happened a year earlier, on January 10, 1977, when both men, piloting separate boats, responded to the Mayday of a 282-foot coastal tanker, the *Chester A. Poling*. The similarities between the *Poling* rescue and the Blizzard of 1978 are striking: both involved tankers in jeopardy, the same group of boats (the *Can Do, Cape George,* and *Cape Cross,* the forty-one- and forty-four-footers) went to the rescue, and some of the same people responded.

On the morning of the *Chester Poling*'s fateful voyage, the tanker was in port in Everett, Massachusetts, having just offloaded her cargo of kerosene. Captain Charles Burgess heard a weather forecast calling for winds of ten to twenty knots, increasing to twenty-five to thirty-five. Burgess was an experienced captain in his fifties, and he anticipated the need for ballast (for better stability) and ordered the filling of cargo tank number 3 with salt water. With fourteen thousand gallons of diesel fuel still in its bunker tanks, the ship left port at 6:15 a.m. and steamed north, en route to Newington, New Hampshire. Rain and sleet made for miserable conditions, with seas of ten feet and wind gusts of twenty-five knots. Almost immediately, Burgess felt the ship needed better stability and ordered more ballast added to cargo tanks number 3 and 5.

Only an hour into the trip the vessel was pounded by waves larger than the ten-footers the weather service had forecast for the morning. By 8:00 a.m. the ship was constantly rolling and pitching, and Burgess noted that the winds had increased to thirty knots. More ballast was added, completely filling tanks 2, 3, 4, and 5. There was no discussion about aborting the trip, however, because Burgess thought the ship was handling relatively well given the difficult conditions. His decision to continue was influenced by the morning weather forecast, which called for winds to gradually increase, leading him to believe he had a window of opportunity to make it to New Hampshire before conditions worsened.

Wind velocity, however, quickly increased from thirty to thirty-five knots, with seas growing to 15 feet. The pounding of the waves forced Burgess to continually adjust speeds in an effort to minimize the rough ride. By 9:00 a.m. seas had reached 20 feet, with approximately 150 feet between crests. An hour later, while standing in the wheelhouse, Burgess was startled by a loud banging sound; he concluded something had come adrift and was striking the hull. Crewman Harry Selleck was with the captain and carefully inched his way out on the deck in the cold, slicing rain but could see nothing amiss.

Thirty-five minutes later Selleck looked out a forward porthole and saw "a sea of enormous proportions . . . pick up the ship." Selleck later described what happened next: "The bow came down and buried into a wall of sea that was twice the size of the normal seas that had been reported. The ship vibrated. She shook as she was coming down as if someone was pulling her back and forth like seesawing. She shook and then she came up . . . that is when the captain, who was doing some work either on the chart or at the chart table, slowed her down. The stern had been up and then when she came back I heard a large bang like a piece of steel hitting the deck."

Captain Burgess immediately placed the engines at clutch speed, and Selleck checked the deck to ascertain what had caused the second bang. Again he saw nothing and returned to the pilot-house. Then it happened. Another wave hit the ship, followed by a sickening crunching sound and a grinding reverberation of twisted metal. Selleck and Burgess looked aft of the wheelhouse and could not believe their eyes—the ship had broken in two.

The bow and the stern section tilted toward where the break occurred, but each stayed afloat. With an alarm sounding, the five men on the aft section ran from below up to the sloping deck and stared in horror as they, too, saw that the ship had split. A segment of deck plating was the only thing connecting the two sections, preventing them from drifting apart. Crew members rushed to get life jackets on, fearing the sections of the *Chester Poling* would sink within seconds.

In a stroke of good fortune, the VHF-FM radio in the pilot-house still worked because it was battery powered. Captain Burgess immediately called out a Mayday message on channel 13, followed by a desperate plea: *"We are six miles off Cape Ann! Don't know how much longer we can stay afloat!"*

"Be advised the cutter Cape George *is on the way,"* replied Coast Guard Group Boston.

"We split in two," shouted Burgess, *"and don't know how long we can stay afloat. Not sinking yet, but we might be any minute."*

"Are there any persons onboard the other section?"

"We have five members aft!"

"Can you see the aft section?"

"No, too much seas coming over!"

While Captain Burgess could communicate with the Coast Guard, he had no way of doing the same with his men on the aft section. Selleck tried to use a battery-operated megaphone, but the screeching wind and booming seas drowned out his shouts. Both men on the bow realized the ship's life raft was on the stern and decided the best course of action was to stay in the wheelhouse, hoping each half of the *Poling* would remain afloat until the Coast Guard arrived. If the boat started to sink, they would have to jump ship, but they knew they could only survive in icy waters for ten to fifteen minutes.

The nearest Coast Guard station was Gloucester, where the cutters *Cape George* and *Cape Cross* were temporarily berthed at their heavy weather mooring at the State Pier. Upon receiving the Mayday, Gloucester Coast Guard asked all nearby vessels to proceed to the scene and dispatched both ninety-five-foot cutters, as well as its forty-one- and forty-four-foot patrol boats to the rescue. Frank Quirk heard the Mayday as well and radioed the Coast Guard that he was heading to the *Poling* to assist in whatever way he could. Quirk was accompanied by Bill Lee and the wild but beloved Herb MacDonald, known as "Captain Mac." Mac, like Lee, was an experienced mariner, making much of his living taking yachts down the eastern coastline from Gloucester to Florida in the fall and then bringing them back up in the spring, often alone. Lee says all three men aboard the *Can Do* never hesitated to head out into the storm. "This was something you just do when other fishermen or mariners are in danger of drowning; it's like firemen responding to an alarm. Mac and I trusted Frank, and we knew he'd make the right decisions."

Coast Guard Group Boston radioed the *Can Do:* "Can Do, *what's your ETA for the vessel?"*

"An hour from my position here," replied Frank. *"We are just coming by Ten Pound Island* [in Gloucester Harbor]."

"You are proceeding, is that correct?"

"Roger, correct."

The *Cape George* was able to get under way within ten minutes of receiving the call, but the *Cape Cross* had just come off patrol and was undergoing maintenance, slowing its departure for forty-five minutes. (Cutters usually spend a week in "Alpha Status," either patrolling or ready to leave berth in fifteen minutes. This is typically followed by two weeks in "Charlie Status" when the cutter is in port, often for maintenance.) Aboard the *Cape Cross* was eighteen-year-old Larry Zaker, just three weeks out of boot camp. On that January day he received a harrowing initiation into his new profession: "Our crew of fourteen was in Charlie Status at the State Pier in Gloucester, having just done a week's patrol. The call came in that a tanker was breaking up a few miles out from Gloucester. The *Cape George* was in Alpha Status and they immediately went out. It was dog-crap weather, so I was glad we were in Charlie Status and probably wouldn't go. But a couple minutes after the Mayday we were also told to get ready. We got under way in a little more than an hour and as soon as we passed the breakwater we were slammed. The seas were so bad I said to myself, 'This is the day I'm gonna die.' I had just come out of boot camp, and this was way more than I bargained for. The winds were howling at sixty miles per hour and some of the seas topped thirty feet. Waves were crashing over the boat and the XPO [executive petty officer] told a few of us to get down below to the mess deck. I was also told to put on a wet suit in case I was needed to help get crewmen aboard the cutter. Even though all the items on the ship had been secured, there was still stuff flying around the galley. In no time I got seasick, and so did everyone else. Guys were puking in anything they could find. Most of these guys had never been sick before, but they hadn't encountered conditions like this. It was so rough I remember the refrigerator was ripped right off the bulkhead. We couldn't see

anything down below, but we were getting tossed around so violently we wondered what we were getting into. Most of us were
half-conscious, we were so ill. I don't know how the skipper and
the XPO were able to stay up on the bridge. They had to be as
sick as the rest of us, yet they still piloted the cutter. In my
twenty-four years in the Coast Guard since then, I've never been
out in conditions like that, and I served for three years in Alaska,
where the waters of the Bering Strait have some of the most severe weather on the planet."

✳

The *Can Do* was slowed by the huge seas but continued east to
the *Chester Poling*. Frank was in communication with all the boats
as well as with the onshore Coast Guard coordinators, telling
them, "*We are taking a real beating, but making progress.*" Frank
was also able to raise Captain Burgess on the radio, offering encouragement, knowing that Burgess faced death at any moment.

"Can Do to Chester Poling."

"*This is* Poling."

"*The ninety-five* [Cape George] *is up ahead, and we are going by
the number two buoy. The forty-four is also up ahead. Help is on the
way; hang in there.*"

"*When you come,*" said Burgess, "*get the crew off first, and I'll
stand by. We might have to get a towline. . . .*"

Ever pragmatic, Frank responded, "*Well, let's just worry about
people first, and then we'll see about that.*"

While Frank was making progress, the forty-one-footer was
being tossed about like flotsam. Skippered by coxswain John
Burlingham, the boat had lost most of its electronics, and the
shrieking wind made it difficult to be heard on the radio. Burlingham could not head back to port because he was afraid the boat
would capsize if a wave caught them broadside before the turn
was completed; if that happened, he and his crew were as good as

dead. Even the largest of ships never try to be beam-on in huge seas, and the forty-one-footer was the smallest boat trying to aid the tanker. Burlingham's only option was to motor all the way to the tanker and then try to make the turn on *Poling*'s lee side, where he hoped the waves might be a bit smaller.

Commanding Officer Paradis at Station Gloucester understood their predicament, and he radioed the *Cape George*, "*Be advised that the forty-one-footer is just holding its own and is trying to turn around and come back in. The forty-four is still out there and trying to find you.*"

Frank was monitoring these communications and was on the lookout for both the forty-one and forty-four, knowing they were vulnerable. Frank felt a little vulnerable himself and radioed the *Cape Cross*, "*Don't run me over on the way out; you might not see me with seas so big.*"

When Boston heard this, they asked the *Can Do* for an update on weather conditions. Frank responded, "*Twenty to twenty-five seas. It's really howling; we are two miles east of the number two buoy.*"

While the *Cape Cross*, the *Can Do*, and the other boats were making their way to the scene, the *Cape George* arrived at the stricken tanker in just under an hour. The temperature had risen to forty degrees, but heavy rain kept visibility to an eighth of a mile. Sea conditions had deteriorated further since the original Mayday, with waves at twenty-five feet and the wind at sixty knots, as measured by the anemometer attached to the *Cape George*. James Loew, commanding officer of the *Cape George*, attempted to maneuver his cutter alongside the bow section of the tanker. He quickly abandoned the effort, however, realizing the seas were so violent that his own boat might be crushed or swamped by the stern of the *Poling*.

Loew radioed Captain Burgess, "*Your bow is really swinging around. Is there any way that your crew could get into a life raft and get away from the boat? Then we could pick them up?*"

Burgess replied this could not be done, and Loew considered his next option. He radioed Gloucester, *"She's breaking up more than ever,"* and requested a helicopter be flown to the scene. Gloucester relayed the message to Boston, but no one was optimistic a chopper could fly in that weather. Loew next tried using a throwing gun to fire a projectile attached to a light line that could then be used to guide a life raft to the tanker. Twice the *Cape George* fired the gun, and each time the strong winds and the unsteady platform conspired to send the line into the ocean, short of its target. Loew considered floating a raft toward the tanker, but the two sections of the *Chester Poling* were finally pulling apart the narrow deck plating that connected them. The bow and stern suddenly separated, then pounded upon each other, with the bow listing heavily as seas poured into the wheelhouse portholes.

The forty-four-foot patrol boat arrived on the scene with Charlie Bucko as the coxswain. He radioed to the other boats that his radar had been knocked out but he could see the tanker. The *Cape George* asked if the forty-four, given its smaller size, could get alongside the tanker. But the forty-four had the same problem as the cutter: the tanker sections were rising and falling in heavy seas, making it impossible to get closer. Bucko maneuvered his boat as close as he dared and held position, ready to act if any of the tanker's crewmen leaped into the sea.

Soon Frank on the *Can Do* and Burlingham on the forty-one arrived on scene. Burlingham recalls that his mission was complicated when a particularly large wave hit the boat, causing a crewman to do "a free fall," injuring his back and neck. Burlingham couldn't turn around because he needed to get out into deeper water. The waves were systemically ripping everything off the forty-one from the antennae to the life rings. Men on the *Cape George* who saw the forty-one thought for sure it was going to flip over backward. "The bow did go straight up a couple times," says

Burlingham, "and it seemed like it would just keep on going over, right back on itself, which would have driven the stern under."

Burlingham and his crew made a decision and announced it on the radio: *"I'm going to attempt to get back. I've got a man down with a pretty good back injury—he says his legs are going numb."*

Gloucester asked, *"Who is the injured man?"*

"It's the new seaman, Cavanaugh. He has not moved, but he's conscious."

Bill Cavanaugh remembers the fall he took as if it happened yesterday: "We would climb up these twenty-to-thirty-foot waves and then at the crest go ripping and crashing down, because the wind made the back of the wave steeper than the front. I was down below preparing a Stokes Litter [a wire basket to scoop survivors out of the ocean] when we climbed up a huge sea. Then the boat fell off the crest like an elevator would drop if it lost its cables. I was literally weightless, being pushed up against the ceiling for a couple seconds; then when the boat smashed down I slammed into the deck. I remember looking at this pair of legs beneath my body wondering whose they were because I couldn't feel anything. I later found out I had broken my neck. On the ride back in I thought I was paralyzed for life. In fact, it took several days of being in traction before there was any movement or sensation in my legs. When the nerves first started responding the pain was almost unbearable, and that went on for almost two weeks."

Frank heard the communications from the forty-one. Knowing they had an injured man onboard and were without navigational electronics, Frank radioed the forty-one and told them he would be looking for them to guide the boat back to Gloucester, adding, *"I've never seen seas like this."* Quirk escorted the boat back and then turned right around, steaming back to the tanker, making better time because the wind had blown the tanker sections toward land.

Meanwhile Captain Burgess knew the bow wouldn't stay afloat much longer. He radioed the *Cape George: "As soon as she starts to go down we are going to jump. She's breaking up now more than ever. The bow will sink first if anything does happen. If worse comes to worst we're going to have to jump, I guess."*

Loew shouted for the captain to hang on a little longer, because his crew was going to try to float a life raft to Burgess and Selleck and then haul them back. Again, however, conditions prevented success. Loew was relaying this latest setback to Gloucester when he suddenly barked, *"Both men are in the water! Don't have time to talk."*

Five minutes later Loew shouted, *"I just picked up one man in the water and have another man in the water! Stand by."*

The man the *Cape George* picked up was Captain Burgess, but they were unable to get Selleck on the first pass. The freezing water all but paralyzed Selleck, and he was unable to swim toward the cutter. Instead he managed to kick off his sea boots and roll over on his back, drifting upwind from the submerged bow. Selleck later told the Coast Guard, "The only thing that kept me alive was that I knew the cutter *Cape George* knew they had missed me and that I was still out there. There were times when I was going to give up. I was going to take off my life jacket and forget it, but they came back and threw heaving lines. I couldn't grab the heaving lines because my hands were pretty well frozen and I didn't have the strength. I got hold of the net they had over the side. I grabbed it the first time and let go, and then I grabbed it the second time . . . they dragged me aboard." Selleck was fortunate the *Cape George* had a scramble net aboard. (Such nets are about five feet wide, with mesh in six-inch squares.) Because Selleck's fingers were frozen, he was unable to grasp the net, but he somehow managed to thread his arms through the mesh before being hauled up like a stunned fish.

Bucko, on the forty-four, stayed on the scene to assist the *Cape George* if needed. But his boat suffered the same fate as the forty-one, losing its navigational equipment. Moreover, the seas had taken a toll on his crew. Engineer Charlie Krocker had been knocked unconscious while making an adjustment in the engine room, and Bucko knew Krocker needed medical attention fast. Bucko also was very aware that he was putting his entire crew at risk if he kept the boat out without an engineer in extreme seas. Should the engines die and not be immediately restarted the forty-four would capsize. Once Bucko heard that the much larger *Cape Cross* would arrive within a couple of minutes, he made a decision to return to port and get the injured man medical attention. First, however, he needed to turn the vessel. He motored in close to the lee side of the *Poling*'s stern, carefully watching the waves while judging the distance separating the waves. He made his move between waves, working the wheel and the throttle, turning the boat as quickly as possible, then dashing back toward Gloucester and a waiting ambulance.

While Burgess and Selleck were being rescued, the wind was blowing the stern section toward the rocky shore of Gloucester's Eastern Point. This was fortuitous, because it meant less travel time for the cutter *Cape Cross* to arrive on scene, but it also posed a hazard—if they didn't get the men off quickly, the stern would smash into the rocky coast where churning surf would make a rescue impossible. Jim Loew expressed his concern: *"We are blowing really fast toward Eastern Point; the tanker may hit the breakwater soon."*

Luckily, a Coast Guard helicopter from Coast Guard Air Station Cape Cod—whose pilot and crew risked their lives flying in such conditions—and the *Cape Cross* arrived on the scene just after Loew picked up Burgess and Selleck. *Cape Cross* crewman Larry Zaker recalls it took approximately two hours to get to the tanker, "but it seemed like an eternity. When we got on scene the skipper told us to get up on deck. It was absolutely horrendous outside. Through the rain I could see a section of the ship [the bow] sticking straight up, and there were fifty-gallon drums all over the place."

The *Cape George* suggested that the *Cross* try to get a life raft to the stern while the *George* turned toward the harbor to get the two *Chester Poling* mariners medical treatment. Loew's voice crackled on the radio: *"The first person wasn't too bad, but the second one we picked up is in bad shape. We have no more life rings, no more projectiles* [for firing line], *so we'd appreciate it if you give it a try. The captain says he thought the stern would float longer than the bow. But it's drifting pretty fast."*

The stern presented even bigger problems than the bow, because there was no radio communication with the five trapped men. As the *Cape George* departed, the *Cape Cross* maneuvered closer, and the helicopter, piloted by Lieutenant James B. Wallace, hovered above the stern, struggling to maintain position in the sixty-knot winds. Wallace kept the helicopter approximately eighty feet above the water and only twenty feet above the stern of the *Poling*. "We wanted," says Wallace, "to be as close as possible so I'd have some kind of visual reference with the tanker. The conditions were absolutely awful, and I even radioed my base that if they didn't hear from us for a while that meant we had crashed. I knew if we went down we'd all die, but since we could see the men on the tanker there was no way we were going to abort."

The helicopter hoist operator, Petty Officer Reginald Lavoie, lowered a steel rescue basket with a guide line attached, doing his best to get the basket in optimum position while the chopper was being buffeted up and down and from side to side. Joao Gilmete, the *Chester Poling*'s cook, was the first to enter the basket, but the basket—with the cook hanging on inside—was pushed by the wind into the deck awning pipe framework and then spilled over the side of the ship and into the sea. Fortunately, the cook held on and Lavoie was able to raise the basket from the water, bringing the cook into the helicopter unharmed.

The basket was lowered again, and this time it was Able Seaman Joao daRosa's turn to be rescued. Earlier he had changed out of his wet clothing, but in his haste to get back on deck he forgot to put his life jacket back on. DaRosa was especially anxious to get off the tanker, as the seas had pushed the stern to within two thousand yards of Eastern Point, where the surf smashing against the rocks made a thunderous clamor. Instead of waiting for the basket to reach an open part of the deck, daRosa climbed atop some oil drums and tried to step into the basket as it hovered on the outside of the ship's railing. As daRosa reached for the basket and raised one leg, the basket swung away, and daRosa fell on the outside of the railing. Amazingly, he gained a partial grip on the wet railing and struggled to hang on. The bouncing action of the next wave, however, loosened his grip and he was unable to hold on. DaRosa tumbled into the ocean, surfaced once, then sank again. He reappeared a second time, only now facedown, floating with arms spreadeagle, drifting away from the stern. Pilot Wallace immediately banked the helicopter lower toward the floating seaman and Lavoie positioned the basket downwind of daRosa, just below the water's surface. The pilot inched the helo closer to the victim and Lavoie attempted to scoop daRosa up by trailing the rescue basket beneath him. The waves kept the unconscious sailor in constant motion, rising and falling, and the basket could not be aligned for the scoop. Wallace was faced with a difficult decision: keep trying to scoop daRosa or return to the stern of the *Poling* before it went down with the remaining men onboard. Looking below at the facedown floating body of daRosa, Wallace knew the man was dead, and he turned the helicopter back toward the living.

Frank heard that daRosa's body was drifting from the scene and radioed that *"we are at the breakwater and we'll try and pick up that last man as soon as possible!"*

Three men were now left onboard the stern, knowing that both jumping overboard toward the *Cape Cross* and trying to enter the rescue basket were fraught with risk. It was a crapshoot either way, and the wrong decision could cost them their lives. At first it seemed they had chosen the basket as the chief mate, Charles Lord, attempted to enter it. He, too, almost fell into the sea as the basket swung away. The aft section was now listing more than forty-five degrees to starboard, and the crewmen feared it would roll any second, taking them with it into the vortex below.

The trio made sure their life vests were fastened, then grabbed life rings and jumped overboard.

Larry Zaker says, "We saw the men jump and the skipper was able to get the *Cape Cross* near two of them. One minute they were right next to the cutter and then a wave would carry them off. I remember the next thing that happened like it was yesterday. Charlie Hart, the master chief, came to me and shouted, 'Can you swim?' When I said yes he then said, 'I'm gonna put the swimmer's harness on you.' Again I thought I was gonna die. I wasn't really afraid of the waves, but I thought for sure I'd get sucked under the boat and cut into pieces by the prop. When I was younger I'd seen a friend almost get his arm severed by a boat's motor, so maybe that's why I was more worried about that than drowning."

While Zaker was placed in the harness two of the drowning men were able to grab onto a rope and wooden ladder hanging over the side of the cutter. Crewmen reached over the side and began hauling the men, whose saturated winter clothes and jackets added an additional one hundred pounds of weight. Zaker helped haul the men successfully aboard and avoided being low-ered into the seas himself.

The third man still in the water was Chief Mate Charles Lord, a nonswimmer. He had floated away from the other two men and was about to be lost in the swirling seas when Wallace spotted him. Lord wasn't moving, but he was floating faceup on his back. The chopper pilot ordered the rescue basket lowered again, and he flew slowly over Lord, towing the basket behind in the water. "We lowered all two hundred feet of cable," says Wallace. "I re-member one of the crew said there was a good chance that the ca-ble might get wrapped around the victim's neck, and I shouted back, 'That's the chance we take; if we don't get him right away he's dead from the cold.'" On the third pass the basket aligned perfectly with an immobile Lord, and he was scooped in and up-ward to the safety of the helicopter. "Of all the people I've res-cued over the years," says Wallace, "that guy was the closest to death of them all. I wonder if he knows how lucky he was. Get-ting him in the basket in those kinds of seas was like threading a needle in a hurricane—we all got lucky."

Aboard the *Cape Cross,* one of the two survivors was on the edge of death. To stabilize and warm the hypothermic man a crew member was wrapped in blankets with him. Zaker says they raced back into Gloucester to get the crewmen to emergency care: "It was just as bad heading in, but quicker since the wind had blown us and the tanker section back toward land. The XPO later told me that when we first got on the scene we went right by the tanker because he couldn't see it over the waves. We never saw the *Cape George* or the *Can Do,* but I had heard of Frank's reputation as someone reliable. It's amazing that he even went out there in a forty-nine-foot boat—we were in a ninety-five-footer and it was awful."

The helicopter and the *Cape Cross* left the scene, but Quirk and his crew continued looking for the body of daRosa. Frank gave a final update: "*Seas are twenty to twenty-five with some up to thirty. Seeing some debris but not spotting the stern section* [it had sunk]. *We'll keep looking, but the radar is not doing too good because half the time the antenna is almost in the water. It's a miracle anyone got off alive; you wouldn't believe it out here.*"

✳

Frank Quirk hated to leave anyone at sea, even the dead, thinking of the effect on the family. In his career as a pilot boat operator, he often searched for missing sailors, without pay, just because it was the right thing to do. Warren Andrews said, "That was Frank, always thinking about others. I recall when a diver drowned off Magnolia, Frank spent forty-eight straight hours looking for the man—a man he never even knew."

For their actions in aiding the mariners aboard the *Chester Poling,* Frank, Charlie Bucko, Jim Loew, and the other skippers involved received Gloucester's prestigious Mariner's Medal. Frank also received the Coast Guard's Public Service Commendation. In a letter to Frank, Rear Admiral J. P. Stewart wrote: "Your humanitarian interest and concern for the plight of a fellow mariner is in the true tradition of those who follow the sea. Your preparedness and willingness to offer assistance, especially in the face of such adversities, are heartily appreciated and most welcome." Jim Loew, *Cape George* skipper, expressed the sentiments of all the Coast Guard personnel involved that day: "Just to know Frank was heading out to the *Poling* was real comforting because any one of us could have gotten into trouble and needed help. The *Can Do* was aptly named."

Later, in a formal service at the Gloucester Coast Guard Station, Frank was honored personally by the admiral. The press was there, and a picture was taken that, in retrospect, is rather chilling.

In the photo, Frank Quirk and Charlie Bucko are shaking hands in the warm spring sunshine, discussing that terrible storm that split the *Chester Poling* in two.

A year later, the next storm that drew these two men together for a rescue was just as ferocious and twice as dangerous.

| 6 |

A STORM LIKE
NO OTHER

The intensity of the Blizzard of 1978 surpassed that of any other winter storm ever experienced in southern New England in the last one hundred years. This monster was not just a blizzard but really a winter hurricane, with winds officially clocked at 92 miles per hour and unofficial recordings exceeding 100 miles per hour. (Meteorologists refer to this storm as an "extra tropical hurricane," which has a cold core distinguishing it from the usual autumn hurricane.) Satellite photos taken throughout Monday, February 6, show the cloud mass of the storm becoming more and more organized, taking on the well-defined look of a hurricane as the storm intensified and moved up the eastern seaboard, parallel to the coasts of New Jersey, Long Island, New York, and Rhode Island.

The storm developed when an upper-level low-pressure system moved southeastward out of Canada and intercepted a sea-level low-pressure system off the mid-Atlantic coast. The upper-level system tapped the potential energy resident in the offshore low and in a sense breathed new life into the relatively dormant sea-level low-pressure system. The result was an explosively intensifying counterclockwise circulation that drew in surrounding air currents and blew them straight up and out of the organizing mass. A sleeping lion had begun to stir.

The storm headed north along the coast, strengthening rapidly as it picked up moisture and heat energy from the Gulf Stream–fed ocean while pulling in arctic air from the northwest. As the storm approached Long Island late that Monday night, it stalled due to a blocking ridge of cold, heavy polar air to the north. This caused the storm to gather all its strength and hurl it at the Bay State's coast for hours upon hours, time for the wind to generate great waves and drive the ocean ashore. In fact, as is common with such nor'easters, the strongest winds were some distance north of the storm's center, placing them off the Gloucester coastline. Analysis of weather charts showed isobars radiating out from the storm's center in all directions but packed closest together to the north of the storm. Each isobar represents a line of pressure, and lines close together depict great pressure changes over a short distance, or what meteorologists refer to as a tight pressure gradient. The clashing of pressure systems causes the most severe wind. The isobars on a weather map are reminiscent of the contours on a topographical map. Just as the elevation lines of a topographical map clustered together indicate the steepest hills, the presence of isobars close together on a weather map depicts the greatest pressure gradients. And just as water flows faster down that steep slope depicted on a topographical map, the air flows that much faster where the pressure gradient is tight on the weather map. The air is trying to rush from the dome of high pressure to the deep valley of a low-pressure center, albeit in a more circuitous spiraling motion due to the earth's rotation. On that fateful night in February 1978, Gloucester lay under the steepest part of that atmospheric slope, between a behemoth high-pressure area centered near Hudson Bay and a very intense low-pressure system just south of Long Island. The resulting winds churned the sea into mountains of water.

Snowstorms can pelt New England anytime from November through April, but February has often been the month for the most severe snowstorms, in the form of nor'easters. Commonly, December and January have a jet stream that runs directly across the country, but in February variations to the jet stream occur more frequently, causing arctic air to plunge southward and collide with low-pressure systems and the fuel of subtropical air off the southeast United States coast. The offspring is a coastal nor'easter with the potential to intensify explosively, a process meteorologists term *bomb genesis*.

Adding to the potential for a significant snowfall along coastal New England is the fact that ocean temperatures usually reach their coldest during February. Had the *Chester Poling* sinking and rescue occurred in February rather than January, it's likely there would have been more than one casualty. The storm that broke the tanker in two was vicious enough, but rain rather than snow was falling, keeping the temperature just high enough to prevent icing on the decks of the *Cape George* and *Cape Cross*. Although the helicopter crew that rescued several of the seamen risked their lives going out in such conditions, they never would have even considered flying had it been snowing during that gale.

An analysis of a report conducted by the National Oceanic and Atmospheric Administration regarding the Blizzard of '78 reveals that overall, most weather models were fairly accurate, predicting that the storm would be major and produce blizzard conditions. Coastal wind forecasting, however, was the one area that was cited for inaccuracies, and the report called for better coastal equipment to monitor wind speeds, saying: "There are not enough surface wind reports to support detailed coastal marine forecasts." One region where underestimates of wind velocity occurred was the Massachusetts coast: "Model Output Statistics forecasts underestimated the sustained wind in the Boston area by a significant amount." The men aboard the *Can Do*, the forty-four, the *Cape George*, and the *Decisive* found this out firsthand.

Along the coast the storm exploded just as the forty-four and the *Can Do* set out to sea, which was about the time when coastal communities began experiencing the havoc created by a surging ocean advancing far beyond its usual shoreline levels. In Rockport, cars were flung into the Old Harbor along with a house. Bearskin Neck houses were crushed, then ripped by the seas, including the red wooden building known as Motif #1, a popular subject for artists. Car-size granite blocks protecting nearby Pigeon Cove, which had stood for a century, were knocked over as if made of Styrofoam. A few miles south, Marblehead Neck was cut off from the rest of the town as boulders the size of armchairs were hurled onto the causeway. In Nahant a man drowned as seas flooded his basement apartment. On Boston's south shore, communities such as Scituate, Hull, and Marshfield were hit equally as hard as boats were ripped from their moorings and dumped on streets, in front yards, and sometimes right on top of houses. The scene was chaotic, with cars, boats, furniture, and appliances all mixed together, bobbing in the rising water that surrounded entire neighborhoods.

Up and down the Massachusetts coast, seawalls were flattened and hundreds of residents became trapped in their houses, encircled by swirling water that prevented them from running to higher ground. Police and fire departments were inundated with calls but often could not reach the danger areas because of flooded and snow-clogged roadways. The National Guard was called in to bring heavy equipment, such as front-end loaders and amphibious vehicles, to the affected towns, but it took several hours for them to arrive. In the meantime, trapped residents waited out the night without heat or power.

One resident described how the evening conditions steadily worsened and with each passing hour her fear increased: "At first the house was shaken by the howling wind; then it was the spray off the ocean. Later the ocean itself was banging on the house. But what really shook me was when the sea started flinging fist-size cobbles into the walls, making sounds like gunshots. We knew our home's walls were starting to give way, but we just had to wait until help arrived—there was nowhere we could go."

Particularly hard hit was Revere, just north of Boston and south of Salem. Fires broke out in several houses due to electrical problems and flooded cellars, but firefighters could not reach the homes due to impassible streets. Three homes were totally leveled and several others suffered extensive damage from fire. However, it was the breaching of the seawall that did the most damage, and that occurred at 8:30 p.m., about the same time McIlvride and crew lost their engines.

"I thought I was going to die," reported Revere resident Anthony Chiarella to *Time* magazine, describing how he retreated to his attic with his dog, wondering when the house would be swept away. Other families slept in shifts so they wouldn't be caught unawares if the walls gave way. One elderly woman sat up on her kitchen sink as the water rose around her. All the doors were blocked by chunks of ice, so she started to go out the window to try to swim for higher ground. Luckily a neighbor saw her and told her to hang on. He then put on his scuba gear, swam over, and helped her swim with him to his house.

The Beachmont section of Revere saw the worst devastation. Homes were bobbing down the streets, and many people thought they would literally be swallowed up by the sea. Ginny Deveau huddled with her family crying, praying, and sipping whiskey.

She described her experience to the *Boston Globe:* "When we looked out, we saw the water was up to the level of the sea wall, which in my whole life, I had never seen. I looked at everyone and said, 'We're goners.' I never thought we'd get out of there alive."

All across Revere people huddled in dark attics, living in utter terror that their houses would collapse beneath them. Although they could not see anything, the sounds of rushing water surrounding the houses were terrifying and every now and then they would be startled by a loud thud. The noise was from either a boulder or car hitting the house or, in some cases, floating houses bumping into each other. Lucky residents were saved by huge front-end loaders, which picked them up from their windows with its bucket.

The ordeal had a lasting impact, what we would now refer to as post-traumatic stress syndrome. A woman at a shelter was interviewed on TV and asked if she was anxious to get home. "I'm scared to go home," she said. "I don't want to go home. I don't want any part of that house. I'm terrified. I've got a thirty-thousand-dollar mortgage and pay two-thousand-dollars in taxes. For what? I've got an indoor swimming pool in my house now." Another Revere woman added, "Our home is gone. We feel like refugees, with our little plastic bag of clothes. It took something like this to make us realize how helpless we are against the elements. The ocean just took over." These women had plenty of other "refugees" for company: in Revere alone, two thousand helpless and homeless people were sheltered at the high school.

The storm surge that pounded Revere and other coastal communities was being assisted by a new moon tide, often called a spring tide, which creates tides higher than normal. On the night of February 6 the moon was also in perigee (closest to the earth), which means the sun, earth, and moon were aligned in such a way that both the sun and the moon were pulling on the oceans. The largest astronomical tides occur when both spring tides and perigee tides occur simultaneously, which was exactly what happened during the blizzard. Couple that phenomenon with the onshore hurricane-force winds produced by the Blizzard and you have a recipe for disaster. In essence, the moon, sun, and wind were aligned, in perfect sync, to produce the most damage possible. If one was so inclined as to look beyond coincidence, it was almost as if the storm had celestial help, in a sinister plot to do harm.

Inland the problem was snow. Snow falling harder than anyone had ever seen. Commuters were lulled into thinking they could make it home without too much trouble, because they had just been through a record-breaking snowfall three weeks earlier with no major traffic headaches. But on February 6 people were caught off guard. Weather forecasts had called for snow to start in the early-morning hours, and when commuters awoke to snow-free skies some figured the storm had gone out to sea or would be relatively benign. Employers thought the same thing, and even though it started snowing in the Boston area around 11:00 a.m., most employers were reluctant to release their employees. The lucky workers—or perhaps the smart ones—didn't wait for permission to leave when they saw how hard it was snowing by noontime. Those who left between noon and 2:00 p.m. generally made it home, while those who waited for an official office closing (which in most businesses came between 2:00 and 3:00 p.m.) found themselves in gridlocked traffic. Rush hour came early, but traffic wasn't moving, because the snow had caused enough spinouts to clog the highways. Two of the worst areas were Route 128, the main artery that encircles Boston, and Interstate 95, connecting Massachusetts and Rhode Island. Thousands of people were stuck in their cars, waiting helplessly as snow and drifts entombed them. Many were rescued Monday evening by police, National Guard, or private citizens on snowmobiles, but scores of others spent a harrowing night trapped in their cars. Some died of exposure when they ran out of gas trying to keep the car warm or while walking for help, and others succumbed to carbon monoxide poisoning caused by buildups of the deadly fumes in the cars.

The governors of Massachusetts and Rhode Island found that even with the aid of the National Guard, their emergency personnel were overwhelmed, and federal troops and equipment were called in. Every effort was made to keep one runway open at Boston's Logan Airport and another at Providence's Green Airport to allow the giant army cargo planes to land. Snowplow operators worked around the clock to keep sixty-foot-wide strips snow-free the length of the runways, but these efforts were hampered by the wind—eight-foot drifts were piling up as fast as they could push the snow aside. When the federal troops did arrive, they were able to relieve some of the National Guard and local police who were needed to establish order in Boston and Providence where looting was occurring.

The American Red Cross reported ninety-nine deaths and more than thirty-nine thousand people stranded or forced from their homes by the storm. More than seventeen hundred homes were destroyed or damaged. Most of the deaths and destruction occurred in Massachusetts and Rhode Island, which took the full brunt of the storm. However, Maine, New Hampshire, Connecticut, and New York were hard hit, especially eastern areas, and as in Massachusetts the coastal areas saw the seas turn furious in just a short period of time. On Monday morning two men from New York thought they had plenty of time to run their seventeen-foot Boston Whaler across Long Island Sound before the storm hit. The area of ocean they had to cross was a relatively protected stretch of the sound between southeastern Connecticut and Suffolk County, New York. The men were experienced boaters and figured that if the seas were bad they would simply turn around. They took an extra precaution in case of trouble, telling a friend who was a marina owner that they would call when they reached the other side. If they did not make the call something was amiss and he and his crew should come out and get them in his much larger boat.

Despite bouncing through choppy seas and slicing through a biting wind, the men made good time and visibility was adequate enough for the boaters to see coastal markers and channel buoys. They had almost reached their destination and the warmth of home when the engine quit. Working on the small components of an engine in cold temperatures is never easy, but the increasing wave size made it a real challenge and nothing the men tried could make the engine turn over. Adding to their problems were mounting waves, which were pushing them offshore, occasionally breaking over the transom, and forcing the men to bail. As they fought back the sickening feeling that they had made a terrible mistake, they debated dropping anchor but were afraid the bow would ride high and a gust of wind would catch it and flip the boat. And so they drifted, fighting not just the sea but also their own mounting fear.

After an hour they were stunned to hear the blare of a horn, immediately recognizing it as the New London Light that marks the mouth of the Thames River. They were far off course, and the wind was pushing them into open water. They took a gamble and dropped anchor but quickly brought it back up when the boat took on too much water. Now, with night falling, the seas were taking them toward the open ocean, and they knew no one would ever find them in the darkness. They shivered as the boat pitched wildly through the raging night, and bailed as best they could, unable to even see each other. A creeping numbness spread through their bodies, and they felt the urge to give in to the cold and simply lie down in the boat and let death carry them to sleep.

At dawn, lady luck shined on the men, barely alive. They had drifted fifty miles but had been pushed to Long Island's North Fork and Mattituck Inlet, and instead of crashing into the rocks, the men were propelled toward a sandy section of beach and safety. Although conditions in the sound were nothing like those in the open seas off Gloucester, it was a miracle that they were alive.

※

Just before the forty-four hit the underwater obstruction, Warren Andrews had made a series of telephone calls to members of the Northeast Surf Patrol. He explained the forty-four was lost somewhere in Salem Sound, and he asked Surf Patrol members to take up positions along the coast of Beverly, on the northwest side of Salem Sound. He wanted them to keep a lookout for the lights on the forty-four and if they should see anything radio back immediately. Warren would then radio the forty-four crew and be able to tell them exactly where they were and, with the aid of the Surf Patrol spotters, help guide them into Beverly Harbor.

Around 9:00 p.m. a Surf Patrol shore spotter thought he saw the lights of the forty-four and excitedly called Warren: *"Unit one-seventy-two with possible sighting! I'm at Hospital Point Light* [in Beverly] *and looking due east and I just caught three flashes of a light. It might be the Coast Guard boat. If it is it's in close to shore. It's a white to white-green light, kind of a high-intensity type light.*

A few minutes later the spotter called Warren again: *"Warren, I just saw a flash, and if he's heading in, he's close enough."*

The spotter was concerned because the shoreline is a jumble of jagged rocks and with fifteen-foot seas within the sound the forty-four would be crushed on the rocks if it got too close. Using his handheld FM radio, the spotter was able to talk directly with McIlvride and warn him away from the shore. The forty-four crew now kept an extra-sharp lookout and made sure they didn't veer any closer to the north where the spiked granite shoreline lies. They still believed they could grope their way into safety, avoid having to drop anchor, and attempt to ride out the storm. McIlvride also knew that if worse came to worst—if the engines quit and the anchor wouldn't bite—they might be able to survive by going below and letting the boat crash into shore. "One of the men who trained me," says McIlvride, "used to say if your worst nightmare comes true and the forty-four is heading into rocks or the shore, go down below and batten all hatches. He thought that since the boat was built like a tank, we might be bloody and bruised, but we'd have a shot at surviving."

The one weakness in this approach was that the crew had to have *time* to get below and secure the main hatch. And since they would only resort to this tactic as a last-ditch effort to save themselves, that meant the four men were going to stay up on the bridge as long as the engines were running. In the dark, however, they could be fifty feet from shore and not know it until it was too late, when there was no time to scramble below. They could not see the shoreline or hear the crashing surf on rocks because of the shrieking wind.

The crew of McIlvride, Krom, Desrosiers, and Mathurin figured they had made it this far and, with a little luck, would find their way to safe harbor. In fact, they staked their lives on their ability to maneuver their boat in ledge-infested waters rather than leaving their fate in the hands of the anchor or locking themselves below.

SWEPT OVER WITH
A CRASH

The news that the forty-four had been sighted was certainly good, showing that progress was being made, and if they were east of Hospital Point in Beverly, they were just a couple miles away from safety. The spotter, however, reported they were just two hundred yards off the rocky ledge of Hospital Point, and Paradis immediately considered the shallow water. He stood up in the communications room, running his fingers through his white hair while massaging his temples to relieve his headache. Then he barked a question to McIlvride: *"Is your fathometer working?"*

"Not clear, repeat again."

"Is your fathometer operable?"

"It's working but not accurately."

"I suggest you take your lead line out and sound the bottom and find out what your depth is. If you have shallow enough water or water that will hold your anchor, I suggest you throw it over. Let me know before you do."

"Roger."

Just as before, the crew was reluctant to throw their anchor over. "We did not want to drop anchor so close to safety, nor did we want to tie up to any buoy," says McIlvride. "We wanted to get the hell in on our own." They held off on sounding the bottom, which would be near impossible with the boat rolling and pitching, and instead continued plowing west as slowly as possible. Luckily, they were never faced with the choice of directly disobeying their commander: "The radar came back a little," says McIlvride, "maybe from less snow clutter since we had some protection now that we were well inside the sound and hugging the north shoreline."

"We have our radar back at this time. We are attempting to navigate into Beverly Harbor."

This was the best news Paradis has had all night, and the relief was clear in his voice: *"Ahhh, am I to assume you are a little out of jeopardy and are seeing your way clear?"*

"That's a roger. For the time being. As long as we have radar, I'm going to try to work my way into the harbor."

"Do you have your blue light energized?"

"Roger, we have our blue light on."

"Remain to the eastern side close to shore, and I'll see if I can get Salem Control to send some vehicles down there to see if they see a blue light and give you some direction to some dock to tie up to."

"It appears we've blown quite a ways south, and appears we've gone quite a ways west, further west than the tanker."

"What do you estimate your position? Marblehead area?"

"Negative, we're right in the middle of Salem Harbor and Salem Sound on the western side. About three-quarters of a mile from Salem Willows. We don't have a chart. They are water soaked and not much use to us. Can you tell us about how much water we have here?"

"About ten feet of water. Use your chart as much as possible. Identify three landmarks ahead of you if you're heading in the northwest

direction. And get yourself into sheltered waters, but make sure you identify three landmarks."

"Roger. We got a light dead ahead. Stand by and we'll get back to you when we identify it."

Warren Andrews then broke in: *"The light that the forty-four is seeing is probably the big searchlight at Jubilee Yacht Club in Beverly Harbor, which would be on the starboard. We requested they turn it on and point it out to the channel."*

Paradis responded to Warren, *"As soon as we can identify their position we will need your help to vector him in to some safe mooring."*

Paradis to forty-four: *"Is your radar still functioning?"*

"That's a Charlie."

"I want you to head into Beverly."

Just as Paradis completed this sentence Frank came on the radio and addressed Paradis. In a calm, matter-of-fact voice Frank said, *"Pilot boat* Can Do."*

Paradis responded, *"Pilot boat* Can Do, *this is Gloucester Station, over."*

"I have to turn around. My radar went out for some reason, plus the AM antenna. That went overboard with a big crash. So if I can get turned around, I'll be a while getting back. I've got no radar to work with, so I'll be taking it slow."

"Roger, Frank. Probably a good idea to call us in fifteen minutes."

"If I don't get back to you, give me a call. We're going to be busy here for a while."

Paradis must have thought he was caught in a nightmare he couldn't wake up from. First the *Global Hope* issued the Mayday, then his forty-four was almost lost, and now Frank was somewhere off Baker's Island without radar. Although Frank's voice made losing the radar sound like no big deal, both he and Paradis knew they had a serious problem. All Frank had now was a compass for navigation. Without radar, however, he had no landmarks to determine his speed or exactly where he was. And when he turned around he was running into seas that might be moving faster than the boat, effectively negating any forward movement. His control panel may have indicated the propellers were doing ten knots, but that means nothing when seas are twenty feet and screaming along.

The only meaningful position was his last radar fix, which indicated the *Can Do* was just to the northeast of Baker's Island. If he could stay north of Baker's there was plenty of deep water, but if he got pushed near the island or just to the south of it he would be in a maze of ledges, which would sink the boat as they had dozens upon dozens of others.

❋

Baker's Island and Great Misery Island, separated by a mile, stand guard at the entrance to Salem Sound, with a narrow shipping channel running between them. Although the granite islands are similar in size—approximately a half mile long—Baker's has summer homes and a fifty-nine-foot granite conical lighthouse and keeper, while Great Misery is uninhabited. In the summer they are welcome sights for pleasure boaters returning to homeport after a long trip to Boston, Cape Cod, or north to New Hampshire. And at night the lighthouse, known as Baker Island Light, is especially welcoming, serving as one of the few illuminated navigation aids in the region, marking the approach to Salem Harbor. However, on fog-shrouded nights and in snowy conditions mariners without radar want to stay far away from the lighthouse and the jagged granite shoreline of the island. The sound of its air horn on a foggy night, particularly if it blasts from a close proximity, sends shivers up the spines of even the most seasoned mariners.

The first lighthouses built on fifty-nine-acre Baker's Island were erected in 1798, and the pair was known as Ma and Pa Baker. Early pilots would station themselves in a nearby pilot shack and scan the seaward side of the island for approaching ships that would need guidance through the labyrinth of rocks and shoals in Salem Sound. Pilot Joseph Perkins gained local fame in the War of 1812 when, from the island's east side, he watched the frigate USS *Constitution* (*Old Ironsides*) struggling to find safe entrance to the sound as it was pursued by two British warships. Perkins hopped in his dory, rowed to the American ship, and safely guided the frigate into Marblehead Harbor, eluding the British. In those days, pilots were not ferried to the ship but rowed out alone in small dories and then climbed up the ship's netting to get aboard. Perkins's son Joseph II entered the piloting trade, as did his two grandsons Asa and Joseph III, who drowned in 1898. The Perkins clan lived in what is now known as the Old Pilots Retreat, a simple home they had framed in Salem in 1848 and shipped out to the island, where they erected it east of the lighthouse. Reports that the pilot's house is haunted and that the ghost of a pilot prowls the island still persist today. One long-standing legend has it that the ghost is the drowned pilot Joseph III, who became lost in the fog while rowing back to the island after guiding in a ship.

Despite the presence of lighthouses, Baker's Island and the bare rock slabs known as the Gooseberry Islands, located just south of Baker's, have sunk many vessels. It's as if these islands conspire with the myriad of submerged ledges to form a maze of hull-busting traps. One such accident was caused as much by man's creations as by the elements and the rocky islands. In 1817 the two lights at Baker's Island were replaced by a single light, but no one told Captain Osgood of the cargo ship *Union*, which was returning to the port of Salem during a heavy snow squall. Seeing only one light where he thought there should be two, Osgood became confused, and the *Union* smashed into the ledge of rock at the northwest side of the island. The crew abandoned ship and all made it safely to the island, but the *Union* was lost. (Its figurehead, however, was salvaged and it can still be seen, now mounted atop a home on Norman Street in Marblehead. The two lighthouses on Baker's Island have been replaced by a lone lighthouse at the island's northern end.)

Other crews who ran aground near Baker's were not as lucky as the men aboard the *Union*. The little schooner *Lady Antrim* apparently ran aground at night near Tinkers Island, just south of Baker's, killing all three aboard, in 1710. Like so many wrecks where there are no survivors, we will never know exactly what happened, but judging from the small bits of debris that washed up along Marblehead, it appeared the vessel ran aground and then was torn apart by the waves. The captain's body was never found, but the two crew members' bodies washed ashore.

With so many ledges scattered throughout Salem Sound, boats often were lost even in relatively calm seas. Such was the case of the *Norseman*, a 392-foot steamer that ran aground in fog on a March night. The captain immediately shot off flares and sounded the distress whistle, and fortunately, a member of the Humane Society lifesaving station at Marblehead heard the alarm and briefly saw the flare. Men from the station launched their lifeboat and when they reached the steamer began erecting the Breeches Buoy. First, they passed a line to the ship and then secured the other line to shore. One by one, passengers were hauled off on a pulley fastened to the line connecting ship to shore and carried above the surf to the safety of the shoreline. The process took several hours, and had the weather been stormy, it is unlikely all one hundred passengers would have been rescued—the ship would have broken apart on the rocks before the job could be completed.

In one wreck, which occurred in January 1855, a pilot boat went to the aid of a stricken vessel and managed to save most of its crew. The schooner, the *Favorite*, found itself wallowing in the seas southeast of Baker's Island without any wind to aid in its effort to steer free of the jagged rocks. The swells swept her into a ledge and then subsequent waves started to slowly demolish the ship. Two lifeboats were lowered, and while the first broke apart before any men could scramble onboard, the second one safely carried five crewmen to the island's more protected waters at its western side. They ran to the lighthouse station and sent word to Salem that men were still on the *Favorite* and in grave danger. The pilot boat *Effort,* operated by Stephen Powers, immediately steamed out toward the stricken schooner. Rather than risk bringing his boat too close to the ledges, he anchored some distance from the *Favorite* and used his dory to evacuate six of the crew in three separate trips. Other boats soon arrived, and all crew members of the *Favorite* were safely taken off the vessel.

In greater Salem Bay, which covers an area from Manchester south to Nahant, over 400 wrecks have occurred in the ledge-filled waters since records were kept in the early 1700s. Most of the accidents occurred at night, during the winter, in the midst of a storm. Frank Quirk was doing his best to avoid being added to this tragic total.

❋

As Frank's situation on the *Can Do* was worsening, McIlvride's was getting better with each passing moment. Not long after Frank had said he'd lost his radar, the forty-four's radar started to clear, and McIlvride spotted a familiar buoy outside Beverly Harbor.

He radioed Paradis that he spotted the buoy, adding, "*We believe we have the problem solved.*"

Paradis responded, "*Calm down now. Assure yourself you are following the channel.*"

"*Roger, we believe we are navigating pretty good.*"

"*Give me a call every five minutes, every five minutes, over.*"

Paradis then radioed Warren to make sure he knew the forty-four was in the vicinity of Beverly Harbor. Warren replied, "*Roger *sir, we have several units along the shoreline that are watching the forty-four, and we'll bring him into Beverly Harbor Marina."*

Tom Desrosiers remembers that once the crew found the buoy, they knew they were safe. "We used dead reckoning to head toward Beverly, and we tied up at the Jubilee Yacht Club. Later, I remember looking at the propellers of our boat: They were folded over, almost like a squashed tin can. And everything that could be stripped off the boat from the waves was gone—life rings, wooden boat hooks, drop pump canister, you name it."

Six-foot-seven-inch Bob Krom recalls being dog tired and bone cold from the ordeal but, above all, just plain relieved once he stepped on land. For a nineteen-year-old seaman, he's seen more life and death action in a single evening than most Coast Guard men and women see in their entire careers. Yet even after the blizzard, Krom had another brush with death on the forty-four when he was qualifying for the Coast Guard designation known as "Bar Conditions." He was doing his qualifying drills at the mouth of the Merrimack River in Newburyport, where sand bars, the outgoing river, and incoming waves create treacherous, boiling seas when the wind is howling out of the northeast. These were the conditions present when Krom was at the wheel of the forty-four. To help stabilize the boat and slow its descent on the downside of the huge waves, a drogue or sea anchor was set behind the boat. At the time, the drogue used was a canvas tube with a wide wire mouth where the water entered, and then it exited at a narrower opening in the back. The drogue was attached to the boat by a hundred feet of nylon rope.

"There were twenty-foot breakers," says Krom, "and we had just finished doing man-overboard drills when we were heading into the river mouth in following seas. We rode a few waves and the boat was handling nice. Then we came down the face of a particularly large wave when I heard a loud *pop!*" The line to the drogue had parted, and without its drag, Krom felt the boat accelerate as it raced down the wave, and he watched in horror as the forty-four's nose buried itself in the trough below. Then he felt the motion of the stern of the boat coming right over his head. All he had time to do was grab a bite of air and hold on to the wheel. The boat had flipped in a shallow area and sand was churning all around it. Krom described the experience as like being in a giant washing machine with the water pulling at him with a terrific force. He was afraid his last gulp of air wasn't enough, because the boat's mast got caught in the sand and he was upside down for thirty terrible seconds. Finally the mast came free and the forty-four rolled back over to the port side and now it was pointed back out to sea. More big breakers were bearing down on Krom, so he punched the engine into gear and shot out through the waves into deeper water. Of the four people onboard, incredibly, the only injury sustained was a broken nose to one of the crew members.

Krom had just pitchpoled, where the weight of the seas held the bow down and the following wave lifted the stern and flipped the boat end over end. In the history of the Coast Guard this was only the second time a forty-four had pitchpoled. Krom owes his survival to the fact that he and the others onboard were wearing surf belts clamped to the boat. Without the harness they would have been drowned by the waves, crushed by the boat, or shredded by the propellers.

Krom was either very lucky or very unlucky, depending on how you look at the situations thrown his way. Like many men in the Coast Guard, he loved the sea, despite the risks, and found work on the ocean even after leaving the Coast Guard. When Krom was twenty-two he joined Peter Brown as a crew member aboard the *Sea Star*. (Peter is the son of Bob Brown, who owned the *Andrea Gail* of Perfect Storm fame.) The *Sea Star* was a seventy-two-foot steel-hulled boat that fished for lobster out on Georges Bank. "It would take us eighteen hours just to reach Georges Bank, and then we would stay there and fish for four or five days. Peter Brown was a very good captain, always monitoring the weather. I fished on the *Sea Star* for a year and we saw some nasty weather but never anything remotely approaching the seas we experienced in the Blizzard."

※

When Bob McIlvride stepped off the forty-four, he remembers, that was the first time the gravity of their situation hit him. He had been so busy on the boat he didn't have time to think that he might not make it. It wasn't until one of his crew confided that he'd been praying onboard that McIlvride reflected just how close they had come to being killed.

McIlvride also recalls that within minutes of their securing the forty-four at Jubilee Yacht Club the wind ripped the cleats right out of the dock and they had to tie the boat with several lines to the pilings on the pier. Paradis sent two vehicles down to the yacht club, one a camper driven by fellow Coastie J. R. Murray, who had the unlucky assignment of guarding the forty-four alone for the next few days.

With the second car the crew started the long drive back to Gloucester. The wind had started drifting the snow, and just minutes after a section of road was plowed it was covered again. McIlvride was happy he wasn't "skippering" the car—he left that to Tom Desrosiers because he was from Maine and had the most experience driving in snow.

On the ride back McIlvride thought of the *Can Do* out there alone in the dark, storm-whipped seas: "I thought the *Can Do* would make it because Frank and Bucko had been through so much. And unlike our boat, the bridge of the *Can Do* was enclosed. To me, Frank was the original 'old man and the sea,' and seemed to have done it all. If anyone could make it, he could."

PART II

PART II

A FAMILY'S
ANXIOUS WAIT

If you were a crew member on a boat at night without radar off Salem Sound and you could choose any captain in the world to pilot that boat, you'd be hard-pressed to choose a better captain than Frank Quirk. Quirk had made the run from Gloucester to Salem and back again hundreds of times in all conditions. Equally important, he stayed calm under pressure, as many mariners from the Gloucester area will attest.

Don Lavato was a Peabody police officer and neighbor of Frank's who often helped Frank on piloting jobs when conditions warranted an extra hand. Lavato explained that Frank was very cautious, even at the docks, where he'd walk from bow to stern, port to starboard, to make sure the *Can Do* was shipshape before he started the engine. If conditions were bad he would ask Lavato to accompany him for extra safety, because once the pilot left the *Can Do* Frank was alone. His concern also helped the pilot, says Lavato: "I remember one time in bad weather the pilot started climbing up the tanker's ladder and slipped. I was standing right below, and I was actually able to catch him and break his fall—if the pilot had landed in the water between us and the tanker he would have been crushed. I was out with Frank in some pretty rotten weather at night. He always stayed cool and seemed to have a knack for sizing up a situation. He almost never got mad or frustrated; he just tried to solve the problem."

Frank's love of the sea came from his father, who was in the merchant marines and had traveled the world before starting a plumbing contracting company in Peabody. Frank's brother, John, said that when they were just five and six years old their father would take the boys exploring in an old rowboat off the Beverly coast. Their dad had a unique way of teaching them how to swim—he'd toss the boys overboard, and they learned fast.

After Frank's stint in the navy, which he thoroughly enjoyed, he returned to Peabody to join the family plumbing business. "He was unbelievable with anything mechanical," says John. "We used to say, 'If Frank can't figure it out, nobody can.' He had this special way of looking at a problem, studying it, then figuring out how it could be solved." But Frank missed being on the sea, and it wasn't long before he started buying boats and taking on side jobs such as replacing moorings and doing underwater salvage, which required diving.

It was through his diving that Frank's relationship with the Coast Guard first blossomed. In the 1970s Station Gloucester did not have a diving unit and because Frank was a diver he would volunteer for jobs—without pay. He often got calls from fishing draggers saying, "We've got something in our net and can't raise it." One time, just outside Gloucester Harbor, Frank dived down and found a torpedo and depth charge tangled in the trawler's net. When he freed those the net still wouldn't budge and he went down again. This time at the other end of the net he found a small reconnaissance plane attached to the netting. He cut the net, then towed the plane to an area where the fishing fleet would not ensnare it again. Other diving adventures included a call from the Coast Guard that a recreational diver was in trouble off the coast not far from where Frank was motoring the *Can Do*. Frank quickly donned his wet suit and scuba tanks, and a Coast Guard helicopter flew to the *Can Do* and lowered its basket nearby in the ocean. Frank swam to the basket, and the helicopter raised him up, transferring him to the diving accident scene. Unfortunately, they were too late, because after Frank dived down to the diver he returned to the surface with a lifeless body.

Over the years, Frank bought progressively bigger and better-built boats, always naming them the *Can Do*. When Quirk began piloting he became good friends with many of the foreign captains of the ships he helped to bring in. John Quirk recalled how Frank would show the pilots around the North Shore and then bring them home for dinner. When these captains came back into port, they would keep the friendship going by inviting Frank onto their ship for breakfast or dinner. The captains all liked Frank not only for his good-natured manner but also because the *Can Do* could help their ships dock. Sometimes the captain would radio down, "Just give us a little push."

John also remembers Frank for his generosity: "Frank helped me when I was looking for a house on the North Shore just before I was going to be married. One day he said, 'Have you ever thought about building?' I answered that buying land was expensive. And he said, 'Well, I've got a lot and it's yours. Consider it a wedding gift.' The lot was part of his own land where his house was. He just subdivided it and gave it to me. He then helped me clear the land, pour the foundation, and build the house."

In 1972 Frank became a full-time pilot boat operator, giving up his plumbing snakes and wrenches to buy the forty-nine-foot *Can Do*. His business grew fast and he was soon on-call seven days a week, twenty-four hours a day, sometimes handling five ships a day. His typical job started with a call from a shipping agent, letting him know what time the ship would be approaching one of the harbors. Frank would call the pilot and the pilot would drive to the *Can Do*. The ship would arrive outside the harbor, holding position about two or three miles beyond the harbor's entrance. Frank would then ferry the pilot out to the ship, assisting in its guidance into port by spotting the buoys that marked the channel and communicating this information back to the pilot by radio. Most of the ships were of foreign origin, often with a cargo of coal or oil. Sometimes the captains did not have a good command of English, yet another reason—besides the shoals and ledges—that a local pilot was needed to work in conjunction with Frank.

Both his sons, Frank III and Brian, assisted their father during summers and on weekends and enjoyed their time on the *Can Do* while learning the trade. "Dad was a perfectionist," says Frank III, "but he didn't get on you when you made mistakes. He was very patient. He had great trust in me because he knew I paid attention to detail. Under his supervision, I was guiding four-hundred-foot ships into port when I was just seventeen. Dad wasn't just my father but my friend. We were very close. I could talk about anything with him because we were together so much working on the boat."

Gloucester area boaters often saw the *Can Do* heading in and out of port with Frank at the wheel giving a wave as if he hadn't a care in the world. They might have felt a little envy, wishing they could call their own shots and make a living on the water by simply motoring pilots back and forth to tankers and freighters. The boaters, however, were usually out in good weather, when the full reality of a pilot boat operator's duties are not apparent. As often as there were piloting jobs on fine warm days, there were the jobs at 3:00 a.m. when the temperature was five degrees, in seas that would make most of us nauseous, wishing to be anywhere but on the ocean. In challenging conditions, getting a pilot safely on and off the ship wasn't a layup. During heavy seas it would often be safer to perform the pilot transfer while the tanker was doing five or six knots rather than at anchor when the ship was pitching and rolling against the anchor chain. Frank would pull the *Can Do* alongside the ship with almost no space between them, then synchronize the *Can Do*'s speed without bumping the ship. The pilot could climb or descend the forty-foot rope ladder as safely as possible. For the pilot, the critical part was getting on or off the *Can Do*; should he fall, death would occur in seconds from being either crushed, sucked under the tanker and drowned, or hacked by the ship's propellers. In thousands of piloting transfers, Frank never had a pilot injured.

The *Can Do* and Frank had a union, a partnership, that came from spending so much time together on the ocean. He was fond of saying the *Can Do* was like a little submarine: "Batten down the hatches and she'll go through anything." It was no surprise to any of Frank's friends or family when he left the plumbing business for piloting. The sea holds an attraction for some men the way mountains do for others; it gets in their blood and the work they do becomes not just a job but a way of life. Whether it's commercial fishing or shipping goods from one continent to another, mariners usually find it difficult to even think of another line of work that takes them away from the ocean. Many who have tried to make the switch are miserable, the experience best likened to that of nineteenth-century Native Americans taken from the vast western plains and put on dusty reservations and told to grow crops. The wide expanse of the sea, the elbow room it affords, and the independence it fosters simply cannot be duplicated. For certain men there is a magnetic force in those green waters that captures their souls, giving them a sense of freedom and purpose. Men and women who feel this connection to the sea do not fight it, nor do they curse the storms and elements that put more lines in their weather-beaten faces, but instead let the briny world around them be what it is. They adapt; the sea does not.

Mysterious, savage, and elemental, the sea can capture a man, making almost everything else seem either dull or petty. To be on the water with the bracing tang of salt air awakening your senses, and looking out at a horizon that is both endless and ever changing, is a tough thing indeed to give up. Frank was no different from thousands of other men and women who willingly let themselves fall under the spell of the sea and ultimately, perhaps, let it define who they are.

Frank told friends he respected the sea but didn't fear it. He knew there was inherent danger in his work and his rescue involvement, but he also knew, from recent experience, danger could find you anywhere, not just on the ocean. On the day of the Blizzard, when he was at the Cape Ann Marina with Gard Estes, he told his friend about a car accident he had a week earlier. His big Cadillac El Dorado went skidding on a sheet of ice and crashed into a bridge abutment and was totaled. He surprised Gard by offering a piece of introspection he rarely showed: "Gard, I don't know why I'm alive. When I saw that concrete abutment coming at me I said, 'I'm all done.' I shouldn't be here now." Gard says he is haunted by those words, coming just a few hours before the *Can Do* went into the Blizzard.

❄

Audrey Quirk did not begrudge her husband his time away from home, nor was she jealous of his attachment to the *Can Do* and the sea. She, like Frank, was smart enough to adapt, and from early on she figured if Frank couldn't be home very often, she'd go to the *Can Do*. With kids in tow, that's just what she did every weekend, even in the winter. While Frank would head out to a freighter, Audrey would be in the galley cooking up a pot of fish chowder or preparing lobster. In warm weather, when no piloting

jobs were scheduled, the family would take the *Can Do* out to islands for picnics, swimming, or diving for lobsters. Often they'd
motor under the drawbridge and up the canal connecting Gloucester Harbor to the Annisquam River. They might stop at the Cape
Ann Marina to see friends who worked there, such as Gard Estes
and Louis Linquata, and perhaps connect with Bill Lee, David
Curley, Don Wilkinson, and Kenny Fuller, either stopping in for
a drink or inviting the men to join them on the *Can Do*. The marina itself was quite an attraction, as it was a hive of activity in
warm weather, hosting sailboats and yachts from around the
world. When it was first built in 1972, the Cape Ann Marina
helped inject new life into Gloucester, which was known as an old
fishing port in decline. With its motel, restaurant, and docking facilities the marina attracted boaters and tourists who had never
been to Gloucester before. It also became a destination for the
rich and famous, with such notables as Bobby Orr, Robert Red-
ford, Tip O'Neal, Luis Tiant, and the Kennedys stopping in.
Some would drive up for dinner, others would come by yacht,
and still others would land a seaplane on the Annisquam River or
even a helicopter behind the motel.

More often than not Frank would motor the *Can Do* past the
marina and head north up the Annisquam River, using it as a
shortcut to take his family up to Ipswich Bay and avoid having to
go all the way around Rockport. The kids would bring friends on
board and would have special sleepovers on the boat, and Frank
might anchor in the river or in the protected waters of Essex Bay.
When Frank's daughter, Maureen, got married and Frank III
joined the marines, their places on the boat were filled by family
friends such as young Mark Gelinas or Fred Delourchry, now
known as "Uncle Fred" since helping in the Michael Almeida rescue at the state pier. Occasionally Charlie Bucko, Chief Brad Willey and wife Betty, and Dave Curley would come on board for an
outing, as well as Maureen's new family. Frank III was not

forgotten, and the family would use a tape recorder to make tapes of recent events and send them to the young marine stationed in far-off Okinawa. On one tape Frank tells his son that he had seventy piloting trips in January and describes how he pulled a disabled boat off the rocks at Coney Island Ledge in Salem Sound (the very ledge the *Global Hope* had hit). In the background gulls and terns squawk and cry, giving the recording a real touch of home. On another tape he lets young Frank know who's onboard: "Your mother's here making chow and Brian and Uncle Fred are off running errands. Brian bought a Honda motorcycle and already had his first flat. About the only news to report is that the *Decisive* brought in a Russian trawler caught within the two-hundred-mile limit." He then offers Frank III congratulations on his promotion to lance corporal, adding, "Keep up the good work. I'm very proud of you. Well, this is dear old Dad signing off."

On yet another recording we hear the voice of Dave Curley, who went out on the *Can Do* the night of the Blizzard. Audrey starts the tape by saying, "We're all going over to Chief Willey's for Sunday dinner and Dad's clear with ships, so we should have a good time without having to go out for ships. Yesterday Dad helped Billie Lee free his barge and a load of lumber from a ledge. Dave Curley is onboard with us and wants to say a few words." In a gentle voice Curley says, "How are you, Frank? Hard to figure out what to say 'cause I haven't seen you for a while, but I'm sure when you get back you will have some great stories. I hope you're getting to see the country and you're getting to see what it's all about. Being away from home is a good experience, although it can be hard to be away. When you get back, I'm sure you will have good things to tell us. I'll be looking forward to seeing you, so I'll just say happy Easter. Good luck to you and all your buddies."

Dave Curley was frequently on the *Can Do*, but he had a boat of his own, a twenty-eight-foot Sport Fisherman, and the Quirks would often join him for a day of fishing and exploration. Frank III says Curley was "a real gentleman. I don't think I ever heard him say a bad thing about anybody. Hell, I never even heard him swear!"

※

Frank III was still in Okinawa the night of the Blizzard, which is unfortunate, because he would have been a real comfort to the rest of the family, who were in an agonizing wait for the *Can Do* to return back to Gloucester. Maureen remembers how she was working at Mello's Bakery the afternoon of the storm but left early when the snow started to pile up. From her apartment she called her mother to see if everyone got home OK, and Audrey explained that "Dad went out to help the Coast Guard." Maureen didn't think anything of it, because her father was always working with the Coast Guard. She put on her CB radio and listened to her father converse with Paradis, and as the storm worsened she began to become concerned. Maureen wanted to be with her mother and younger brother Brian, but the streets were impassible, so instead she called Audrey every half hour and told her everything was going to be fine.

For Audrey, the waiting must have seemed an eternity. Throughout history, the wives of mariners wait for their safe return, and the term *widow's walk* derives from wives anxiously pacing back and forth when ships are overdue, sometimes actually wearing grooves in the floor. But Audrey's predicament was the exact opposite of that of those women who have to face the unknown. Audrey knew exactly what was happening on the boat and this added a more intense concern—as if she were on the boat with Frank but unable to do a damn thing to help him. Since Warren Andrews telephoned her at Frank's request to "call my base and advise her that I won't be in touch for a while" Audrey had been sitting in Frank's home office with Brian, both glued to the radio. She was surrounded by all the things Frank cherished, including his nautical books, artifacts found while diving, and photos of himself and her onboard all the earlier *Can Do*s. On the door of his office was the original wheel from the current *Can Do*. She tried to stay calm for Brian, reminding him how resourceful Frank was and that with Bucko onboard it was almost like having two Franks piloting the boat. Even when she heard the sickening news that Frank had lost his radar, she tried to stay positive, but the shrieking wind outside the house served as a constant reminder that this was no ordinary storm.

※

There were several minutes of radio silence since Frank's last transmission to Paradis before Warren Andrews, at about 10:00 p.m., could no longer take the suspense and radioed the *Can Do*, *"How far out were you when you turned around?"*

"I'm not quite sure. We've got problems here without the radar, and everything else is down, just about. We're banging our way up to Gloucester."

At least this response showed that Frank successfully turned the boat 180 degrees from a southwest bearing into the northeast, no mean feat in hurricane-force wind and waves. He would have had to time his turn in the trough between two waves and have it completed before the next wave crested on the boat. If the turn was incomplete and the *Can Do* was broadside when the next wave hit, it would capsize under a mountain of frigid, rampaging sea.

※

Audrey Quirk was not the only wife agonizing over radio transmissions, wondering if the ocean would claim her husband. Just thirty-five miles south of Audrey's Peabody home, Ellen Fulton was anxiously monitoring the rescue efforts of her husband, Herb, along the shoreline of Scituate, Massachusetts.

Huge waves, coupled with the astronomically high tide, had deluged coastal communities such as Scituate, cutting off many oceanfront homes from higher ground. In some homes the people trapped inside were in danger, as walls and roofs collapsed under the onslaught of wind and surging seas. As in Revere, those caught in homes close to shore were terrified by the staccato bursts of small rocks cast up by the waves peppering their homes' walls. "Sounded like a machine gun," said a Scituate resident. "We were afraid if we stayed in the house the walls would crumble and we might not have a chance to get away from the rising sea."

Fleeing by foot, however, was not an option, and residents had to wait until police and fire department personnel could evacuate them using small rowboats and skiffs. Herb Fulton, a call captain with the Norwell Fire Department (a neighboring town of Scituate's), was asked to help in the rescues. His wife, Ellen, begged him to stay home, pointing out he was needed right in his own town. "I pleaded with him not to go down there, because I had this feeling something was going to happen. But he went anyway, so I sat by the fire radio, listening to what they were doing."

Arriving at the coast around 11:30 p.m., Herb and other firemen waded along oceanfront streets, dragging a fourteen-foot aluminum skiff behind, going from house to house to check if anyone was trapped inside. Occasional lightning flashes illuminated the swirling snow, giving the night an eerie hue. A little after midnight, as conditions worsened, Herb was called to Jericho Road, which goes out to Lighthouse Point, a small peninsula of land that separates Scituate Harbor from the ocean. Thundering waves crashed over the seawalls, collecting in a natural swale, covering a section of Jericho Road. Over the course of the evening the swale of water expanded into an inland pond, turning

Lighthouse Point into an island that faced the full fury of the howling gale.

When Herb arrived on the scene he was met by several Scituate firefighters. They gathered on the lee side of a fire truck so they could be heard. A Scituate fire captain shouted that two of their rescue boats and crew had already paddled across to Lighthouse Point but had not been heard from in forty-five minutes. The fire captain requested that Herb and nineteen-year-old volunteer fireman Brian McGowan accompany two Scituate firefighters to check on the missing crews. The four men carried the Norwell skiff down to the water, paddled it across the flooded area, then beached the boat on dry land. They soon found the missing firefighters, who were still knocking on doors, asking residents if they wanted to leave. Herb and Brian assisted in this effort, stopping at the home of Sally Lanzikos.

Sally had been waiting in her home with her five-year-old daughter, Amy, for several hours wondering if help would ever arrive. The electricity and heat had gone dead about four o'clock, and the surf was coming over the seawall as if it weren't there. Sally recalls how the waves went right over the roof of the two-story house facing the ocean across the street, and that's when she called the fire department to see if they could take her daughter, Amy, and herself to higher ground.

Sally packed a suitcase for herself and Amy, then stood by the door with a candle, growing more alarmed by the roaring wind that was shaking her house. When help did not arrive she called the fire department again, and they said they would be there as soon as possible. "About nine o'clock," says Sally, "water started coming in through our kitchen window. Outside I could see the house across the street breaking apart. I stayed by the door with the candle because I was afraid the rescuers might miss us."

While going house to house, Herb and Brian saw Sally's candle and they went to her aid. The blasting wind was so strong Herb decided to carry Amy, and the group trudged through the blinding snow and knee-deep water back to the boats. As they walked, Sally stared in disbelief at boulders the size of compact cars strewn along the roadway, flung there by the sea. Upon reaching the boats they joined with others who were waiting to make the crossing. Passengers and rescuers split into groups of from four to six, and Sally, Amy, Herb, and Brian were joined by a couple in their sixties, Mr. and Mrs. Edward Hart. This group boarded the Norwell skiff, with Brian rowing and Herb using a pike pole to push along from the stern. In the confusion Amy was seated in the bow with Mr. Hart while Sally and Mrs. Hart sat in the stern.

About halfway across the flooded area the group saw a man signaling with a flashlight from a porch of a nearby house surrounded by water. Deciding to help him, they turned the boat toward the man. Then catastrophe struck. A portion of the seawall facing the harbor collapsed, and water that had been trapped inside now raced out, like a raging river that had breached a dam. "It was churning white water," says Sally, "and all of the sudden the boat was flying toward the broken seawall and the harbor."

Brian tried to stop the boat by using an oar against a submerged car, and Herb attempted to hook a telephone pole with his pike pole. The current was too strong, though, and the skiff went careening into the side of a house. The jolt knocked Amy out of the boat and into the frigid waters. Mr. Hart immediately leaned over to grab the girl, and that motion caused the boat to capsize in the dark, swirling vortex. Water was being sucked out to the harbor, taking the six struggling victims with it. "I grabbed Amy several times," says Fulton, "but the current tore her loose. On the way out into deep water I tried several times to stand but found myself pushed out into water over my head."

Back in Norwell, Herb's wife, Ellen, heard screams on the fire radio. "I could hear the firemen shouting, 'We've lost a boat!' I knew Herb was on that boat. The power at our house went out just after that happened, so I sat there in the dark thinking I was a widow."

All six people in the water were now battling the waves, current, and ice in the darkness of the harbor. Herb's strength was ebbing and he thought, *This is the end.* He decided to float rather than fight the current, and when he found an area where the flow wasn't too strong he swam for shore. Finally he reached a shallow area and struggled out of the water. Slowly making his way along the beach, he came upon Mrs. Hart, who was still floundering in the water. Dressed in heavy winter clothing, Mrs. Hart could not claw her way out the water, and Herb grabbed her, yanking her to shallow water.

While Herb and Mrs. Hart reached dry land, Sally and Mr. Hart were being swept deeper into the harbor. "When the boat capsized, my leg became entangled in a rope hanging from the boat," says Sally. "The boat just dragged me out into the harbor, and I remember screaming for Amy. I thought, *This can't be happening.* Then I had this terrible flash in my mind that my parents were reading a newspaper headline saying they found my body. Maybe that gave me the push to act. I reached down and freed my leg from the rope. That's when I felt Mr. Hart grab my neck from behind. He was drowning. It was awful, but somehow my emotions became detached and I was able to think clearly—I needed to live to find Amy. I asked Mr. Hart to let go, telling him we'd do better by ourselves, and he did."

Sally considered whether or not she should stay with the boat, but within seconds an extremely strong gust caught the boat and she watched it flip end over end, skimming away across the harbor. She then saw a post nearby and swam for it, but it turned out to be nothing more than flotsam. Although she didn't feel the icy water, hypothermia was sapping her strength, and the next few minutes were critical for survival. Treading water—expending extra energy because her winter clothes were weighing her down—Sally got her first break when there was a lull in the snowfall, briefly allowing her to see a house onshore.

"It was odd how my mind seemed to process things for a few seconds—almost like a computer. I wasn't panicked but instead started to swim toward the house. I quickly tired, however, and thought, *This is it*. Then for some strange reason I thought of John F. Kennedy, and how when he was swimming from *PT-109* he floated on his back when he was tired. So I floated on my back to rest a minute and then resumed swimming the rest of the way.

"When I reached the rocks I crawled up a ways and rested, but I was worried a wave was going to wash me back in. Then I thought of Amy and became frantic, running as best I could, screaming for her. I saw people standing down the shore and they hollered, 'Stay there.' I didn't know what was happening—I thought about going back into the water to try and find her. A strange thing happened next. A tall man in a parka was at my side and he just hugged me. I couldn't see his face and he didn't say a word, but it calmed me for a few seconds and prevented me from going in the water. Then two firemen arrived and the man in the parka was gone. I never found out who . . . or what he was."

The people Sally saw standing on the shoreline were police and firefighters, gathered around the lifeless body of Amy. Sally was taken to an ambulance, pleading with the two firemen assisting her to tell her where Amy was, but neither answered. Inside the ambulance, medics wrapped her in blankets. Now the full effects of the freezing water hit her, and she shivered uncontrollably, her whole body shaking. No one wanted to be the one to tell her about Amy, and Sally began to suspect the worst. "I kept asking, 'Where's Amy?' But no one would answer. Then Fireman McDonough was next to me and I said, 'Please tell me. She's not OK, is she?' He started crying and shook his head."

The hypothermia that gripped Sally was so bad she didn't even know that her legs had been cut to ribbons by the seawall and the rocks. Between spasms of shivering, she cried out over and over, "This can't be happening!" Making matters worse, on the ride to the hospital the ambulance became stuck in the snow and the men were unable to free it. Sally thought, *After all this, I'm going to die in an ambulance.* "But it didn't matter," says Sally. "I didn't care anymore." Although it's hard to measure time in such a situation, Sally thinks the entire trip to the hospital took two hours because of the snow-clogged streets.

Herb Fulton, Brian McGowan, Mrs. Hart, and Sally all recovered, at least physically. But Amy died and Mr. Hart was missing and presumed dead. Three months later his body was found under the Scituate town pier.

Ellen Fulton later stumbled on a chilling discovery. While reading *Warnings Ignored: The Portland Gale of 1898,* by David Ball, she came upon this passage: "A huge wave swept the woman out of the grasp of her husband and into Scituate Harbor." The location was the exact same spot where Amy drowned.

The Blizzard of '78 hit the Northeast so suddenly that cars and their occupants were trapped on highways. (Courtesy of Vince Horrigin)

The power of the waves collapsed seawalls, allowing the waves to demolish many homes. (Courtesy of the Massachusetts National Guard)

At Coast Guard Beach, the storm-generated waves swept away the bath house. (Courtesy of Cape Cod National Seashore)

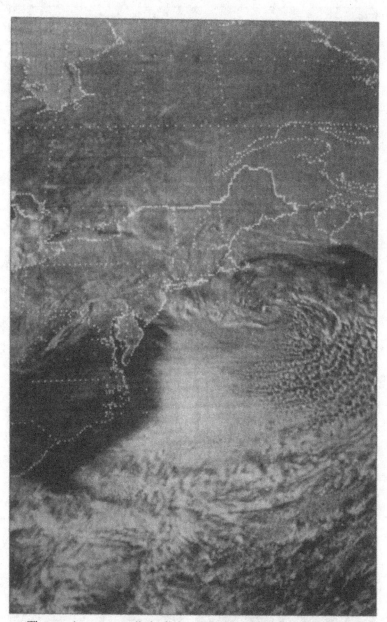

The massive storm stalled off the coast, hurling its most destructive winds at Boston's North Shore, where the *Can Do* was caught.
(Courtesy of the National Weather Service)

Frank Quirk receives an award from the U.S. Coast Guard for coming to the aid of the sinking *Chester Poling*. (Courtesy of the Quirk family)

Charlie Bucko received two purple hearts while serving with the U.S. Marines in Vietnam. (Courtesy of the Bucko family)

Bob McIlvride, the young coxswain of the forty-four-foot motor lifeboat, kept a cool head under terrible conditions. (Courtesy of Robert McIlvride)

The oil tanker *Global Hope* dragged anchor during the storm and started to take on water in the engine room. (Courtesy of Mel Cole and the U.S. Coast Guard)

The 685-foot *Global Hope* dwarfs the tugboats in the foreground. (Courtesy of Mel Cole and the U.S. Coast Guard)

The Coast Guard's forty-four-foot motor lifeboat was designed to take a pounding. (Courtesy of the U.S. Coast Guard)

The *Chester Poling* was in conditions similar to these when it split in two.
(Courtesy of the U.S. Coast Guard)

Even the 210-foot-long cutter *Decisive* had some close calls during
the blizzard. (Courtesy of the U.S. Coast Guard)

The *Can Do* was a forty-nine-foot pilot boat with a steel hull. It worked the ports of both Gloucester and Salem. (Courtesy of the Quirk family)

The *Can Do* was such a solid vessel that mariners referred to it as a "fortress" or a "surface-submarine." (Courtesy of the Quirk family)

| 9 |

TIME IS THE ENEMY

Although the *Cape George* and the *Decisive* were slowly approaching the vicinity of Baker's Island, where the *Can Do* was lost, they had trouble of their own. The *Decisive* was four times bigger than the *Can Do*, but the power of the seas made its size almost irrelevant. First commissioned in 1968, the *Decisive* had patrolled through the worst of conditions, including a stint in the International Ice Patrol in the North Atlantic, but it had never been battered as on the night of the Blizzard. The 210-foot cutter took several rolls in the sixty-degree range and the men onboard could only hope the next big roll didn't put it completely on its side at ninety degrees, from which they wouldn't recover. "Picture looking at a wall of water," says Jim Quinn, "which is the size of a three-decker home. That's what it was like with each oncoming wave." Quinn says that he didn't even have to climb up the stairs from the engine room but instead just time a wave, and jump, and the motion of the ship would catapult him to the next level. He knew the *Can Do* was now in trouble, but the *Decisive*'s radar wasn't much good because of all the snow, and the men up on the bridge only had brief periods at the top of waves to get a look ahead—most of the time they were surrounded by those walls of water.

Frank and the crew must have surely known that the chances of the *Decisive* or the *Cape George* finding them on the open ocean were so poor it was not even worth hoping for that to happen. Yet Frank continued to remain calm, as is evidenced when Paradis tried to get a fix on his position: *"Pilot boat* Can Do, *how far out were you, Frank, when you lost your radar?"*

"Not quite sure. When the radar went out, I was taking a reading on Baker's Island. When the AM antenna came down I don't know if it hit the radar on the way down. We're trying to nurse along here, best we can. So can't tell you just where we are right now. Once in a while I'll get a blip on the radar. Trying to make the mouth of the harbor. Hang in there for a few minutes and I'll give you a better position when I find out where I am."

"Roger. I'd appreciate it if you give me a call every fifteen minutes. If you want I can send the forty-one out there to see if they can pick you up on radar."

"Yeah, OK, well, you call me back, 'cause I'm going to be losing track of time here, so give me a call in fifteen minutes and we'll let you know how we're making out."

Chief Paradis didn't have a lot of options; in fact, the only boat at his disposal was the forty-one, the same forty-one that got beyond the breakwater earlier and had to turn back. He offered its services now because both he and Frank thought the *Can Do* would soon be at the mouth of Gloucester Harbor. However, in just the brief period of time since the *Can Do* left Gloucester the winds increased more greatly still, screaming at 70 and 80 miles per hour, and some gusts reached a terrific 100 miles per hour.

The *Can Do* was now going directly into the teeth of these bitter winds wailing out of the northeast, and the twenty- and thirty-foot breaking seas were pushing the boat backward faster than it could motor forward. On the way down toward Salem, Frank was going full throttle to give himself a bit of maneuverability in the racing seas. Now, heading into the waves, he needed to find a slower speed to minimize the spray and water taken over the bow and give his boat and crew a little less wear and tear. Icing was an additional concern, and the spray was freezing on the deck, rails, and pilothouse. It was essential Frank make forward progress, but he must do so at a snail's pace, while still keeping approximately a half mile to a mile offshore in deep water. Hugging the shore any closer would put him in jeopardy of striking Great Egg Rock and Kettle Island off Magnolia or hitting Norman's Woe and Round Rock Shoal just before the mouth of Gloucester Harbor.

The forty-one did go back out, and onboard was Bill Cavanaugh, who had fully recovered from his broken neck injury sustained in the *Chester Poling* rescue. "I was off-duty down in Marblehead," says Cavanaugh, "but I still got the call to come to the station. I explained that my car, a Gremlin, would never make it through all the snow, but they said, 'Don't worry; we have it all arranged for you to be brought back up.'" Station Gloucester had lined up a series of snowplows from different towns to transport Cavanaugh back to the station using a relay approach. Each plow would carry him to the northern end of their town line, where the next town's plow would be waiting to continue the relay.

"When I arrived at the station," recalls Cavanaugh, "it looked like it was floating—there was seawater entirely encircling it. I joined the rest of the forty-one crew, and Paradis instructed us to try and get a radar fix on the *Can Do* from just outside the break-water. He made it clear, however, that we were not to put ourselves in jeopardy. As soon as we were onboard and departed we knew we were in for a long night. It was a battle just to get to Ten

Pound Island within the harbor. Conditions were unbelievable. We hadn't even reached the breakwater and our radar was out. The waves were so big, even with our radar it wouldn't have helped much, because each time we went down in a trough the radar would have just picked up the seas in the front and back, and above the troughs it was all snow. Our bow was submerged a good part of the time—we call that green water because it's not just cutting through crests of spray but is actually in the sea. I had learned a lot from when I was a rookie on the *Chester Poling* rescue, and that was to make sure I knew when the waves were going to hit. Most of us, over the course of time, develop a built-in sense of timing so you know when to brace yourself so you're not airborne like I was when I got injured."

Cavanaugh says they made it to the breakwater, but the seas beyond it were breaking, and the twenty- and thirty-foot waves surely would have overwhelmed the utility boat: "The forty-one wasn't designed for those kinds of seas, and we couldn't get beyond the breakwater without being killed. At that time there was no escape hatch in the forty-one's enclosed area."

The lack of an escape hatch was a real weakness in the boat, exposed just three months earlier in a terrible accident at Cape Disappointment, Washington. Coxswain Roger Albrecht was in command of a forty-one-footer that was being used in a nighttime training exercise at the mouth of the Columbia River. Ten men were aboard the boat when a twenty-foot breaking wave caught the vessel on the port side, causing it to capsize in the frigid November seas. Two men who were outside on the deck were immediately thrown into the water. One managed to hold on to the overturned hull, but the other was swept away by the waves and drowned. The other eight men, including Albrecht, were pushed by the force of the water from their position in the wheelhouse into the forward cabin, where they were trapped.

Albrecht later told the United Press that he first tried to calm things down and then, as the water was rising, told the men they would each have to swim to safety and it would be an individual effort. The swim would involve trying to negotiate several turns in total darkness. First the men would have to go downward through the cabin hatch (only thirty inches wide), then through the cabin itself and out its door, and finally swim upward to the ocean's surface and onto the overturned hull. There were no guarantees that one could hold his breath long enough to make the swim, but with water rising in the cabin space they knew there were no other choices. Albrecht decided to go first, telling the men to follow his lead. Five men followed. Boatswain's Mate Steve Salo made it about halfway but then became disoriented, struggling in the darkness to find an escape. He managed to grope his way back into the cabin. "I was badly scared and had to wait another fifteen minutes to muster enough courage to try it again," he said.

After Salo tried a second time and made it, there were just three men left in the cabin: Boatswain's Mate Gregory Morris, Seaman Albin Erickson, and Seaman Michael Lee. Morris and Erickson said they'd never make it. "I pleaded with them to follow me," said Lee, "but they had completely resigned themselves to their fate and the fact that they simply couldn't make it." When Lee made his swim, the water in the cabin had risen to the waists of the two remaining men.

Helicopters were immediately dispatched to the scene, and the men clinging to the hull were rescued. Other Coast Guard boats battled the seas to reach the overturned forty-one before the air supply inside the cabin was gone. The waves, however, had pushed the utility boat far out from the original scene of the accident, and in the darkness it could not be located, sealing the terrible fate of the two men inside.

Bob Gesking was on board a lightship anchored seven miles off the mouth of the Columbia River and remembers his commander calling all the crew up on deck to be on the lookout for the hull of the forty-one. About an hour later it floated by, heading southwest, just twenty yards away. Gesking and crew threw all their life rings with illuminated float lights at the hull to mark its location. The *Triumph,* a fifty-two-foot motor lifeboat, sped out and found the forty-one and began towing it back to port. The towline, however, became tangled in the *Triumph's* screws and the capsized forty-one was adrift again, eventually sinking nine miles off the coast.

About a year later the Coast Guard began alterations on all forty-one-foot utility boats to provide better escape routes if there should be another capsizing. In the forward section of the cabin a two-foot-square "sun roof" hatch was installed, and inside the wheelhouse the aft windows were modified so that they could be kicked out in an emergency.

These changes, however, had not been made when the Blizzard hit Gloucester, and if Cavanaugh's forty-one-footer capsized it would be certain death.

※

Back in Salem, Warren Andrews was dying inside, listening to the *Can Do*'s worsening situation. Frank was not just his friend but more like a brother. Warren had been on the radio with Frank for so many years he sometimes felt as if he were on the boat himself, able to see clearly everything Frank described. He knew Frank had made it through dozens of severe storms, including the one that split the *Chester Poling* in half, yet still there was something different about this night. The combination of snow, incredible winds, and monstrous seas was making this storm a killer, particularly for any boat caught in its grip at night. Warren had heard what was happening on the Coast Guard's largest cutter in the area, and he knew that if the 210-foot *Decisive* was rolling sixty degrees—her deck almost at a right angle to the seas—the *Can Do* must be faring far worse.

Finally Warren couldn't wait any longer, and he broke in on the radio, concern giving his voice a clipped and tense quality.

"This is Salem Control. Pilot boat Can Do, what's the situation?"

"We've got problems here without the radar and everything else. Boy, I'll tell you it's some wild out here. So we're just poking along. I've got plenty of water. I'm just trying to pick up something to go by."

Bucko was probably standing—as best he could—by the helm with Frank, hoping to pick something up on the malfunctioning radar. Judging from the comments of the crew of the *Decisive* and the *Cape George*, the two men were probably already exhausted just from the energy expended trying to keep their balance and from being knocked around. For the other three men on the *Can Do*—Curley, Fuller, and Wilkinson—the return trip was even worse, because they could only hang on and wait. At this point whatever tasks needed to be done, such as securing any equipment that was jarred loose, would have been completed. Now they could only hope the *Can Do* could struggle back to Gloucester without popping a hatch or splitting a seam—and each wave that pounded the boat made that scenario less likely. If they didn't know it before, they now realized they were in serious trouble. The murderous seas and the howling gale didn't give an inch and instead were trying to claw their way inside the boat and get at the men.

The three men were wedged in a sitting position between the table and the cushioned benches, likely seasick and vomiting from the endless rising and falling, as if trapped on a roller coaster that had no "off" switch. They were totally spent from bracing themselves for each jarring impact the *Can Do* made after cresting a wave. *Pow! Pow! Pow!* they heard over and over.

The men were struggling to push the fear back, keep it in the pit of the stomach, keep it from taking over. They could only pray that Frank would make it to the breakwater and see it before they were slammed into it and crushed. Maybe the thought that they were losing ground and actually going backward toward the shoals of Baker's Island crossed their minds, but it was a thought too terrible to contemplate and best kept to oneself.

Even if they could hear one another above the growling sea and demonic wind, there was nothing to say at this point. Each man was likely lost in his own thoughts, just trying to make it through the next minute. Dave Curley, the soft-spoken man who gave young Frank III the encouraging words on the tape, could have been thinking back to that afternoon at the marina. Dave usually only went there at night and almost never in the day-time, because his electrical work took him all over the North Shore. Had he headed home rather than to the marina, he wouldn't be stuck in this heaving black void. How odd is the na-ture of life, that one seemingly insignificant decision can set in motion events that spin out of control. Just a few hours earlier he and his friends were safe and warm, laughing and maybe even glad for the storm because it gave them a break from the daily grind of work. At that time Dave Curley's biggest immediate worry was whether the drive home would be a long one in the snow. Now, instead of watching the news of the blizzard on TV, he was in it, wondering if the next wave to break on the bow would be the one to bury them. Being an electrician and familiar with the *Can Do* from several trips with Frank, Dave likely wracked his brain trying to figure out if there was some way he could get the radar going. Most likely the antennae were lost as Frank said, but even if the problem was an electrical short there was not much wiring work he could do with the boat riding up twenty feet, then slamming down twenty feet into the next trough. And at the bottom of each wave green seas covered the bow, shaking the boat from end to end, like a cat would shake a mouse. Before escaping from its grip, water cascaded off the *Can Do*'s bow, and then the terrible process was repeated. Dave could only wait it out; the ocean, not Frank, would call the shots.

Commercial fisherman Kenny Fuller knew the toll the punishing waves were taking on the *Can Do*, and, from his experience fishing far out at sea, he also realized time was their enemy. If they didn't get into the harbor quickly the vessel would eventually—perhaps piece by piece—succumb to the unrelenting waves. And if a rogue wave hit or a sea slammed them from a slightly different direction, Fuller knew, it could be all over in a matter of seconds. Every fisherman from Gloucester knows someone who didn't make it back after being caught in a storm. Still, it's ironic that Fuller had successfully made dozens of high-risk trips—over a hundred miles offshore searching for bluefin tuna—and now he was in the battle of his life just a mile from the coast.

Facing the possibility of death leads some to contemplation, and Kenny Fuller might have thought what a rough couple of years he'd had. Before trying his hand at fishing he owned the Patio Restaurant in Rockport, but mounting debt, some from his gambling habit, forced him to sell. Friends said Fuller had a bigger problem than gambling: his own generosity. "He was too good-hearted," says Gard Estes, "to be a businessman. Any friend that came to the restaurant would have drinks and food on the house. And just about everybody was his friend."

If Fuller wasn't cut out for business, Wilkinson was the exact opposite, using his shrewd management skills to increase profits at the Cape Ann Marina and the Captain's Bounty Motor Lodge, both owned by his good friend Dave Warner. As dedicated as Wilkinson was to his job, he took time out for his children, a daughter and two sons. "My father could be demanding," says his son, Donald, "but he cared about us kids and put us first. Two or three times a week we had 'game night,' where we would each take turns choosing what game we were going to play together. Dad always picked Monopoly, and of course usually won." Wilkinson's business savvy and outgoing personality produced friends and connections all over the state. "If somebody was being treated unfairly," says Gard, "Don would make a few calls and straighten things out. Of course we never called him Don—his nickname was Uncle Al, because we thought he looked like the Boston Strangler, Albert DeSalvo."

If business was Wilkinson's talent, his passion was powerboat racing. Wilkinson and friend Dave Warner competed in power-boat racing and together sponsored charity races to benefit the Lions Club Eye Research Program. A photo in a 1977 edition of the *Gloucester Times* shows a smiling Wilkinson pumping his fist from the cockpit of a powerboat after he and Dave Warner won a race in rough seas off Gloucester. Not all the participants of the race, however, were smiling at the end. During that race, one boat sank and two men were hospitalized. Speeding at 70 miles per hour, their boat slued sideways, pitching one contestant thirty feet in the air and slamming the other into the boat's super-structure, smashing the vertebrae in his back in the process. At the finish line was the *Can Do,* and Frank helped get the men to safety before they drowned.

Wilkinson's powerboat racing experience probably helped him through the unnerving experience of being lost in the storm without radar—but not much. Groping blind in terrible condi-tions was something only Frank and Bucko had any real training and experience in. It's likely one of the men asked Frank if he'd ever experienced seas like this, and Frank would have found a way to answer without making things worse, saying something like, "Not quite, but Bucko and I have been in jams before."

Gard Estes summed up the five men as the best of friends, always together: "We were family, and like family there wasn't anything we wouldn't do for each other." And now there was nothing the friends could do for one another except keep their emotions in check and silently pray.

| 10 |

HEADING NORTHEAST

Bob McIlvride referred to Frank as the "original old man and the sea" but wasn't the only person to view him this way. Although Frank was only forty-nine at the time of the Blizzard, the young Coasties were half his age, and to them Frank—with his gray crew-cut and Popeye arms—did look like a grizzled sea captain. He also had many of the traits of fishing boat captains who were born to be at sea, no matter what the risk. Gloucester either breeds these staunch individualists or attracts them, and over the years some remarkable tough-as-nails mariners have hailed from the nation's oldest fishing port. One of those men was Howard Blackburn.

Blackburn first came to the attention of the nautical world in 1883 at age twenty-three when he was trawling for halibut aboard the schooner *Grace L. Fears* on Burgeo Bank off Newfoundland. Here the warm waters of the Gulf Stream meet the cold Labrador Current, creating an ideal fishery in the nutrient-rich waters. On a cold and blustery January day the captain of the

Fears steered the ship over this fishing ground and ordered the anchor dropped at his favorite spot. The crew then lowered six eighteen-foot dories and Howard Blackburn and Tom Welch climbed down into one. Rowing away from the mother ship, the two men went to their assigned area, where they set the trawl line with hundreds of baited hooks dangling toward the ocean's floor at fifteen-foot intervals. After the job was completed they returned to the ship, looking forward to a rest before heading back out to bring in the lines, hopefully heavily laden with fish. The captain, however, sensed a storm brewing and ordered the dorymen back out to collect their trawls after only a couple hours.

Blackburn and Welch were hauling in the trawl lines when the squall suddenly hit, its snow and driving winds pushing their dory away from the ship. Within minutes they were in whiteout conditions, and try as they might, they could not reach the *Fears*. Exhausted, they lost sight of the ship and decided to drop anchor and wait for a break in the storm. A few hours later, at nightfall, the snow stopped and the two men could see the dim light of a torch on the distant mother ship. They hauled up anchor and rowed with every ounce of strength. But they were heading into the wind, and the seas were so rough they were forced to drop anchor once again, having made little headway. Spray hit the dory and instantly froze, coating it in a thick sheet of ice while waves crashed up and over the bow, forcing Blackburn and Welch to bail the entire night. When dawn broke, the *Fears* was gone and the two exhausted men were utterly alone, sixty miles from Newfoundland.

The seas gave them no quarter and threatened to capsize the dory, forcing one man to pull on the oars to keep the bow pointed into the oncoming waves while the other bailed. Blackburn took off his mittens and dropped them in the bilge so he could use his fingers to fashion a sea anchor from a buoy keg. The improvised sea anchor worked, helping to hold the bow to the wind. Water still came up and over the gunnel, and as Welch bailed he inadvertently scooped up Blackburn's mittens, pitching them overboard. A couple hours later both of Blackburn's hands had a sickly gray hue, the blood and tissue having frozen to the bone. Knowing he'd be next to useless if he could not row, he wrapped his fingers around the oars and let his hands freeze solid in that grip, like two claws. In this position he could use his hands for both rowing and bailing.

Sometime during the second night, the cold sapped Welch's will to live and he stopped bailing. He lay frozen, huddled in the water-soaked bow. Blackburn grabbed his mate and said, "Tom, this won't do. You must do your part. Your hands are not frozen and beaten to pieces like mine." Blackburn then showed Welch his hands, with one finger attached only by a piece of skin. Later Blackburn acknowledged this was a mistake, writing: "I have always been sorry that I showed him the hand, for he gave up altogether then and said, 'Howard, what is the use, we can't live until morning, and might as well go first as last.'" By dawn, Welch was dead.

The following day the seas calmed a bit and Blackburn used the opportunity to begin rowing north, hoping to make Newfoundland before the cold crept closer to his vital organs, killing him as it had his dory mate. His frozen hands were disintegrating before his very eyes, and Blackburn later described the grisly details: "The end of the oar would strike the side of my hand and knock off a piece of flesh as big around as a fifty-cent piece, and fully three times as thick. The blood would just show and then seem to freeze." Somehow Blackburn made it through a third night and at dawn commenced rowing, even though he had not had so much as a sip of water in the three days passed on the dory.

Late on the fourth day Blackburn's tenaciousness paid off when he spotted land and forced himself to bend to the oars harder still, directing the boat toward the mouth of a river. "I would give ten years of my life for a drink of water," Blackburn later wrote, describing his feelings at the time. He soon spied an abandoned shack at the shoreline and made for it. There he spent his fourth night, not daring to sleep for fear the cold would claim him. Instead he paced the floor of the shack the entire night, eating snow, which did nothing to quench his merciless thirst.

At dawn on the fifth day, having found there were no other cabins in the area, he returned to his dory with the thought that he would row until he found a harbor or came upon a house. As he climbed in the dory his spirits hit rock bottom when he realized there was a crack in the hull from where the vessel beat against some boulders during the night. Blackburn's willpower was giving out: "I looked all around me but could see no escape and said to myself, 'It is too bad that it must end like this after such a struggle.'" Still he was not ready to admit defeat and he decided to chance rowing the cracked dory eastward along the coast. In the leaking boat Blackburn miraculously managed to row five miles, often stopping to bail, and almost intercepted a schooner. But no one onboard noticed the small dory bouncing in the seas, and amid this bitter disappointment of almost being rescued Blackburn was forced to acknowledge that he needed to survive a fifth night. He rowed back to the same river mouth he entered the prior night, only this time he somehow struggled farther upriver to a cove.

This decision saved Blackburn's life. He was spotted by fishermen and taken to a cabin owned by the Lishman family. Mrs. Lishman tried to remedy his frozen feet and hands by placing them in a tub of cold water. "In a few minutes I was wishing myself in Welch's place. I will say no more about the agony . . ." Blackburn's fingers could not be saved, and over the next two months dry gangrene set in. He eventually lost all his fingers, half of each thumb, and five toes. His flesh, however, grew out from the stumps of his hands and feet and covered the wounds with scar tissue.

Most men, after surviving such an experience, would understandably curse the sea and never again set foot in a boat. But not

Blackburn. Returning to Gloucester that spring, he opened a saloon but still spent time on the water. After several more nautical adventures, he decided, at age thirty-nine, to sail a thirty-foot sloop, the *Great Western,* solo to England. After two months of being bedeviled by fog, calms, and easterly winds, Blackburn astounded the world by entering Bristol Channel and stepping aboard land in Portishead, England. Still, he was not satisfied. Two years later, as if to prove his voyage was not a fluke, he did it again, this time making Portugal in an even smaller boat, the twenty-five-foot *Great Republic.* It took him just thirty-nine days to cross the Atlantic, recording the fastest single-handed (or in Blackburn's case no-handed) nonstop voyage across the Atlantic ever sailed.

❋

Frank Quirk was going to need the toughness of Blackburn and, perhaps more important, a little of his luck if he was to guide the *Can Do* to safety without radar. The one thing he had going for him was experience; both Frank and Charlie had had their radar knocked out before in heavy weather. Charlie lost his navigational aids during the *Chester Poling* rescue, and his experience was quite similar to McIlvride's during the Blizzard. The citation that accompanied Charlie's *Chester Poling* commendation medal explained his predicament:

> Proceeding toward the pending disaster, Petty Officer Bucko's unit (a 44-footer) suffered a radar casualty followed shortly by the loss of his fathometer and FM radio. With all navigational aids down and communications severely limited, Petty Officer Bucko expertly maneuvered and navigated by dead reckoning to the scene of the distress. Upon arriving on scene, Fireman Crocker was injured and appeared to be unconscious below decks. His unit was further impaired by the loss of the starboard engine, making maneuvering in the overwhelming seas virtually

impossible. Sensing the immediate danger to his crew and potential of becoming a distress case itself, Petty Officer Bucko withdrew the CG 44317 for return to Gloucester Station to seek medical assistance for his crew and repair sustained damage. His precise navigation and calm assurance while engulfed in turbulent seas and battering winds directly contributed to the safe return of his unit.

Bucko's dead reckoning (determining position based on distance, time, and speed) used during the *Chester Poling* worked because he had some visual references and knew where he was when the radar went out, but now, caught at night in blinding snow, he couldn't see beyond the *Can Do*'s bow. His assistance to Frank at that point was largely symbolic—both men knew they were groping blind, heading northeast and doing their best to stay offshore in the deeper water. With such a strong wind it was difficult to steer a steady course, and with waves battering the boat their engine/propeller speed might be giving them a reading that was entirely different from their actual boat speed. At some point they must estimate where the mouth of Gloucester Harbor was and move closer to shore, angling the *Can Do* more to the north for safe entry. If their estimate was a bit south of the harbor they might hit Kettle Island, Norman's Woe, or the Magnolia shoreline. Should they overshoot the entrance they would hit the breakwater or the coast of Eastern Point and end up sinking in almost the exact same spot where the stern section of the *Chester Poling* lies in its watery grave.

While Frank and Bucko tried to inch northeastward, the ninety-five-foot *Cape George* had finally reached the outskirts of Salem Sound. At approximately 11:00 p.m. Paradis asked them for a status report on their position and their radar's effectiveness. The *Cape George* responded, but Skipper Glen Snyder's voice could barely be heard above the howling wind: *"Negative on the loran and navigation. We think we are three miles southwest off Marblehead. Making four knots. Wind is blowing sixty-two knots. Seas about twenty feet. We're taking a real beating out here. Lost fathometer."*

Paradis replied, *"Be advised the forty-four ran aground and is presently tied up in Beverly. We don't know how much damage she sustained on the bottom. She lost her radar and fathometer and she couldn't navigate. The tanker is aground, but we do not have a good position on her."*

"Is there any assistance to her at this time?"

"Negative. There is no assistance on scene."

"Is there any chance of that tanker breaking up?"

"We do not know at this time. As far as we know all POBs are onboard and they're OK, but we do not know for sure; all we know is the tanker is aground."

In Boston, Jim Loew was monitoring this exchange. This was the same Jim Loew who skippered the cutter that saved several men from the *Chester Poling*. Now he was a Rescue Coordination Center (RCC) controller for the First Coast Guard District in Boston, which covered an area from the Maine–Canadian border south to the Rhode Island–Connecticut border and offshore. At the time, the RCC was a branch of the Coast Guard Search and Rescue Operations and its primary function was to coordinate cases that crossed group or district boundaries, using aircraft or larger cutters. Jim had the watch for RCC that night, and it was he who sent the *Cape George* out when he learned that the *Global Hope* was in trouble. "It was tough," says Lowe, "to send the *Cape George* out into that storm, because I knew exactly how dangerous it would be for them. But the vessel had a good skipper in Glen Snyder, and he knew that I had 'been there' with the *Cape George* and he trusted my judgment that we needed him to go out on this mission. If the *Global Hope* was sinking we were going to need more than the patrol boats that went out from Gloucester. Glen knew he'd be entering unpredictable conditions. Before setting out he took the extraordinary, but prudent, measure of 'setting material condition ZEBRA,' requiring all watertight doors, hatches, fittings (except those needed for ventilation) to be closed and kept closed."

This proved a wise decision, because without navigation equipment the cutter was in increasing peril as it approached the ledge-filled waters of Salem Sound. Seaman apprentice Vern DePietro was on the bridge, watching his superiors discuss where they might be. "Myron was studying the charts," says DePietro, "trying to memorize where the hazards were located. His memory saved our bacon, because just a few minutes later we took water in the bridge, and the charts turned into mush, so we had nothing to go by. Things were getting pretty tense, but I kept my mouth shut."

Loew learned the latest news from the *Cape George*'s first class boatswain's mate, Dennis Hoffer, because Snyder was so busy. Besides the lost radar and charts, Hoffer reported, they had no high-frequency radio, the anemometer (wind speed/direction) wasn't registering, and they had zero visibility. Hoffer then gave Loew his loran C readings and asked if he could plot their position and provide them a course to both Salem Sound and Gloucester. Loew did so and then decided he had heard enough. He released them from the case and told them to get to safety, basically making it their option to attempt to proceed to Gloucester or turn around and reenter Boston Harbor. Snyder chose to avoid the danger of turning and decided to continue north-northeast for Gloucester.

❀

In Gloucester, Paradis was cursing the tanker captain. Had the *Global Hope*'s captain checked his position when he was first asked if he was dragging anchor, none of this would have been happening. The captain could have set an additional anchor, added more ballast, or started up his engines and held his position with his bow into the wind. Instead he did nothing and later cried that he was taking on water, which set in motion all the events that followed, including the near loss of the forty-four. Paradis now had additional worries about the *Cape George*. He knew that if the *Cape George* was without navigational aids, they wouldn't be able to locate the *Can Do* or the *Global Hope*. And if it turned out that the *Global Hope* had broken apart and there was loss of life, every newspaper and politician in the region would be asking why the Coast Guard wasn't able to do what they were supposed to do: save lives. Every decision Paradis made would be analyzed later, when hindsight would be twenty-twenty.

Now, however, his immediate task was to get the *Can Do* to safety. He radioed Frank and again asked if he had any idea where he might be.

Frank responded, *"Position unknown at this time. Radar's down. We're trying to stay offshore and find the entrance to Gloucester. It is some howling out here and not having any luck."*

"Roger, if you would like an escort we'll be standing by."

"OK. If your radar is on, you might try to pick us up outside the harbor. We have nothing to work with and we are just trying to fish around at the present."

"Roger, if you want an escort we'll be standing by at this time."

"OK, roger."

"We'll see if we can pick you up on radar and maybe you'll see the blue light."

What both men knew, but it went unsaid, was that this scenario was a long shot. The forty-one was battling to hold position at the entrance to Gloucester Harbor, and the only way they were going to be able to pick up the foundering pilot boat on radar was if it made it to the breakwater.

| 11 |

PURSUING LIFE'S
PATHWAY

While Frank had the rugged character of a Howard Blackburn, Charlie Bucko was cut out of the mold of the Coast Guard's first hero, Joshua James. Prior to the Coast Guard's formation in 1915, the first organization to aid shipwrecked mariners in the United States was the Massachusetts Humane Society, established in 1786. The first boathouse and rescue surfboat station was in Cohasset, Massachusetts, and was followed by other rescue stations. When a shipwreck occurred, volunteers rushed to the surfboats, which looked very similar to the dory that saved Blackburn. Due to lack of training, sometimes the volunteers themselves were drowned when the surfboats capsized during their attempts to reach stranded ships.

Huts were also built along the beaches to serve as shelters for shipwrecked mariners who managed to swim ashore. These were stocked with food, clothing, and firewood. The huts were an effective means of survival—provided the surviving seaman could find the hut after being hurled up on the shore. During storms, volunteer surfmen maintained beach patrols by walking the shore both night and day, on the lookout for wrecks. If the patrolman came upon an offshore wreck he would light a flare to let the surviving mariners know they had been spotted; then he would race back to the station to summon help. In populated areas, the surfman would also pound on the doors of nearby homes and awaken the occupants, and they would spread the call for assistance using a tag-team type system.

This was the state of sea rescue during Joshua James's early years. Born in 1826 at Hull, Massachusetts, Joshua was the ninth of twelve children. While James was still a young boy his mother died, and he was raised by his beloved sister Catherine. His life was then shaped by a tragic accident when Catherine and his baby sister perished during the sinking of the schooner *Hepzibah*. After that incident he made it his life's work to do whatever he could to save shipwrecked crews and passengers. As early as age fifteen he participated in a rescue while on board one of the Massachusetts Humane Society lifeboats from Point Allerton, at the northern edge of the Hull Peninsula. As a volunteer, James participated in countless rescues and at the age of fifty he was appointed keeper of four Massachusetts Humane Society lifeboats at Point Allerton, Stony Beach, and Nantasket Beach in Hull. In 1886 James was presented with a special silver medal for "brave and faithful service of more than 40 years." The report that accompanied James's medal said: "During this time he assisted in saving over 100 lives."

James's most famous rescue, however, was still to come. On the morning of November 25, 1888, a heavy gale tore northward along the New England coastline, prompting James to race to the top of Telegraph Hill in Hull to scan the horizon for vessels in distress. He saw several and noted that at least three were dragging anchor and being pushed toward the rocky shoreline. James estimated where the vessels might come ashore and then gathered his men, who carried a lifeboat to the position. The schooner *Cox and Green* soon ran aground at the predicted spot west of Toddy Rocks, but James felt the seas were too heavy for the lifeboat's capability. Instead his men fetched the breeches buoy. Using a cannonlike device, they shot a line out to the stricken ship. Then a thicker line, the main hawser, was hauled out to the ship by the stranded crew members. One end of the hawser was secured on the ship and the other fixed to the beach using a sand anchor. The breeches buoy was then attached to the hawser. It worked like a pulley running along the hawser, and a whip line was used to haul the breeches buoy back and forth from ship to shore. James was able to successfully rescue all eight men onboard the *Cox and Green* without exposing his own crew to any danger.

As the last man was being taken off the *Cox and Green*, the coal-laden schooner *Gertrude Abbott* struck the rocks just an eighth of a mile from where James and his crew were working. This vessel was too far from shore for the breeches buoy, and darkness had descended on the distressed *Gertrude Abbott*. James was in a bind. The tide was up and seas were so furious he dared not send the lifeboat into the tempest. Instead he instructed his men and the huge crowd that had gathered to build a large fire high on a bluff to cast light on the vessel and to let the shipwrecked mariners know their distress flag in the rigging had been seen. Then he told his men to wait, hoping conditions would abate as the tide fell. Instead the opposite happened and James knew the *Gertrude Abbott* would not hold together much longer. Rather than order his men to launch the lifeboat, he asked for volunteers, explaining that they only had an even chance of returning from the rescue attempt. Every one of his men stepped forward, including his own son Osceola, and together they launched, pulling on the oars for all they were worth to get past the worst of the crashing breakers. Although the lifeboat was taking on water and two men had to bail while the others rowed, they made it to the floundering ship and all eight men onboard slid down ropes into the arms of the waiting rescuers. But now the lifeboat was heavy and crowded, making it exceedingly hard to manage. Approximately six hundred feet from the beach the boat struck a rock and filled with seawater while rolling on its side. James describes what happened next: "The men shifted to windward and straightened her up. One of the crew got overboard but was hauled in by the rest. I called to the men as loudly as I could to stick to the boat, no matter what might happen."

Now the lifeboat was bouncing off rocks like a Ping-Pong ball, first turned one way, then the other. Most of the oars had been lost and the remaining ones were used for steering and pushing the vessel off rocks. The breakers were propelling the boat at incredible speed toward more rocks, and James said it was nothing less than a miracle she wasn't smashed to bits. Somehow they made it past the rocks, despite having the starboard side "stove in," and all onboard made it safely to shore.

James and his men then fanned out along the shoreline on patrol, and five hours later they spotted the floundering schooner *Bertha F. Walker*. The captain and the mate had been swept overboard and drowned, but the remaining crew of seven had climbed up into the rigging to escape the waves washing over the deck. The stranded men were too far out for the breeches buoy, and the lifeboat had been wrecked in the earlier rescue. James's men rounded up some horses and pulled a different lifeboat four miles overland to the scene. At first light James and his volunteers rowed out to the vessel and held position just beyond the rigging. One by one the crewmen let go of the rigging, timing their falls to land between waves, and James managed to haul each one into the lifeboat.

Next James was summoned to Nantasket Beach where the schooner *H. C. Bigginson* was floundering. Again he repeated the process of maneuvering a lifeboat abreast of the schooner. A line was thrown to a sailor in the mizzen rigging and he tied it around his waist, worked his way closer to the sea, and jumped. James and his crew pulled him into the lifeboat, then threw the line back to the floundering ship, where four other seamen took turns jumping and being hauled to safety.

At the end of those two days twenty-eight mariners had been saved. The damage and loss of life from that storm prompted the government to erect more stations with better equipment and trained crews who were paid rather than volunteers. James went on to be appointed the keeper of the Point Allerton Station operated by the U.S. Life-Saving Service, the vanguard of today's Coast Guard. Although at age sixty-two he was past the maximum age limit, a special exception was made and the requirement was waived. James continued to assist in several other rescues, including the terrible Portland Storm (November 26–28, 1898). Even James's death was in keeping with his desire to be in action. On March 17, 1902, seven crew members of the Monomoy Point Life-Saving Station drowned in an attempt to rescue the stranded coal barge *Wadena* off Cape Cod. When James learned of this tragedy, he decided even more vigorous training was needed by his own crew. Two days later, on the morning of March 19, a northeast gale was blowing, and James decided the conditions were perfect for heavy weather training. The seventy-five-year-old leader joined his men in the maneuvers, and when he was satisfied of their ability he ordered the boat to shore. He stepped onto the beach, turned to the sea, paused, and said, "The tide is ebbing," then dropped dead on the sand.

Using a lifeboat instead of a coffin, James's funeral procession wound through the streets of Hull, and he was laid to rest beneath a tombstone that reads: "Greater love hath no man than this—that a man lay down his life for his friends." Sumner Kimball, the superintendent of the Life-Saving Service, wrote of

James's quiet courage: "Here and there may be found men in all walks of life who neither wonder or care how much or how little the world thinks of them. They pursue life's pathway, doing their appointed tasks, without ostentation, loving their work for the work's sake, content to live and do in the present rather than look for the uncertain rewards of the future. To them notoriety, distinction, or even fame, acts neither as a spur nor a check to endeavor, yet they are among the foremost of those who do the world's work. Joshua James was one of these."

✳

Charlie Bucko knew the story of Joshua James, as did every Coastie who served at Point Allerton. Perhaps Bucko's own opinion about staying with the boat, no matter what the situation, was reinforced when he read how James told his own men to do the same during the *Gertrude Abbott* rescue. But Bucko didn't mold himself to be a Joshua James; he was born that way. As early as eight years of age he found a neighbor trapped under a car that had fallen off a jack and ran and told his mother, who called the police. When he was eleven a similar thing happened when a neighbor fell asleep while smoking and a small fire ignited inside the house. Charlie happened to notice smoke coming out of a window and pounded on the door, waking up the neighbor and potentially saving her life. When he was thirteen years old he made his first full-blown rescue. Charlie's sister Janice recollected how he had been skating on a pond when another boy fell through the ice and disappeared. Charlie went in after the boy and dragged him up, saving his life. That night the boy's parents came over to the house to thank Charlie, and Janice, just seven years old at the time, listened in on the conversation, amazed to learn how Charlie went under the ice and didn't come up until he had found the boy.

Pete Lafontaine, Charlie's commanding officer at Point Allerton, says Bucko was "a natural leader and rescuer." Lafontaine saw Charlie mature from a brash and reckless youth who spent time in the brig for punching an officer while stationed in Newport, Rhode Island, to a mature, confident young man: "He really found his niche when he became a coxswain. He never had to raise his voice to his crew and they really responded to him. We had him out on so many rescues I lost count. He had a whole lot of heavy weather experience under his belt when the Blizzard struck. Charlie would have gone a long way in the Coast Guard."

Charlie Bucko's toughness was first forged and tested in Vietnam. Janice remembers that the first time he was wounded two marines came to her parents' house and she thought for sure they were going to say he was dead. Instead they said Charlie had been wounded in the arm, but that they thought he would make a full recovery. The marine representatives brought the Buckos a Western Union telegram that stated Charlie "sustained a gunshot wound to the left elbow from hostile rifle fire while on an operation." He had been in Vietnam for all of one month.

Charlie's arm did heal, but just a month later his other arm was hit, this time by shrapnel during a firefight at Quang Tri Province. He was airlifted to the aircraft carrier *Valley Forge* for treatment and later sent to a hospital for further recovery. After his arm healed he was stationed at Marine Headquarters in Okinawa and upon completion of his duty there he received an honorable discharge. "When Charlie was released from the marines," says Janice, "he took the train back to New London. I remember it was winter and I was walking home from school and Charlie came trudging through the snowy streets. I ran over and hugged him and then we quietly walked the rest of the way home together as if it was just a regular day. About a week later one of our cousins, Donald Walsh, told Charlie he was going to enlist in the marines as a medic, and Charlie said don't go, he'd seen enough new recruits killed fighting over there. Don still decided to join. When Charlie heard this he actually went to the Marine

Corps recruiting office to reenlist, figuring that he could get assigned to Don's unit and look out for him. The recruiting officer turned out to be the same marine who came to our house when Charlie was injured and he was able to talk Charlie out of reenlisting. Don went over there, though, and within a month of arriving in Vietnam he was killed."

Although Bucko's Vietnam experience led him to advise his cousin not to join the marines, Charlie was proud of his service and of the Marine Corps. Back home he watched the war protesters and wondered if they really understood the situation in Southeast Asia. Being the curious type, Bucko drove down to Washington, D.C., to observe a demonstration that took place in front of the Washington Monument. He later wrote about his experience, and his article was published in a newspaper near New London, the *Norwich Bulletin*. "The crowd was singing protest songs and laughing," wrote Charlie, "somewhere among them I could hear the chant 'D.C. for V.C.' I struck up a conversation with a girl holding a sign which stated, *Bring our boys back now.*' As we talked, I found her to be quite intelligent yet very irrational. She spoke of all the things wrong with America and Americans, but failed to shed any light on the good of our nation. She mentioned many problems but failed to offer any helpful ideas that might illuminate the social enigmas of our society. The undoing fault of the Yippies lies in the fact that they offer no constructive criticism or concrete replacement for the society they wish to pull down."

Bucko went on to write of his perspective on the protesters and their interaction with the nearby riot-control police, which was quite different from the usual views of that time. He describes a scene where the demonstrators marched on the Smithsonian Institute where Vice President Agnew was to make a speech. The police had thrown a protective cordon around the building, and the demonstrators formed a line paralleling the helmeted police:

"The Yippies grew impatient with the calm attitude of the police and started to taunt them . . . to provoke them into making a move. Suddenly a rock landed among the police . . . an officer was helped into a squad car, his ear bleeding. My respect for these officers of the law grew as I observed these harassed, mature men 'keep their cool.'"

Charlie clearly found the demonstrators' motives as bewildering as the situation in Vietnam, but he moved on, letting his spirit of adventure be his guide. He took a few college courses but grew restless and started traveling, experiencing all he could. In New York City he took acting classes and did some theater, only to pack up and move again after a few months. He wound up working on a cattle ranch in Idaho for a few more months, then pushed farther west to Seattle, where his sister Janice was living at the time: "Charlie just blew into Seattle and spent several weeks with me. He was just so full of life, and he had the attitude of not sweating the small stuff. In fact, while he was living with me I cracked up his car, and it was a total loss. He said, 'No big deal. You're OK and that's all that matters.'"

Charlie had an active imagination and he especially enjoyed reading Ernest Hemingway and Jack London, particularly their stories about the remote and isolated places. While at Janice's apartment, he started reading about Antarctica and he quickly made up his mind to somehow get there himself. He figured the only way he'd ever do it was if he joined the Coast Guard, and sure enough, he enlisted and got himself assigned to an icebreaker, which went to Antarctica for six months. A picture shows Charlie standing on the deck of the ship with jagged ice floes behind him. He is tall, six-foot-four, handsome, with sparkling blue eyes and brown hair, and his smile shows how happy he is, living his dreams of adventure.

In a letter to his parents, Charlie wrote: "I should have joined the Coast Guard years ago. It's unbelievable! Compared with the

Marine Corps the Coast Guard is, well—there isn't any comparison actually. The guys are a lot friendlier and you can actually have a conversation with an officer. I'm aboard the *Staten Island*. The Navy built her after WWII, and we gave her to the Russians during the Eisenhower Administration. And get this—the Russians got fed up with her in the Arctic and just left her there. Well, the Coast Guard went up there and claimed her. On the engines, some of the pressure valves are in Russian!" He goes on to show his literary side with the following observation: "If you looked at the *Staten Island* berthed at the pier—the laundrymen working with shirts off, beards, laughter, knowing she was headed on an exciting voyage, you could only think of *The Sand Pebbles* [a novel by Richard McKenne]."

Charlie was named after his uncle Charles, who was a private in the U.S. Army Airborne Infantry during World War II. Uncle Charles was with his lifelong friend, Henry Apanaschik, on a transport ship in the Atlantic when it was hit by a torpedo. Charles assisted his friend Henry as they struggled in the water, and while Henry was later rescued, Charles was lost at sea, his body never recovered.

Like his uncle before him, Charlie loved the water. And after his Vietnam experience, speeding on a Coast Guard patrol boat to save people rather than kill them was welcome change. The ocean offered him the ultimate freedom, and the Coast Guard gave him the adventure he craved, along with the occasional adrenaline rush when on a rescue. Unlike in the marines, real action in the Coast Guard is not dependent on the nation being at war but rather is the result of someone's need for help. Often that need has nothing to do with adverse weather conditions but rather a boater's incredibly dumb decisions or alcohol-induced mistakes. The reasons for a boater's distress are analyzed *after* the rescue is made, however, and Charlie was no different from the thousands of other Coast Guard men and women who risk their lives for total strangers.

After serving on the West Coast and making the voyage to Antarctica, Charlie returned east and was assigned to Coast Guard Station Point Allerton, in Hull, Massachusetts. By all accounts he was both a born leader and really knew how to have fun. Charlie trained several younger Coasties to be coxswains, one of whom was John Halter from Minnesota. "I was assigned to Charlie's crew," says Halter, "aboard an old forty-foot patrol boat, the *40419*. As most of the crew at Point Allerton were native New Englanders, their distrust of someone from landlocked Minnesota training to be a coxswain became obvious. Charlie quickly put them in their place. One afternoon we towed a broken-down boat to the city dock in Hull. After it was secured, Charlie turned the *40419* over to me and ordered me to take it back to the station. There were a number of 'townies' fishing from the city dock, and I proceeded to back the boat over their lines, my props cutting about a half dozen of them in the process. The boat engineer, a young downeaster from Maine, began screaming at me about what a stupid fuck I was and what a complete embarrassment I was to both Point Allerton and the CG in general. Charlie grabbed him by his shirt and dragged him down into the cabin, where he informed him in no uncertain terms that my training was none of his 'goddamned business' and that he'd be better suited to minding his engines. When Charlie finally reappeared on deck he was grinning and reassured me that in the future the townies would know better than to leave their lines in the water when a CG boat approached. 'Now let me show you what I would have done in that situation,' he said, and he very patiently instructed me in the art of close-quarter boat handling. He knew a thing or two about boats."

Halter and Charlie became close friends, and Charlie confided that he wanted to be a writer and was working on a story set in Vietnam called "Guardian of the Rain," in which a young soldier's entire unit was ambushed while he sat alone in the rain on sentry duty. Halter thought Charlie looked a little like a young Ernest Hemingway: "He was a tall, powerful-looking man with dimples and laughing eyes." Charlie liked to tell a story as much as write about one, and many a night he held court over a gathering of Coasties at Mike Burn's Tavern telling stories of life at Point Allerton, in Vietnam, and in Antarctica.

Halter recalled Charlie had "a built-in bullshit detector" and was not afraid to use it. While serving aboard the Coast Guard cutter *Chase* he was busted down to seaman apprentice over an altercation he had with the ship's executive officer, who Charlie thought reeked of bullshit. The officer wasn't too wild about having Charlie on his boat and, to prove his superiority, one day ordered him to paint the deckplate bolts in the engine room. Charlie did as he was ordered, but at the next crew muster he walked up and punched the executive officer in front of everyone, an action he never regretted.

After Halter completed his coxswain training, Charlie transferred up to Gloucester Station, but the two friends stayed in touch, with Halter making frequent visits to Gloucester. Charlie told Halter that Gloucester was the best station he'd ever served at: "No bullshit up here," said Charlie. "Everyone is treated like a professional, without any of that Mickey Mouse crap." Halter recalls one visit where Charlie, on the spur of the moment, convinced a bunch of fellow Coasties to pool their money and head up to Montreal for the weekend. They drove all night, singing songs and laughing, arriving the next morning in Montreal, where they rented a cheap hotel room to sleep in. As it turned out, that night was Halloween and all the downtown bars were packed. The contingent of Coasties entered one of the rowdier-looking French-speaking taverns and settled in to a corner table. Halter explains that before long "someone accused us of being Americans and Charlie boldly stood up and confirmed that indeed we were. With anyone else a huge fight might have broken out, but not with Charlie Bucko. Within minutes, he had the whole bar singing *'God Bless America,'* and afterward everyone in the place was our friend."

Another young Coastie from Station Point Allerton, Elmer Borsos, remembers a night that he and Charlie almost got in a fight. Boros explains that when he first arrived at the station he was a naive young man from eastern Ohio, and the Coast Guard was his first taste of the real world. Charlie had been teasing Boros during his first couple months, and one night at Mike Burn's Tavern in Hull Charlie started in on him again. "Both of us had had a few beers," says Boros, "and when Charlie started teasing me I grabbed his beer and poured it out right in front of him, saying, 'This is what I think of you!' I figured he would pound me into the ground. Instead, he laughed till he couldn't laugh anymore. Everyone else was in shock."

As time went on, Charlie gave Boros more respect and Boros in turn began to understand that Charlie's service in Vietnam put him at a different level from the younger men at the station. "He tried really hard to blend in with the station," says Boros, "but his service in Vietnam set him apart. He had been to hell and back in Vietnam, and at Point Allerton he was looking to do something productive. He wanted to have fun and not fight for his life."

When Charlie decided to leave the Coast Guard his fiancée, Sharon Watts, wondered how he would adjust to civilian life. To her surprise he did just fine, simply focusing his energies on his dozens of other interests. "He was beat coming home every night from his new job at the shipyard, but he truly liked his work and fellow coworkers. I loved watching him come through the door of our apartment with his ratty old jeans and flannel shirt." After dinner the couple would take quiet walks, often sneaking up to the Eastern Point Lighthouse to sit by the breakwater and watch the sunset over the harbor. At the breakwater the couple would talk of their future together, which, of course, still involved the water.

Charlie had picked out a boat, and he talked about how someday Sharon and their kids would all enjoy it together. He also sketched out a design for his dream house that he wanted to build overlooking the coast. He envisioned the family room to have nautical furnishings and feature his restored furniture, with a window looking out to sea.

When Charlie retired from the Coast Guard in 1977, his family was relieved, especially after learning about the sea conditions during the *Chester Poling* rescue. Sister Joan says, "Charlie had that marine mentality 'to leave no man behind,' and we knew he would do anything to help someone in need. So we were glad when he settled down with Sharon, and not on a Coast Guard patrol boat, figuring life would be a lot safer."

Once a marine, always a marine—and for that matter once a Coastie, always a Coastie. The Coast Guard has their own saying: "You have to go out, but you don't (necessarily) have to come back." The phrase goes back to the early 1900s when lifeboat oarsman Patrick Etheridge was leading a rescue to a floundering ship off Cape Hatteras. One of the crewmen looked out over the angry seas and shouted out, "We might make it out to the wreck, but we'd never make it back!" Etheridge shouted back, "The Blue Book says we've got to go out and it doesn't say a damn thing about having to come back!" At the time there was some truth to Ethridge's interpretation of the regulations because they read: "The statement of the keeper that he did not try to use the boat because the sea or surf was too heavy will not be accepted unless attempts to launch it were actually made and failed." Although today's Coast Guard takes a more pragmatic approach, with risk assessment analysis, many of the Coasties from the 1970s and earlier tended to literally follow the motto. Bucko, being both a former marine and a Coast Guard coxswain, definitely had this mind-set, and he could not listen to the communications of the struggling forty-four during the Blizzard without at least trying to help.

By all accounts Charlie was content in his new life after the Coast Guard, using his newfound freedom to spend more time with Sharon and enjoy frequent visits with Frank on the *Can Do*. He also sat down in earnest and channeled his energies into his latest writing project, the manuscript about a sea rescue that he hoped to have published as his first book. "It was remarkable how it mirrored the night of the Blizzard," says Sharon. "He had the book about ninety percent complete, all handwritten in a spiral notebook. The book was about five men who set out during a winter storm to help some friends whose boat was in trouble." Unfortunately, the manuscript was lost when Sharon's basement flooded several years after the Blizzard. Bucko's sister Janice, however, had saved his preliminary book outline, and it does have some striking, eerie parallels to the night he went out on the *Can Do*. In sketching out the story, he wrote how "no one believes the weatherman who comes to the conclusion that this [approaching storm] is the granddaddy of all northeasters. An intense low pressure system in the Ohio valley is moving northeast with a secondary low forming in Long Island Sound." When the systems converge, he wrote, "a huge storm is developing, hurricane winds, with twenty foot seas. Storm tide with moon tide in excess of fifteen feet (above normal). Heavy snow/sleet."

Bucko's outline notes clearly show how he planned to combine some of his real-life experiences with his own rich imagination. Notations show that certain characters would be modeled after real people in the Coast Guard, events borrowed from the *Chester Poling* rescue, and incidents incorporated from his days at Point Allerton. He also had Frank and the *Can Do* in mind, noting that a pilot boat would join other Coast Guard boats going to the aid of the stricken tanker. His outline goes on to describe two lead characters who have marked similarities to Charlie and Frank, with a notation saying "the reader must feel the chemistry that make these two men get along so well." Bucko then describes

how Salem Shipping Control picks up a Mayday call from a
tanker in distress and how the actions of the two lead characters
during the blizzard will determine whether they live or die.

❋

And now, in the actual Blizzard, Frank and Bucko were side by
side in the pilothouse, drawing on every bit of their nautical
know-how to keep the beleaguered *Can Do* afloat. Their lives had
intersected two years earlier when Chief Willey introduced the
two men, helping to bridge the years. In Bucko, Frank saw a
younger but more gregarious version of himself, and he warmed
to the big man's smile and self-deprecating humor. For Charlie,
Frank was something of a role model, a veteran of the seas. Charlie was heartened by the fact that Frank could make his living on
the ocean and still be involved in helping mariners in distress.
And Charlie took note of Frank's family life, especially how the
entire Quirk family made the *Can Do* their weekend home and
how the boys could operate the boat as if they'd been at sea far
beyond their years. It's no surprise that he told Sharon, "I want
kids, not just a couple but a whole slew of them. Think of the
times we'll have!"

| 12 |

IN SHOAL WATERS

At midnight the storm was merciless in its pelting fury. Both wind and seas had continued to increase, and beyond the windshield of the *Can Do* driving foam, spray, and snow filled the frigid night sky. Each time the *Can Do* crested a wave its propeller was momentarily out of the water, whining crazily, and the boat was out of Frank's control. Then down the wave it plunged, as if going over a cliff. At the bottom of the trough, green water engulfed the bow before cascading off as Frank coaxed the pilot boat up the next wave. Every few minutes he was sucker punched by a confused sea coming at the *Can Do* from a slightly different angle. Frank was like a blindfolded fighter thrust into the ring against an unseen opponent who threw all haymakers and no jabs.

The force of a thirty-foot wave is almost unimaginable, considering that just one cubic foot of water is equal to sixty-four pounds and one cubic yard of water weighs fifteen hundred pounds. To the men on the *Can Do*, each wave felt as if a gigantic battering ram were being slammed into the floundering boat, intent on busting it open. As February 6 ended and February 7 began it seemed like the storm picked the *Can Do* as its target and was trying to stop the boat before it could reach its home port.

The *Can Do,* however, was a rugged boat, and Frank had made many improvements to it. On its modest-sized front windshield he had installed a visor to reduce the glare on sunny days. For snow and sleet he mounted a small motorized revolving circular plate of glass on the main windshield, which helped keep that portion free of ice and snow for better visibility. Frank also wanted to be sure other boats could see him in low light, and just below the wheelhouse he painted a large section bright orange and upon that wrote the word "PILOT in large black letters on the far left and right, with the boat's name in the middle. The hull was black, the superstructure light gray, and the exhaust stack red. A stainless-steel rail went around the hull, and for extra safety Frank added stanchion pipes that supported a thick safety cable that encircled the entire boat. The radio and radar antennae stretched skyward off the back of the pilothouse, and flying above those was an American flag. Inside the boat, Frank had stowed several pieces of safety and rescue equipment, including a ten-man life raft, fire extinguishers, first-aid kits, and wet suits. He had also purchased a Lyle gun that could shoot a messenger line six hundred feet to a disabled vessel, which mariners could then use to heave in the hawser line for towing.

The *Can Do*'s low superstructure both helped and hurt its chances of survival during the Blizzard. It gave the vessel a low center of gravity, which aided in stability against the powerful wind gusts. But the low superstructure also meant the exhaust stack was not far from the ocean's surface, leaving it vulnerable to a deluge of water from a monstrous wave. And the longer the boat stayed out in the storm, the greater the probability that something onboard would fail. Each man onboard knew it was imperative to find that entrance to Gloucester Harbor immediately. Judging from the previous radio communication, when Frank radioed Paradis to have the forty-one-footer try to pick them up on radar, the crew of the *Can Do* believed they were getting closer to safety. After that communication little more was said and Frank put all his focus on feeling his way up each wave while keeping his bow pointed north-northeast.

Suddenly, at approximately 1:00 a.m., a different voice came over the radio from the *Can Do*. It was Charlie Bucko.

"Gloucester Station, Can Do, *Gloucester Station,* Can Do.*"*

At Station Gloucester, a lower-level officer had temporarily relieved Chief Paradis from the communications room, and this man quickly responded, *"Roger, this is Gloucester Station."*

Charlie Bucko, in a remarkably clear and calm voice, then said, *"Roger. This is not a drill; this is not a drill . . . a* Mayday, a Mayday, a Mayday. Over.*"*

"Roger, pilot boat Can Do, *this is Gloucester; we have you at this time."*

There was a long pause and nothing more was heard from the *Can Do.*

Station Gloucester shouted, "Can Do, *keep sending traffic, over!"*

There was no response. The man at the mike immediately had Paradis summoned back to the communications room, and shortly after his arrival Bucko came back on the radio, his voice now out of breath:

"Gloucester Station, Can Do, *Gloucester Station,* Can Do.*"*

"This is Gloucester Station."

"We're not sure what has happened at this time . . . ah. . . . We feel we may have hit the breakwater [outside the harbor]."

Bucko paused for three seconds and then shouted, *"Negative on my last, negative on my last!"*

"Roger, do you happen to know approximately where you might be?"
"That's a negative."

There were several anxious seconds of silence; then Paradis, exhausted and tense, responded, *"This is Gloucester Station; keep on talking to us here."*

"Mike, be advised we are in shoal water—" Suddenly, in the background, Frank's angry voice is heard: *"Look, give me that—"* The rest of Frank's words were cut off.

"This is Gloucester Station, over. Keep talking to us. Let us know the situation."

"We're trying to get into deeper water here." The voice was Bucko's again.

"Keep talking."

"We're in shoal water. Our windshield is out. Position unknown. Action extremely violent."

This last message began to explain what happened. The *Can Do* hit something in shallow water, either the ocean's bottom or a rock ledge, and at the same instant the windshield was blown out, probably from a giant wave. The wall of water, parts of the windshield, and probably the motor for the spinning window crashed into Frank's head, knocking him from the wheel. Because Bucko was likely standing by the wheel with Frank, he, too, would have been sent reeling backward, arms flailing, by the booming fist of water. The pounding of the seas—which was loud even inside a sealed wheelhouse—was now a deafening roar.

Curley, Wilkinson, and Fuller had all accompanied Frank and Charlie to lend a hand—now they were needed and then some. They must have been stunned by the wall of water pouring into the boat, but they had to recover immediately or they'd lose the *Can Do* and their lives.

Frank was temporarily knocked unconscious, and that's why Bucko took over the radio and the wheel. When Frank regained consciousness he wanted to get back to the wheel, despite having severe cuts on his face and head. While the boat was pitching wildly, Frank struggled toward the radio, trying to regain control of the microphone. One of the crew likely held him for a minute, telling him he was badly injured while trying to stop the flow of blood. Two of the others dashed below and frantically searched for something to seal the jagged opening of the shattered windshield. Each cresting wave was pouring more water into the boat, and the crew only had seconds to hold the sea at bay before it was too late. The two men hauled up a mattress and stuffed it in the gaping hole—it didn't entirely stop the icy water from gaining entry, but it bought them more time to stay afloat.

The actions of the men at that time were crucial to whether or not they would perish in the next moments. Quirk was injured, water had poured through the opening where the windshield once was, and the boat continued to flounder in shoal water, with the peril of capsizing or engine failure increasing with each oncoming wave. Charlie Bucko, operating blind and relying on instinctive reactions, had only seconds to maneuver the boat into deeper water before it was too late. But the waves he was encountering were much deadlier than those they were fighting on the open sea.

When waves hit shallow water they are shortened, become steeper, and break more frequently. These chaotic sea conditions were lifting the *Can Do* up twenty feet only to let it free fall down and scrape bottom. In seas of this magnitude the depth of shoal water and the trouble it can cause for boats is relative to wave height. Normally the *Can Do,* which drew six feet of water, had no trouble in sea depths as shallow as ten feet, but the giant waves left a void in their wake exposing the ocean floor. At the time of the Mayday the *Can Do* might have been in as much as twenty feet of water but was still hitting bottom in each wave trough. And although the *Can Do* had been battling breaking seas all night long, the manner in which they broke was now much more violent. Breaking seas occur when the crest of the wave must get rid of excess energy by spilling over, which happens when the wave's face or height exceeds one-seventh of its length. When the *Can Do* was in deeper water the breaking waves were "spillers," which broke gradually and continuously. Now, in shallow water, the waves encountered resistance from the bottom of the ocean and were stacking up, causing them to have steeper faces. These breaking waves were "plungers," which fell much more suddenly. The speed of the water in what is known as the "jet" within the plunging wave can be as much as four times faster than the velocity of advancing waves. This sudden burst of furious energy is every mariner's nightmare, because even the best of skippers usually lose control of their boats in such conditions.

The *Can Do* was encountering a compounding of problems, where one causes the next and the sum of two or three problems can be more devastating than a single major mechanical or structural failure. The lack of radar caused the *Can Do* to be swept into shallow water, and shallow water meant more confused seas, which in turn led to the smashed windshield. To make matters worse, the waves, in both shallow and deep water, were getting bigger, because the third factor in the creation of wave size— besides the wind and fetch—is the duration of the storm. The longer winds blow, the larger the wave trains become. And the Blizzard was locked in place and showing no signs of weakening.

Slowly, the options for the men on board the *Can Do* were being taken away.

❋

Before the *Can Do* went into its Mayday situation, Gard Estes and Louis Linquata, back at the marina, decided they had to do something to help. The men had access to a Jeep that was formerly used as a two-seater mail truck. It had a CB radio inside, and they were briefly able to raise Frank on the radio and he said, "We're in deep trouble with no radar." Frank went on to say that he might be near Magnolia Beach and he wanted them to get searchlights there, thinking if worse came to worst he could try to beach the boat onshore. Gard and Louis then ran back inside the marina and started calling neighboring police and fire departments, civil defense, and friends from the Northeast Surf Patrol requesting them to head to Magnolia. Their plan was to get as many vehicles as possible down to Magnolia Beach and shine their headlights seaward and hope that Frank would see the lights and be able to drive the *Can Do* up on the sand.

The two men hopped back in the Jeep and started heading south for Magnolia. "I don't know how we got there," says Louis. "The streets were either blocked with drifting snow or flooded. It was almost impossible to see more than a foot or two past our headlights. When we got to Magnolia Beach we were relieved to see there were several police and civil defense men gathered on a nearby roadway."

By the time they reached the beach they had heard Bucko's Mayday and knew Frank was hurt. The men parked their cars and trucks as close to the beach as possible and shined their headlights out toward the ocean. Then they broke up into groups of two or three and tried to walk closer to the water, thinking the *Can Do* might have already been smashed in the surf. Gard explains what happened next: "I had moved toward the ocean and was talking with a police officer when a giant wave crashed over the seawall. It sounded like Logan Airport with jets taking off right next to us. The wave knocked us down and rolled us. As the wave receded it started to take us with it. We grabbed hold of the seawall. We were literally hanging on by our fingertips. Once the water went past us we ran like hell. There was a tennis club nearby and after that wave hit, half of it was gone—it looked like a stick of dynamite had been thrown into it."

Two civil defense men were also caught in the same wave but were unable to grab the seawall. Louis, standing just twenty feet away, watched as the two men disappeared beneath a receding wave. Then seconds later another breaker hurled the men back up onshore. Louis, Gard, and several others helped the men who had been tossed ashore back onto their feet and they all ran to a nearby house for safety. Inside the home the men felt safe until a wave came up and over the roof of the house. Louis and Gard stayed inside for a few minutes but thought the *Can Do* might have been pushed farther south, so they returned to the Jeep. "We headed down toward Beverly," says Gard, "and that little mail carrier got us through many sections of waist-deep water. We stopped at several places such as Hospital Point, looking for the *Can Do,* and even searched for debris from the boat. Then we headed north again, stopping now and then to shine our lights out to sea, but there was no sign of the boat."

Trying to determine the position of the *Can Do* became the goal for everyone who knew the pilot boat was in trouble. In 1978 the EPIRB was still a relatively new piece of technology. Its genesis was in the emergency locater transmitters that became required equipment on most U.S. civil aircraft in 1974. These battery-operated transmitters were programmed to be activated by a manual switch or an impact of five g's. The distress signal they emitted upon civil VHF radio frequencies and military UHF frequencies allowed rescuers to home in on the signal. Mariners quickly recognized that this technology would be a lifesaver for boats in distress, and the transmitters were modified to be activated by water immersion. In the mid-1970s, the few vessels that had EPIRBS were those that went offshore beyond range of shore communication, which was usually over twenty miles. The *Can Do,* like other coastal utility boats, did not have an EPIRB, and the Coast Guard, Warren Andrews, and members of the Northeast Surf Patrol continued to try to get a rough fix on its location through its radio communications. But first they had to hear from the stricken pilot boat.

Since the original Mayday communications nothing had been heard from the *Can Do*. Paradis and Warren called the boat over and over, but their queries went unanswered. Bucko's last message rang in their ears like an ill wind: *"We're in shoal water. Our windshield is out. Position unknown. Action extremely violent."*

TROUBLES ON THE
CAPE GEORGE

The windshield of the *Can Do* was likely obliterated by the rampaging seas, but it's possible the windshield's sun visor played a role. The visor extended over the top of the windshield by four or five inches, and as each wave swept over the bow and up the windshield, some of its water was temporarily trapped by the visor, creating extra pressure. This entrapment of water made the force of the wave slightly greater, perhaps giving it just enough power to shatter the extra-thick glass. On most boats, windshields are very vulnerable components during storms. Fishing vessels often have pieces of plywood stowed onboard that can, in theory, be quickly screwed into place should a windshield blow. For the plywood to hold up against large waves a crew member would have to go on deck outside the broken window and drill through the plywood and the boat. Then he or she would have to insert the bolts while someone inside screwed on the nuts.

During gale conditions, however, it's virtually impossible to work outside without being swept over.

Some Coast Guard men on duty the night of the Blizzard offered a different scenario, saying the *Can Do*'s windshield could have been taken out by a log. In the week prior to the storm they had seen logs scattered and stacked about the shore of Thatcher's Island, located just northeast of Gloucester Harbor. They theorized that these logs were washed into the seas and propelled southwest by the northeast winds and one could have been hurled by a wave directly into the *Can Do*'s windshield.

Blown windshields usually mean that a compounding of events—all bad—follows. Besides the inability of the skipper to see clearly, the incoming water, even if eventually stopped, plays havoc with the boat's stability. The water in the boat slops around, and based on the topside weight of the vessel or the wind direction, the water gravitates to one side or the other, causing the boat to list. If the boat is listing, more water might find its way in through a loose hatch on the lower side. Countless Coast Guard Marine Casualty Reports mention that a blown windshield was the first problem reported by captains in Mayday situations.

While some boats eventually capsize after the windshield is gone, others manage to stay afloat, but they are still vulnerable. When the windshield goes, a boat that was trying to ride out the storm by heading into the seas must make a turn to be in following seas so that the next wave doesn't spill more water through the windshield opening. But turning in a storm with barely any visibility has its own set of risks. A fifty-foot wooden lobster boat found itself in this exact predicament off Georges Bank in 1980. After the windshield was blown out the captain managed to turn the boat to go with the seas, but the waves were so huge the vessel broached and one monstrous wave slammed the boat on the port side. The blow was so powerful it sent one of the crew crashing through the wooden wall of the pilothouse and into the sea. The remaining crew members threw the victim a life ring, but the injured man never moved, apparently knocked unconscious by the impact. The next set of waves carried the victim away from the crippled boat, and he was never seen again.

※

When Charlie Bucko radioed the Mayday, Audrey, Brian, and Maureen Quirk all heard it on their radios at home. Concern turned to terror. The radio transmissions were not clear, but the family knew it wasn't Frank on the mike, and that spoke volumes to the seriousness of the situation. Fifteen-year-old Brian immediately wanted to get down to the Coast Guard station, if only to be closer to his father. But the storm had already dumped a foot and a half of snow and the roads were virtually impassable. Maureen wanted to be with Brian and her mother, but even though she only lived a couple miles away, getting to them would not be easy.

In the minutes that followed the Mayday all communication with the *Can Do* ceased and the family was aghast, thinking the worst. Audrey called Paradis, hoping he was still in communication with the *Can Do*. The commanding officer tried to sound positive, but he had to explain that neither he nor Warren Andrews could raise the boat. Audrey's call was just one of many that were pouring into Gloucester Station from people who had been listening to the drama on their marine radios. Machinery Technician Ron Conklin was Officer of the Day, working alongside Paradis in the communications room, and recalled that about midnight "the place became a madhouse. Calls were coming in every minute from family, people wanting to help, and from people who thought they saw the lights of the *Can Do*. Others called saying they thought they heard a boat's engine, and some of these callers were from as far away as Ipswich and Boston. We had ambulances on standby at the police stations, and they were calling to ask if we heard anything more."

Ralph Stevens was a young seaman who was standing by the door of the communications room listening to everything that was happening. He was especially concerned with the situation of the forty-one-footer holding position by the breakwater. Earlier that night he was on board the forty-one when it aborted its trip to aid the *Global Hope:* "We literally could not see a thing and the conditions were unbelievable. I remember asking the guys onboard, what the hell are we trying to do—that huge tanker wasn't going anywhere, and even if we got there it would be impossible to get anyone off. So we decided to turn around near Norman's Woe. I'm convinced that had we gone just a little bit further I would not be here today. So when I heard they sent the forty-one back out again, I thought, *My God, it's suicide to go back out*. In fact, I had already made the decision that if I was told to go back out I was going to refuse. Let them court-martial me. Sometimes I think in situations like this adrenaline takes over, and common sense gets left behind."

For the men standing outside the communications room, the normal flow of time transformed into a surreal zone, as if at half speed. All night they had listened to the *Can Do*'s progress, trying to will the pilot boat toward the harbor. And now there were no incoming messages from the boat and they feared the worst. Some prayed and others discussed what might have happened to the pilot boat after its windshield was lost.

Ralph Stevens says that the men in the hallway talked softly so they could hear what was happening in the radio room: "Things were really hopping in there and we could feel the tension. Paradis was on the radio, a couple other people were on the phones, and another was on the teletype giving situational updates to Boston. The rest of us were just standing in the hallway, hoping we'd hear Bucko come back on the radio. Charlie Bucko was the guy who taught me how to run a Coast Guard boat, and he was a great instructor. I was hoping somehow he'd get lucky this one time and make it. The guys in the hall were just standing there, anxiously waiting for news. We all knew Charlie and Frank, and we knew things didn't look good."

All this commotion was not helping Mike Paradis. His right-hand man, Brad Willey, was unable to reach the station, trapped by the snows at Annisquam light, ten miles away. Any kind of help would have been appreciated, and from where Paradis sat he could look out the window into the swirling snow and be reminded of just how limited his resources were. The station's concrete helicopter pad was just a few feet from the window, and he must have wished conditions would change so a helo from Coast Guard Air Station Cape Cod at Otis Air Force Base could get airborne. From time to time the tall, thin station commander stood up from his chair and rubbed his temples, pushing back his white hair. He'd been handling this crisis for six straight hours and he needed a drink. He probably figured there was a good chance the *Can Do* had capsized, and he wondered if people would blame him for what happened. Paradis was just months away from retirement, and never in his Coast Guard career had he had a night like this, when almost everything that could go wrong did. He may have thought how cruel and ironic it was that Frank and Charlie, who had answered dozens of Mayday calls, had no one to help them in their time of need. The forty-one-footer could not venture much farther than the breakwater, the forty-four was damaged down in Salem, the *Decisive* was still miles away, and the *Cape George* was without effective radar. Still, Paradis hoped that the *Can Do* might get close enough for the forty-one-footer to make radar contact. He radioed the 41: *"Four-one-three-five-three, this is Gloucester Station. The* Can Do *is in Mayday situation at this time. Where are you?"*

"We are outside the breakwater and no radar contact with the Can Do."

Paradis responded as if talking through clinched teeth, *"Get in the best position you can and ride it out."*

"I'll do my best."

Paradis next raised the *Cape George* and asked if they were still heading to Gloucester.

Skipper Glen Snyder shouted back to be heard above the shrieking wind, hesitating between each sentence to be sure he could be heard: *"Station Gloucester, cutter* Cape George, *that's affirmative! We are presently lost! I repeat, we are presently lost! We have lost loran reception. We believe we are two and a half miles east . . . of Cape, of, ah, off, ah, Eastern Point. But we cannot confirm it. We are proceeding toward shore to try and pick up some lights and confirm our position."*

"Do you have any radar?"

"Radar is performing poorly! I can barely pick up any landmasses at all. What I do pick up we are unable to identify."

"Understand that we have the pilot boat Can Do *in a Mayday situation somewhere near Gloucester and Magnolia. We request on your way in to make any sweeps in any area if possible to see if we can pick up the pilot boat."*

Seaman Vern DePietro remembers that conversation as if it happened yesterday: "When I heard Glen Snyder say we were lost, that really scared me, because the seas were still getting bigger. I knew we weren't far from shoal water, and the *Cape George* drew six feet, four inches, aft and about four feet, four inches, forward, so we could have easily hit an unseen shoal."

The *Cape George* and the *Can Do* were not all that far apart, with the *George* just to the south of Baker's Island and the pilot boat to the north. But without functioning radar on either boat they might as well have been in different oceans. Snyder had to worry about hitting the shoals near Baker's Island, and his cutter performed sluggishly, with significant ice buildup causing it to wallow heavily in the pounding seas. Freezing spray hardened as soon as it struck, making the boat top-heavy. Usually when this happens men are sent on deck with baseball bats to pound and chip away at the ice, but that night it was impossible to spend more than a second or two on deck without being swept over.

Executive Petty Officer Myron Verville was concerned about the weight of the ice on the cutter, but it was the ice damage to the radar that really had him worried. He recalls that the radar only worked on a thirty-two-to-fifty-mile scale when he really needed a quarter-mile-to-one-mile scale to get the kind of detail necessary to know what was ahead. What Verville guessed was Gloucester looked like a pin dot. The *Cape George* also took on so much water some of its electronics were shorted out and the crew was without their primary loran. There was an old loran system onboard, however, and that gave Verville something of a fix and he called that in to Gloucester and they would tell him roughly where the cutter was. Verville would then discuss the information with Skipper Snyder and they'd agree on a heading, trying to keep on course for Gloucester but staying off the rocks near Baker's Island.

Dennis Hoffer, a boatswain's mate, was in the *Cape George*'s pilothouse with Verville and Snyder, and at the ripe old age of twenty-five Hoffer was actually one of the older and more sea-soned men on the cutter. "I spent the entire night in the pilot-house," says Hoffer, "on the port side. I was mostly in a sitting position, wedged into my seat by keeping my feet on the door-jamb. We always traveled with the leeward side door of the pilot-house open so that we could hear any other boats in the vicinity. Because the door was open, we took a huge wave through the door, and that's how all our charts got soaked. Myron would give me the loran readings from the old system and I called those into Gloucester and they would suggest a compass course to steer for. Myron would then think it over and make a recommendation to Glen. The loran numbers were all over the place, but every now and then when we crashed down into a trough some ice would break off the loran antenna and the numbers would be steady. I asked Glen what we were going to do if we hit the rocks, and he said, 'If that happens, we're going to go balls to the wall and run this boat as far as we can onto the shore.' I figured if the cutter was about to capsize I'd run to the Boston Whaler we kept on the deck and cut it loose. Then I'd hang on to that as long as I could. Looking back, I know I'd have no time to cut it loose, but that's what I thought. There weren't many options."

Vern DePietro can clearly picture Hoffer and Glen talking, but the visual image that sticks in his mind is that of Bob Donovan at the wheel. "Bob's arms looked like he had been in a car wreck, they were so bruised. I also remember his feet coming out from under him a couple times and him sliding all the way over to the bulkhead of the wheelhouse. That's how steep the rolls were. Worst of all, we couldn't see the waves coming, just feel them. But we could see the snow swirling around because it was illuminated by the running lights. Red snow on the port side, green snow on the starboard side, and above it was white from the mast light. I didn't look at the snow for more than a couple seconds, as it would make me dizzy and I was feeling crappy enough."

Seasickness was a problem for most of the *Cape George* crew. Dennis Hoffer did not normally get seasick, but that night was different: "I was on my knees puking out the starboard-side door. Myron came over and he was sick, too. He was standing above me and his puke and the sea foam covered me. It wasn't much better for the newer guys down below. A couple guys who had no duties to perform during this period figured the safest place was in their bunks. Our bunks folded into the walls, so the guys would trice-up their bunks, rigging them so they were only halfway down from the wall. Then they would lie down in that V and wouldn't be thrown out. Other guys had to just sit in the mess deck, but even that was dangerous when the TV ripped away from the wall and went flying by them."

Gene Shaw was one of those guys in the mess hall dodging both the TV and vomit from fellow Coasties: "The mess hall had two tables with benches and about six of us spent several hours there sitting as best we could and just gripping the sides of the tables so we wouldn't fall. I was one of the lucky ones that didn't get sick, but just about everyone else was as sick as can be. I thought how ironic it was that we were sent out on a search and rescue and now we were a SAR case just waiting to happen. A ninety-five-foot cutter may sound like a big ship to some people, but believe me it's not. For example, to get from the bridge to the engine room or the mess deck you had to go out on the exposed deck. Each area had its own watertight hatch and little entrance shelter above it we called the doghouse. I remember opening the hatch of the mess deck to get to the bridge and the wind was deafening. We had tied a rope from that hatch to the bridge, and I never took my hands off it as I struggled to the bridge. When I got up in the bridge I remember Myron was hunched over what little he could see on the radar. He was only getting a thirty-two-mile scale, which basically shows crap, yet he was confident in giving navigation directions. He had brass balls that night. When people would question his readings he stuck to his guns, and if it weren't for Myron, there would have been thirteen dead sailors from the *Cape George* that night."

Vern concurs that Myron's opinions on their location made the difference between life and death. He also credits Skipper Glen Snyder for following through on Myron's suggestions—and not letting his own ego get in the way.

Dennis Hoffer sums up those tense minutes this way: "The *Cape George* was a proud boat and we were a good team. It had never turned down a mission due to conditions, and we weren't about to be the first crew to do so. I remember hearing with disbelief Bucko on the radio saying, 'This is not a drill, a Mayday, a Mayday, a Mayday.' It was an awful feeling to hear that out in the pitch-black, really a helpless feeling. I was just praying we'd pick them up on what little radar we had, but I knew it was a long shot. I really thought we were all going to die. I went below once and I stopped in the mess deck where a prayer for mariners was posted on the wall. I'd looked at that prayer a hundred times before and it never meant anything to me, but that night it sure did and I said every line. Other guys told me they did the same thing. I kept asking myself, 'Why am I here?' A few years later in October of 1991 I was on a SAR during the Perfect Storm. Even that storm wasn't as bad as the Blizzard. The Blizzard was absolutely terrifying."

| 14 |

SILENCE

Station Commander Paradis's and Warren Andrews's inability to communicate with the *Can Do* harkened back to the days when there was no shore communication with ships that put out to sea. Before the invention of wireless communication, ships in trouble were on their own, with no realistic chance of help unless they were incredibly lucky and another vessel was within sight. For those souls trapped on a floundering ship the last minutes of life were excruciatingly lonely, dreadful, and long because they knew they were utterly alone, yet in many cases they were just a few miles offshore. Ships went down to the bottom of the ocean and took the reason for the catastrophe with them. Friends and relatives on land waited anxiously for overdue loved ones, and each passing day chipped away at any hope of a safe return.

The invention of the wireless changed all that, and the new technology played its first major rescue role on the luxury steamer SS *Republic* on a foggy January night in 1909. Heading from

New York City on a transatlantic crossing to Italy, the *Republic* was a high-speed White Star liner that carried 461 well-to-do passengers who were looking forward to the warmth of the Mediterranean sunshine. Also onboard was Jack Binns, a wireless operator stationed in a small radio shack far aft. The twenty-six-year-old Binns was on lease to the ship from the Marconi Company, founded by Guglielmo Marconi, who sent the first wireless message in 1895.

As the *Republic* left the bright lights of New York astern, it sliced through dark, frigid waters and headed northeast toward the Nantucket sea buoy where she would then turn east to cross the Atlantic. As the *Republic* approached Nantucket, a thick fog enshrouded the luxury liner and Captain Inman Sealby reduced speed and began sounding the foghorn every minute for six seconds. Slowly the ship plowed through the seas, its whistle blasting a low, forlorn *oooogah* into the night.

Suddenly, just before dawn at 5:45 a.m., another ship loomed out of the fog, coming directly at the *Republic*. Sealby had time to send out three quick blasts on the foghorn, but it was too late. In an earsplitting crunching and tearing of metal the *Republic* was rammed on its port side, dead center. Passengers near the point of impact, still asleep in their staterooms, were either killed instantly or trapped in the twisted steel and debris. The sea poured in through the gaping wound, flooding the engine room. Engineer John Hart recalled that there was "a terrible crash on the port side, and an instant later the big stem of a ship crashed through the steel plates, outer and inner, shoving aside frames and forcing its way in to within five yards of where I was standing. The vessel tore away everything on that side for twenty feet aft and then disappeared, and we could see the water rushing in below."

The ship that rammed the *Republic* was the steamer *Florida*, crammed with 742 homeless Italian immigrants coming to America to start a new life after surviving a devastating earthquake that had ravaged their homeland. The *Florida*'s bow was crushed, and it recoiled backward into the fog. Three crewmen in the forward berth were killed instantly, but the ship itself stayed afloat, saved from sinking by a watertight bulkhead. The *Republic,* however, was not as fortunate, and it was clear the liner would eventually go down.

Jack Binns ran to the radio shack and found its wall had been ripped open by the impact. Despite the damage, his equipment was in good shape, and just as he was about to send out a message for help the ship's power went out and the radio died. Binns then scrambled to rig a storage battery to his wireless machine, his fingers freezing from the cold January air blowing into the shack. When auxiliary power was established, after almost an hour of work, he tapped out CQD, the international distress signal at the time. Binns knew that the storage battery would only allow his message to have a range of fifty or sixty miles. He tapped out CQD again and prayed it would be heard.

On Nantucket, at the lifesaving station known as Siasconset, radioman Jack Irwin sat bolt upright in his chair. He tapped back: *"What is the nature of your emergency? What is your position?"*

Binns didn't know. He ran to the bridge and found Captain Sealby, got the information he needed, and sprinted back to the shack, where he typed out: *"Republic rammed by unknown steamship. Twenty-six miles southwest Nantucket. Badly in need of assistance."*

Jack Irwin, on the receiving end of the message, immediately used his stronger signal to bang out a message to all ships in the area: *"Republic rammed by unknown steamship, do utmost to reach her."*

Captain J. B. Ranson of the steamship *Baltic,* over a hundred miles away in the Atlantic, heard the call for help at 7:15 a.m. He had his radioman respond that he was on his way but did not expect to arrive until 11:00 a.m. What he didn't say was that it would be very difficult to find the crippled ship in the fog.

Binns and Captain Sealby wondered if the *Republic* would stay afloat that long. They still did not know what ship had hit her, as the *Florida* had no wireless and therefore no means of communicating with their floundering ship. It wasn't until approximately eight-thirty that the *Florida* reappeared out of the fog and slowly pulled alongside. The two captains conferred by megaphones, and Sealby told Captain Ruspini on the *Florida* that he needed to evacuate his passengers. Sealby, concerned that the passengers would panic if they learned the ship was slowly sinking, announced that the evacuation was merely a precaution. Women and children entered the lifeboats first, followed by first-class-passenger men and then the rest of the passengers. The transfer took place without mishap, but it was a temporary safety measure at best, because now the damaged *Florida* was dangerously overcrowded.

Binns stayed down in the radio shack and by midmorning made contact with the *Baltic*, letting Captain Ranson know that his ship was urgently needed to take on all the passengers from the *Florida*, which now totaled almost twelve hundred. Communications between Binns and the *Baltic* were far from clear. The airwaves were jammed by amateur wireless operators along the northeast coast who were alerted to the collision when the Siasconset radioman originally sent out the request for help. The amateurs flooded Siasconset with wireless messages, eager to know what the lifesaving station was doing to help the ships, and in a sense the entire episode became one of the first live media dramas.

As the *Baltic* steamed closer to the crippled ships, Captain Ranson ordered explosives to be fired. Binns would carefully listen, make a judgment as to where the *Baltic* was located, then try to direct the ship closer. Binns later described the effort, writing: "About 12:30 p.m. *Baltic* is not more than 10 or 15 miles from us, and with the aid of bombs, foghorns and the strength of wireless signals, we tried to get *Baltic* alongside in the fog."

At 6:00 p.m. Binns was still hunched over the radio, having continuously typed out messages to the *Baltic* and Siasconset for twelve straight hours in freezing temperatures. The passengers had all been transferred to the *Florida*, but Binns, Sealby, and six crew members stayed on the *Republic*. The fog was thicker than before and Binns was concerned the *Baltic* might run into the *Republic* just as the *Florida* had done. Equally as troublesome was that each ship had only one bomb left and the *Republic* was drifting.

At 7:00 p.m. Binns heard a loud cheer. He said: "I knew of course that it couldn't come from the members of our own ship, as there were only eight of us. I looked out the cabin. There was the *Baltic* coming up right alongside of us. Her passengers had lined the decks to keep a sharp lookout for us."

Once again passengers were transferred, this time from the *Florida* to the *Baltic*. It took eighty-three boatloads in a driving rain and choppy seas to complete the evacuation, and this accomplishment became the largest transfer on the high seas without a single loss of life.

By Sunday morning other ships descended on the area, and Captain Ranson wired New York that all passengers were safe and that the *Baltic* and the *Florida* were heading into port, escorted by two of the recently arrived ships. Meanwhile the *Republic* continued to sink, and it was decided that two of the revenue cutters (precursors to the Coast Guard) would try to tow it closer to shore in the hopes that some of the ship and its contents could be salvaged. Binns wrote that the cutters could barely budge the ship and that "water was beginning to creep into my cabin." Captain Sealby ordered everyone off, but he and Second Officer Williams decided to stay on the ship in a noble but foolhardy show of machismo. Once Binns and the rest of the crew departed in a lifeboat, they turned back to look at the ship. Its stern was completely underwater, and as its bow sank they watched Sealby climb into the foremast and Williams jump from the bow rail. "We rowed over to the spot where it went down," said Binns. "For twenty minutes we rowed around, earnestly but aimlessly, for we did not know where to go. On all sides we saw the glaring searchlights—but nowhere could we discern any sign of life in the sea. I don't think any more sorrowful moment ever came into the lives of the men in that open boat . . ."

Amazingly, both Sealby and Williams were found alive, the captain hanging on to a floating crate and the officer clinging to a hatch cover. When Sealby and Binns later steamed into New York they were treated as heroes, along with Captain Ranson of the *Baltic*. Three years later Binns was assigned a position on the grandest ship of the White Star lines, but luck was with him and he declined to be the radio operator of the *Titanic*.

※

Communications had improved by light-years from the days of the *Republic* to those of the *Can Do*. Frank's pilot boat was well equipped with the latest communication equipment: two VHF marine radios and an AM radio, all hard-wired to the boat's power source. In case of power failure Frank also had a Citizens Band (CB) walkie-talkie and a handheld VHF radio, both of which ran on portable batteries. (More modern methods of communication such as cellular telephones were not yet available.)

When Paradis lost communication with the *Can Do*, he feared the worst, because he reasoned that if the boat was still afloat Bucko would have transmitted on one of the portable radios. Yet the station commander held out hope, and he encouraged the crew of his embattled forty-one-footer to stay just beyond the Eastern Point breakwater and keep searching.

At approximately 1:30 a.m. the coxswain of the forty-one radioed Paradis that they were one hundred yards off the breakwater and had adjusted their radar for two miles but still had no contact with the *Can Do*. Paradis could hear the trepidation in the young coxswain's voice and knew he was taking a calculated risk keeping the small utility boat exposed to the furious seas. In a night of calculated risks—some wise and some not—Paradis was not ready to call in his forty-one, and he radioed the crew with further instructions.

"Maintain position off the breakwater and around Rock Shoal if you can, and keep yourself heading in if possible and remain in that area and keep scanning."

"Roger, I'm not sure how long we can hang on out here; it's really roaring."

"I understand. We have people in jeopardy."

"I understand, too. Over."

Paradis then tried once again to raise Charlie or Frank: *"Pilot boat* Can Do, *pilot boat* Can Do, *this is Gloucester Station, channel twelve, over."*

Paradis waited for a reply, but only the crackling static of empty airwaves was heard. He tried again, and still no answer. He called Warren Andrews, thinking maybe his location in Salem might yield better results: *"Warren, I'm concerned; how about try- ing to raise Frank on sixteen and twelve?"*

Warren gave it a shot: *"Pilot boat* Can Do, *pilot boat* Can Do, *Salem Control, Salem Control. Sixteen FM. Answer up, Frank."* Warren was almost pleading, as if through the sheer force of his will he could make Frank get on the air.

Next, Coast Guard Group Boston tried: *"Pilot boat* Can Do, *pilot boat* Can Do, *this is Coast Guard Boston; can you read?"* There was no reply.

Paradis continued trying to make contact, then stopped to check on the forty-one: *"How are you maintaining yourself out there?"*

"Be advised, Mr. Paradis, it's getting worse out here; I cannot maintain a position close to the breakwater; every time I come up around I get blown over into Norman's Woe. I'm slowly coming back into the harbor. Making headway just a little bit."

In a defeated tone, Mike Paradis answered, *"Roger, keep an eye out for* Can Do."

"Roger, at this time my port engine is just about ineffective."

The modern technology of radios, radar, and high-performance engines was no match for the storm. As the forty-one limped back into the harbor, the men of Coast Guard Station Gloucester held out little hope for the *Can Do*.

| 15 |

BEYOND THE REALM
OF EXPERIENCE

Coast Guard Group Boston, located on Atlantic Avenue at the foot of Hanover Street in Boston, is the operations coordination center for individual stations from Scituate, Massachusetts, north to the New Hampshire line. Paradis asked Group Boston to assist in trying to make contact with the *Can Do* because Group Boston's radio was tied into a number of antennae strategically placed at high points along the coast.

Suddenly, about 1:45 a.m. the radio operator at Group Boston heard a very weak transmission as if from another planet: *"Be advised we just took a big one over the bow and lost our windshields. Frank's hurt. Do you have any boats in our destination?"*

The *Can Do* was still afloat! The voice, however did not sound like Bucko's or Frank's and might have been that of Donald Wilkinson, talking on the handheld marine VHF radio operated by portable batteries. The main radios were rendered useless when water coming in through the windshield opening covered the vessel's electrical system and shorted them out.

Group Boston responded to the *Can Do* that the *Cape George* was having a hard time and the *Decisive* was on its way.

Then seconds later another stunning surprise: *"Busted out the windshield. I thought we hit bottom, but maybe we took a bad sea. I'm not quite sure. Pretty shallow. Trying to take it easy here now. No idea at the present time of our location."*

The person talking was Frank Quirk. Remarkably, the tone of Frank's voice was no different than before the Mayday: calm, collected, and thoughtful, trying to give what little information he could to would-be rescuers. The stoicism—rather than alarm—expressed by Frank was his natural response to a crisis, but it was also meant to hearten his crew. And judging from the rest of the crew's handling of the Mayday situation, all the men were showing a spirit worthy of the boat's name, the "can do" spirit of doing their best despite the pressure and odds stacked against them. They were not ready to think of the *Can Do* as their casket.

The fact that the *Can Do* was still afloat after a six-hour battle was a testament to the skills of the crew. The enormous waves, now thirty feet and greater, were still the biggest hazards the pilot boat faced, particularly climbing the breaking waves without any visibility beyond the mattress-stuffed windshield. If the vessel starts to climb a wave but cannot make the crest it will slide back down, burying the stern. Then the same wave will push the bow up and over and the pilot boat will pitchpole to its doom.

For the crew of the *Can Do,* the goal of finding the mouth of Gloucester Harbor had been replaced by simply trying to keep the boat afloat.

After receiving the transmissions from the *Can Do,* Group Boston immediately contacted Warren Andrews and Mike Paradis, saying, *"Were you aware that I just had contact with the Can Do? We're picking them up on our remote speakers, believe it or not."*

Warren and Paradis were ecstatic over this news. Just minutes earlier they were beginning to think the worst, and now they learned that not only was the *Can Do* afloat but also Frank was on his feet. Warren was likely thinking; *Hang on a little longer, guys; this storm has got to ease up soon.* It was a realistic thought, based on prior storms' durations, like that of the one that split the *Chester Poling* in two. But the Blizzard and its assault on the Northeast were beyond the realm of Warren's experience, just as they were for most everyone who lived through the events.

A second later Group Boston told Warren, *"I'm going to make another call to them in five minutes. Were you able to get bearings on them earlier?"*

"I took an RDF on the Can Do *just before they lost their main radios and I got a good reading, although very heavy snow static, of one hundred degrees from this station."* (RDF is short for *radio direction finder*. It gave Warren the direction from his base to the *Can Do*. But to get a meaningful location for the *Can Do* another RDF would need to be taken from a different radio position, and where the two lines crossed would yield a fairly good estimate.)

"Roger, was that one hundred degrees from Salem Harbor, is that correct?"

"Roger, that is right; that is from Salem Control. In your last contact I was not able to read the Can Do. *Do I understand someone was injured?"*

"Roger, we believe it was Frank. They patched him up and he will probably need stitches and they are holding their own. They gave us a rough estimate of their position: three miles north of the breakwater, three miles south of the breakwater, or three to five miles out from the breakwater."

"Has the cutter Cape George *had any sightings on her radar regarding the* Can Do?*"*

"They were having a rough time also. If you don't have anything

further I'm going to go back to sixteen and make a call to the Can Do *in a couple minutes."*

The *Cape George* was having more than a rough time—the crew was literally fighting for survival, just like the crew of the forty-one. Bill Cavanaugh remembers that even when the forty-one was in shouting distance of Station Gloucester they were still in danger. They couldn't tie up at the station because they thought they'd be swept into the parking lot, so they went to a more protected pier by the Empire Fish Company. As they tied up at the concrete pier Cavanaugh remembers being awed by the way water was coming through openings in the pier like "geysers."

The *Decisive*, at 210 feet, was a bit safer than the other two Coast Guard vessels but was in a battle of its own, about three to five miles south of Salem Sound. Rich Fitcher, a machinery technician, spent much of the night down in the engine room. "I was really concerned about how much icing was occurring up top, because we took some incredible rolls. No one onboard had ever experienced anything like it, particularly being so close to land. The wind would occasionally come in from a different angle, and it must have been a nightmare for the helmsman whenever the wind and seas weren't aligned. It was challenging just to keep on course. I spent thirty years in the Coast Guard, including time in the North Atlantic, and I never encountered seas that could even compare to that night."

Fitcher was in the engine room with Jim Sawyer, an engineer. "When you feel the whole boat shudder," says Sawyer, "and literally moan, you can't help but be concerned." Fitcher was able to get up to the bridge, but things were no better. "The bridge is about midship, and when I was there I remember looking dead ahead and seeing a wall of water at eye level. That's forty-eight feet. I know the height because there was a little placard in the bridge along a line that said: 'forty-eight feet above the surface.' I have no idea how the smaller cutter and boats managed. The *Cape George* would have looked like a tiny cork out there."

Seasickness made performing even the simplest of jobs even harder. Brian Tully was fresh out of boot camp, and he recalls about 90 percent of the men were sick and a couple were totally incapacitated. Usually when you're feeling queasy, the best thing to do is get on top, get fresh air, and watch the sea. Going out on deck, of course, would be fatal, and so the men suffered with their seasickness, hour after dreadful hour.

Rich Fitcher recalls there were three civilians on board the *Decisive*. They would have been dropped off at Boston, but because of the emergency they had to stay on the cutter. One of them was a fisheries inspector, and of all the people who were sick he was the worst. The corpsman gave him shots of tranquilizers and this man spent the night of the Blizzard alternating between vomiting and unconsciousness. There were also two sea cadets onboard. These were two fourteen- or fifteen-year-olds who were supposed to be onboard just briefly for the experience to complement what they were learning in their classes. "They were terrified," said Fitcher, "but then again we were pretty scared ourselves."

※

When Group Boston tried again to make contact with the *Can Do* the strength of the vessel's radio signal had weakened further.

"This is Group Boston; say everything again; say everything twice. Over."

There was a faint, unintelligible response from the pilot boat. Group Boston desperately tried to maintain contact. Over and over Group Boston said, *"Pilot boat* Can Do, *pilot boat* Can Do, *Coast Guard Boston Group, Coast Guard Boston Group, over."*

Group Boston heard an inaudible response and shouted back, *"Pilot boat* Can Do, *this is Group Boston. I believe I hear you very, very broken; say everything twice."*

Frank could barely be heard: *"Taking a beating. I'm trying to build up some power. I'll call you back in about five minutes."*

Frank did not call back in five minutes, and neither Group Boston, Warren Andrews, nor Mike Paradis at Station Gloucester was able to reestablish contact. It seemed the *Can Do*, alone in the impenetrable darkness, had finally lost its only connection to the rest of the world as a result of the weakening batteries in the hand-held radio. On the pilot boat, it must have been devastating to the men's morale to hear Warren and the Coast Guard calling to them over and over and know that their replies could not be heard. Whatever their fates, they were once again alone in the black void of the tempest. What they didn't know was that high on a hill in the seaside town of Beverly their words were being picked up loud and clear.

A tall, thin, bespectacled amateur radio operator named Mel Cole had been listening in on the plight of the *Can Do* for the last several hours. The fifty-three-year-old engineer and businessman was seated before his radio apparatus in the finished basement of his modest house, hoping the men aboard the floundering boat would make it to Gloucester Harbor.

Cole's house sat high atop Indian Hill in Beverly, just a half mile from the northern shore of Salem Sound. Mounted on the roof was a forty-five-foot rotating antenna capable of receiving and transmitting messages to ham radio operators around the world. The antenna was surrounded by enormous white pines and hemlocks that protected it from the full force of the wind, prob-ably the only reason it was still standing. Mel's equipment was a bit more sophisticated and extensive than that of the typical ham radio operator because of his knowledge of electronics. He had designed and invented several pieces of electronic equipment, and that background had spilled over to his radio transmitters and receivers. In fact, he had so much radio equipment in his basement he called the office the radio shack, where he could sit in a chair on wheels and scoot from one communication device to another. In front of him arranged along a wall-length desk and cabinets were a marine radio, a two-meter radio, two low-band radios, and tape-recording devices connected to the communication equipment. He had his own little "mission control," and that night it proved to be invaluable, as he and his equipment were the only link with the *Can Do.*

Mel had learned about the *Can Do*'s mission to Salem Sound earlier that night from Warren Andrews. "Warren and I were good friends," says Cole, "because we were both radio operators, and we would get together from time to time. Through Warren I also met Frank. It seemed like whenever Frank was in Salem and he had a free minute, he would walk over to Warren's place and say hello. I'd be visiting Warren and Frank would pop in and I got to know him. In fact, it seemed most everyone in the area knew Frank—he was like the hub of the waterfront group. He cast a wide net of acquaintances, and people always enjoyed his company. He had that rare quality of being laid-back and easygoing but was extremely bright. I quickly realized Frank was a true ocean expert in a modest sort of way."

When the *Can Do* first set out for Salem, Mel's phone rang. It was Warren and he said, "Frank and the boys have just left Gloucester and are heading down to Salem." Warren then explained to Mel that the crew of the *Can Do* was going to help the forty-four that was in trouble. Mel recalls that Warren mentioned how the crew on the Coast Guard boat were all young and Frank was really concerned. "I figured," says Mel, "if anyone could get to Salem Sound that night it was Frank."

Just before Frank lost contact with Coast Guard Group Boston, Mel talked with another amateur radio operator, Robert Wood of Topsfield, and they decided to try to get a "fix" on the *Can Do.* Wood, a deputy fire chief and boater, owned a van, and inside he quickly rigged a portable radio direction finder (RDF). He then put chains on the tires and accompanied by his friend William Simmons set out for Singing Beach in Manchester.

Wood's plan was to get a cross-bearing on Frank's signal and with Mel Cole's beam estimate the location of the *Can Do*. Cole could then look over his nautical chart and relay the information to the Coast Guard, with the hope that the *Cape George* or the *Decisive* could move into the area. At that point the only successful radio fix taken on the pilot boat was the one performed much earlier in the night by Warren Andrews, who placed the *Can Do* a couple miles offshore somewhere near Baker's Island.

Wood and Simmons somehow made it down to Singing Beach, slipping and sliding in the driving snow. They parked the van and got their equipment up and running, but Frank's transmissions were not powerful enough to get a bearing on. Wood later said, "Frank must have been much farther south. I couldn't get to him; his signal was too weak for me to pick it up from that point." Wood and Simmons went on to West Beach and tried again but still could not get a strong enough signal to estimate the position of the *Can Do*. While driving in the van, however, Wood did talk briefly with Frank: "A lot of people were shutting down [their radios] and going to bed. We just wanted Frank to know someone was out there. It must be pretty awful to think you're going to die and no one is even listening."

However, many folks monitoring their marine radios could not turn off the drama and a few were wracking their brains wondering how they could help. Some struggled through the snow as close to the shore as they dared, to see if they could hear the *Can Do*'s engines. Others maneuvered their cars near the shore and shined their headlights out to sea, thinking maybe Frank or Charlie would be able to spot the lights and make a run at the shore. But the most desperate of all the people glued to their radios were Audrey, Maureen, and Brian Quirk, absolutely helpless to do anything. The waiting for fifteen-year-old Brian was especially difficult; he repeatedly told his mom that maybe none of this would be happening if he had been on the *Can Do*. Somehow, he felt, he could have helped his father get the vessel to port, and Brian actually blamed himself for not being onboard as he had been during most every minute he wasn't in school. Now, trapped at the house, he wanted to at least get down to Coast Guard Station Gloucester, but the roads from Peabody to the coast were virtually impassible. Imagine his frustration as he listened to the rescue efforts while realizing the situation was worsening and there was nothing he could do to help his father.

❉

At 1:50 a.m. Mel realized he was apparently the only radio operator still able to hear Frank and asked the Coast Guard for permission to intercede and communicate with the *Can Do*. Group Boston approved, while instructing Mel to pass along what he learned. "I broke in and told Frank I could read him. Mr. Paradis and Coast Guard Group Boston could only hear my voice, so I often repeated what Frank said. Warren was on the two-meter radio and that way we could communicate without disrupting anything Frank said. Then on the phone I had Jim Loew at the Rescue Center, so he could give advice. I was basically the go-between, passing communication back and forth. I also made a tape of all my conversations." .

Frank heard Mel clearly and gave him an update: *"We have been aground, but we're off now. Still under our own power."*

Mel decided he had better get information on warding off hypothermia, and while he was making this request of Jim Loew a voice from the *Can Do*—not Quirk's—shouted on the airways, *"We've lost it! It's all gone! We've had it!"*

"*Beverly Base to* Can Do, *Beverly Base to* Can Do, *come in.*

"*Beverly Base to* Can Do, *Beverly Base to* Can Do, *come in.*"

Mel repeatedly called, but no one answered. The time was 1:55 a.m.

| 16 |

THE ANCHOR

Around 2:00 a.m. Mel was taken from the depths of helplessness and despair to one of guarded euphoria and relief. Mike Paradis radioed Mel and said, "*We have had an unconfirmed report that all of the* Can Do *crew have been rescued and have been taken to a hospital in Manchester.*"

Mel allowed himself to relax and responded, "*Roger, that's mighty good news.*"

Paradis used the word *unconfirmed* because the report had come in from an unidentified CB operator with few details other than to say all the men were alive and at the hospital. Mel didn't know the details, but he was jubilant. "I was so tired and grateful," he recalled, "that I didn't stop to think there isn't any hospital in Manchester."

The news was too good to be true. Minutes later, Mel heard a weak, static-filled voice. It was Frank: "*Tell them it isn't true.*"

Apparently Frank had heard the radio chatter about his alleged rescue. He then went on to describe his latest battle: *"Hard aground. No power. Taking on water."*

Throughout the night Frank, Bucko, and the crew had somehow managed to get the boat off the shoals each time they entered shallow water. But now three of the very worst things that can happen to a boat had befallen the *Can Do*—and all three occurred simultaneously.

The pilot boat ran aground on one of the many rock ledges that litter the ocean off Salem. There is a particularly bad section of water just south of Baker's Island that mariners describe as a labyrinth of ledges, many lying just two or three feet below the ocean's surface. This region, which covers about a square mile, is known as the Gooseberries, named after the two tiny islands, North and South Gooseberry Islands, that rise up from the uneven ocean floor. Of all the locations where the *Can Do* possibly went aground, this was the most likely. Although Frank earlier believed he was somewhere outside Gloucester Harbor, the wind and waves were so strong that even though he was under power trying to head north, the seas were actually pushing the boat slowly backward, to the south. Over the course of the night, the *Can Do* likely slipped just to the east of Baker's Island and then into the treacherous waters of the Gooseberries. This location was close to where Warren Andrews made his radio fix on the pilot boat and was consistent with where both Mel Cole and Robert Wood estimated Frank's position to be. Ironically, the *Cape George* and the *Can Do* likely passed within a half mile of each other, but without radar neither could locate the other.

Frank knew the Gooseberries as if they were his own backyard, and he had enjoyed many happy times there. Often when he was out with his family for a Sunday boat ride he would drop anchor at North Gooseberry Island and the kids would swim and dive for lobsters and later the family might picnic on the island.

In the early morning of February 7, 1978, all Frank would have needed was just a speck of light, even the glow of a quarter moon, and he could have steered clear of these shoals. Instead he might as well have been blindfolded, with no radar, no lights, not even a windshield to look through. It was as if the storm conspired with the night and together they had set a trap at the Gooseberries. The Blizzard had been hunting various prey—the *Can Do,* the *Cape George,* and the *Decisive*—and now it had settled on cornering the smallest boat. The enormous waves had finally succeeded in stopping the *Can Do* and killing its main engine, probably by totally engulfing the boat and sending water down the exhaust stack. Located just behind the pilothouse, the exhaust stack was a vulnerable part of the boat because it rose only about twelve feet from the waterline. Water spilling into the pilot boat had likely entered through three different sources: the exhaust stack, the mattress-patched windshield opening, and a hatch or hatches that loosened. The destructive force of six straight hours of battering waves is almost unimaginable, and no matter how well crafted the *Can Do* was, sooner or later a bolt, seam, or hatch would fail.

Earlier the men on the forty-four related how the hum of the engine gave them a certain degree of comfort, and for the men on the *Can Do* it must have been the same. Now, with the engine dead, the full roar of the storm was the only sound they could hear, except perhaps the sickening grinding of the hull on the rocks below. It's little wonder one of the men said, "It's all gone! We've had it!" Whoever uttered that desperate cry knew that without power, the seas would eventually lift the boat off the rocks and the next big wave would probably catch it broadside, driving it over until it capsized. The desperation that man kept contained within himself prior to the latest catastrophe was finally uncorked, and no matter how calmly Frank radioed their latest predicament, they all knew their situation had gone from critical to almost hopeless. The crew was reaching the limits of their endurance. They had been physically battered from the ceaseless pounding of the waves, and no doubt some or all of them had been weakened by seasickness to the point where they were vomiting nothing but gall or racked by dry heaves. Winter's icy fingers were further adding to their discomfort, making them shiver uncontrollably, adding to their exhaustion. Death, it seemed, was just outside the aluminum walls of the pilothouse, and it now had the upper hand.

The men knew that it would be an incredible long shot for the *Cape George* or the *Decisive* to find them at night and their only realistic hope of survival would be if the storm either abated or moved offshore. Then they could hang on until daylight and shoot up the case of flares that was stowed on the boat. But the storm was still stalled south of Nantucket Island, blocked by the high-pressure system to the north where the tightly packed pressure gradients acted like skyscrapers, funneling the wind through their narrow openings. Not only was the storm spinning in place, but also its dry center, called the occlusion, actually wobbled, making a small loop. The Blizzard was like an angry bull, trying to bust out of his corral, and because he was unsuccessful, his rage only intensified. With nowhere to go, the storm spewed out its wrath to the north, concentrating its most destructive force directly at the region where the *Can Do* was floundering.

❄

At 2:15 a.m. Frank came back on the radio: *"We've got an anchor set and are holding our own. Taking a beating but no further injuries. Trying to build up some power and get things started again. Our position unknown."*

Mel answered, *"OK, Frank, we copied that. We understand you are anchored and everyone is all right and things are essentially unchanged. You're getting beat up where you are, but you are apparently in no immediate danger. I presume Coast Guard Boston and Gloucester have copied that. I'll be standing by, Frank."*

Dropping anchor was one of the last options available to the crew, but how did they do it? The anchor was located on the outside deck of the bow, and it could only be dropped if someone actually went outside and unlocked the release mechanism. This would take incredible courage, because the chances of being swept overboard were greater than those of making it back inside. The same scenario was played out earlier on the forty-four when Paradis told McIlvride to "drop your hook." McIlvride gave Paradis lip service, saying, "Roger," but he had no intention of doing so — at least not until it was absolutely necessary. His crew felt the same way. They knew that just one ill-timed wave could have come over the bow and plucked them off the way a shark would snatch a wounded seal.

Unfortunately, the crew on the *Can Do* could not restart their engines as the men on the forty-four did and had little choice but to get an anchor set. The waves probably swept the *Can Do* off the ledge, leaving it wallowing in the sea, where it would be only a matter of time before it capsized. Without engine power there would be no way for Frank to keep the vessel's bow pointed into the waves, unless, of course, the anchor was set. An anchored boat will swing to the wind with bow headed into the seas, thereby avoiding a broadside wave while reducing the surface area hit by the wind. The boat will still have plenty of violent motion, because a vessel with a single anchor set will "horse" on its anchor chain, moving in a figure-eight motion. So as the wind gets on one side of the bow the boat will get forced downwind until the force of the anchor chain pulls the bow around, and then the wind will pull the bow around in the opposite direction. The rougher the conditions, the heavier the "horsing" motion. Under most circumstances in heavy weather a captain would also use the engine to stay under way and relieve the strain on the anchor chain, which was not an option on the *Can Do*. Frank also would not have been able to determine if his anchor was dragging, which was quite possible given the blizzard's winds.

It's unknown who set the anchor, but the decision to do so must have been made within seconds of either the grounding or being swept free. The anchor-dropping person would not have been Frank because he was injured and, as captain of the *Can Do,* had the most knowledge of the boat. Viewed in a cold, analytical way, his life could simply not be spared in such a high-risk act. The person to perform the task could have been any one of the remaining men, Curly, Fuller, Wilkinson, or Charlie Bucko, with the most likely one being Charlie.

Pete Lafontaine, Charlie's commanding officer at Point Allerton, believes the logical choice would have been the former Coastie. "Charlie," says Pete, "was trained specifically in heavy weather seamanship, and that included dropping the anchor." Frank III, who had performed the chore hundreds of times on the *Can Do,* concurs: "Charlie had been out in the soup before, and he was the youngest of the men onboard. I've thought long and hard about who dropped that anchor, and it's almost miraculous that they were able to do so in those conditions."

The *Can Do* had two anchors, and both were on the bow. On a night like the Blizzard the big picket anchor, weighing 75 to 100 pounds, would have been used. The anchor was fastened to ten feet of chain for extra strength when it was down among the rocks. Attached to the chain was an eyehook followed by two hundred feet of inch-and-a-half-thick nylon line, an excellent material for the purpose because of its elasticity and ability to minimize shock.

Before Charlie went out on the open deck a safety line would have been fastened around his waist, although its usefulness was doubtful should he end up in the churning seas. His crew might have been able to haul him back toward the boat, but twenty-foot waves would have smashed him against the hull long before the crew could have pulled the 210-pound Bucko up to the gunnel. Charlie also may have donned a wet suit, which would give him a few extra minutes of life if he went in the water, and more important, the rubberized wet suit would have provided better traction for crawling on the ice-covered deck.

Imagine the anxiety and tension during each of Charlie's moves to get to the anchor. When he was ready to go, the crew members would have opened the pilothouse door and Charlie would face the shrieking wind and stinging snow that felt like buckshot peppering his face. Crawling on his belly, he had to keep one hand on the stanchions as he inched forward, timing his movements between waves as the *Can Do* reared and plunged. Spray would slash at his exposed flesh and the howling wind take his breath away. One misplaced knee or hand would send him sprawling and sliding, and the next wave easily could have taken him before he could recover. Ice breaking off the bow, from either Charlie's weight or the crashing of the boat, would fly like shrapnel, just as the bomb fragments had when he was wounded in Vietnam. Each time a wave came down on the bow, Charlie would be covered by hundreds of pounds of pure fury, trying to break his hold. Once he reached the bow, where the anchor lay, the most difficult part of the maneuver would begin. In the dark, with frozen fingers, he must unlock the anchor release. Then he'd need to break the hundred-pound anchor free of the ice and somehow lift it over the gunnel and steel railing that encircled the boat. Finally, after he let out the proper length of chain and line, he'd have to tie the line to the electric winch, which would be akin to tying your shoes while riding on the back of a rodeo bull.

As difficult as dropping the anchor was, somehow they got it done, and it bought them more time. Now the anchor chain and line had to hold.

✳

Back on Indian Hill in Beverly, Mel told Frank he was still trying to get a fix on his location. Frank in turn gave Mel a quick update: *"No luck on the power. Thirty-two-volt batteries all shorted out. Can't get the engine started. I have a mattress stuffed in the window to keep the seas out, and the boys have me pretty well patched up. Water not building up in the boat at this time."*

"OK, Frank, I copy. Stand by. On your last transmission there was so much snow static that we could not get a cross-bearing on you. Sorry we can't pin you closer. I am telling the story just as you give it to me — sorry we can't do more for you but am conveying your info just as you tell it."

Commander Paradis was listening, but since he could only hear Mel, he was anxious to learn exactly what was going on.

Paradis asked Mel, *"Pass along whatever information you have on them."*

"Roger, the anchor is still holding. They have a mattress in the front window and they're keeping the seas out pretty well. The water is not building up on them intolerably. They are having no luck at all in getting their batteries up and getting their engines on. The thirty-two-volt battery is shorted out. They can't seem to get it back on, so they can't start their engines. They are taking a beating from the seas. But they are in no worse shape, generally speaking. No one's been injured any more than before. Go ahead."

"Roger, appreciate your information. Ah, the next time you are in contact with them try and make an effort to see who has been injured. We're getting an awful lot of phone calls. And also Frank's wife is involved here."

"Sorry we didn't convey that to you; it's Frank that has been injured."

"Serious or not so serious?"

"He says it's cuts and that's about it. I'm assuming he's doing much of the work there, so that it is not serious. He's been cut up with flying glass and he's apparently doing all right; he's doing most of the talking."

Mel's comment about the *Can Do*'s dead thirty-two-volt battery didn't mention the boat's second battery, a smaller twelve-volt battery that powered the boat's lights, the heads, and, most important, the bilge pumps. Earlier Frank mentioned he was "trying to raise some power," which implied all power sources were dead. With inoperable bilge pumps, water would slowly accumulate at the base of the hull and as each new wave slammed the bow, the water inside the boat would slosh around, adding to the instability. There was nothing more, however, the men could do to secure the vessel. Now it was a matter of waiting out the storm and hoping the wounded boat would stay afloat. The men played their last card when they dropped the anchor, and their fate was out of their hands.

| 17 |

THE BREAKWATER

The *Can Do*'s steel hull was one reason the boat was still afloat and the men had a fighting chance. If the pilot boat's hull was wooden or fiberglass it would likely have sunk or broken apart within minutes of running aground and setting an anchor would be useless. Many vessels never give the crew a chance to take corrective action because they sink so rapidly when water enters through the hull. An example is the tragedy that befell the fishing party boat *Comet* five years before the Blizzard. Although this vessel was roughly the same size as the *Can Do,* it was an older, wooden boat and poorly maintained. The *Comet*'s final voyage began on the morning of May 19 when Captain William Jackson and deckhand Ralph Nickerson steamed from Galilee, Rhode Island, toward Block Island with a party of twenty-five eager anglers onboard. Seas were not particularly rough, with waves of three feet rolling out of the southwest. Just forty-five minutes into the voyage, however, passengers noticed that the vessel was taking heavy spray over the stern and that the stern itself seemed to be riding low in the water. A passenger ran up to the pilothouse and shouted to Captain Jackson, "We're taking on water!" In the next instant the engines suddenly stopped.

Jackson hollered for everyone to put on life preservers and "to stay with the boat." Within seconds of these instructions the *Comet* swung to port and broached, sinking farther at the stern. Jackson scrambled to cast loose a box-type buoyant apparatus while Nickerson unsuccessfully tried to send a Mayday on the water-soaked radio. Then the *Comet* sank, taking Nickerson down with it. Just five minutes had passed from the time the passengers first noticed the stern was riding low.

The sea was filled with screaming passengers and pieces of debris. The lucky ones managed to swim to the buoyant apparatus, where they clung to its sides. Captain Jackson also found his way to the apparatus and told everyone to "keep your arms and legs moving as much as possible to keep circulation going." By 10:00 a.m. the frigid water was picking off victims one by one, including Captain Jackson. Hypothermia had sapped their strength, and as they succumbed, the waves carried them away. It was clear to the remaining survivors that they would be next, and they had no way of knowing whether or not Nickerson's effort in sending a Mayday was successful. Two men in the group, Michael O'Reilly and Brian Beaudette, made the bold decision to attempt to reach shore. Using a long wooden bench that had floated free of the boat, they lay on top of it as if it were a surfboard and used their hands to paddle. It was a desperate gamble, but after two hours of paddling their efforts paid off when they were spotted by Captain Lemmerman on the sailboat *Decibel*.

Lemmerman had set out from Stonington, Connecticut, en route to Marion, Massachusetts, and had just altered his course to put the wind more on his stern when he heard the cries of O'Reilly and Beaudette. At first he thought the two men were on a kayak, but as he approached he saw the bench and quickly took the men on board the *Decibel*. Lemmerman alerted the Coast Guard and immediately sailed northwestward, where he found the other survivors still clinging to the buoyant apparatus. Using his auxiliary engine to get windward of the survivors, Lemmerman then let the *Decibel* drift closer. When the *Decibel* reached the group in the water its crew tied the survivors alongside the sailboat, and then, using rope and tackle rigged to the main boom, they hauled the survivors on board, one at a time. Eight passengers from the *Comet* were rescued in this manner before a Coast Guard forty-foot utility boat arrived at the scene. Because the size of the waves had increased, a transfer of survivors was deemed too dangerous, and it was decided the *Decibel* should head to shore, where medical personnel were waiting. The Coast Guard boat continued the search but only found one remaining survivor among several floating bodies.

The Coast Guard investigation into the incident determined the probable cause of the accident was that the seams on the *Comet*'s wooden hull opened, allowing water to enter the hull. The report also found that the captain had violated the law in not registering the vessel with the Coast Guard and therefore it was never properly certified. Out of the twenty-seven people aboard the *Comet,* only eleven lived. Twelve bodies were recovered, and the last four victims were never found.

※

The crew of the *Cape George* didn't have to worry about leaky seams, but they certainly feared running aground as they navigated north past the shoal waters around Baker's Island and toward the breakwater at Gloucester. No matter how thick the steel on the cutter's hull was, it would be no match if thirty-foot waves pounded the boat into granite. And if the men onboard needed a reminder of the cutter's vulnerability they only had to think back on what had started this awful night: the failure of the hull on the giant *Global Hope*.

All night long Glen Snyder and Myron Verville had successfully kept the *Cape George* in deep water and away from land. But now they estimated they were near the entrance to Gloucester Harbor, and finding the opening without navigational aids would be extremely difficult, with no room for error. On the plus side, the harbor mouth opens to the south, and with a little luck they might be able to grope their way toward the opening and not have to make any dangerous turns. But they still had to contend with the breakwater, which extends across a third of the entrance, providing one last treacherous obstacle before safety.

Dennis Hoffer says this was the part of the voyage that he will never forget: "Myron had relieved Glen for a few minutes so he could go below. I was on the bridge with Myron and Bob Donovan, trying to find the harbor entrance, but the buoy (marking the entrance) had been dragged off station. Glen was just climbing the ladder back to the bridge when he shouted, 'Turn! Turn!' I just had time to look out the starboard window and all I saw was an enormous wall of white water. I didn't even have time to shout. The wave hit us and the whole boat seemed to fly and shudder at the same time. Glen shouted, 'What did we hit?' I hollered back, 'It was a wave!' I later learned Glen thought he saw the breakwater directly ahead of us when he shouted, 'Turn.'"

Myron says the wave picked up the ninety-five-foot cutter and tossed them airborne at least the length of the boat. When the commanding officer shouted, "What did we hit?" Myron shouted back, "Nothing," but Snyder couldn't believe the seas could toss a boat as big and as heavy as the *Cape George* that far. To this day Myron remains convinced that had they made that tight turn in the open sea and not at the harbor entrance they would have rolled.

Although Dennis, Myron, and Bob Donovan believe it was a wave near the breakwater that made the boat shudder, others onboard, such as Gene Shaw, think they actually hit the break-water before being hurled *over it*. Gene was down below, closest to the hull: "When we were somewhere close to the breakwater I went down to the engine room to see what help I could give Mike Leonard. Mike was the engineer and he had been down there all alone in that tiny space. Suddenly this mountainous wave picked us up, then slammed us down so hard all four engines tripped off-line. Mike and I immediately hit the compression release and starter button on each engine to get them back going. I think that big wave had lifted our propellers out of the water and the force of the fall was so hard the engines died. A couple seconds later, I heard a loud bang, unlike any of the noises the boat had made from the waves. Then we were suddenly in calm water. We had gone over the breakwater and a section of the hull actually hit it. Once we were on the other side the seas were much calmer. It's amazing Myron and Glen got us there." Vern DePietro concurs, recalling they got slammed harder than he thought possible and still have the boat stay afloat. He believes a second wave then picked the cutter up and hurled it over the breakwater, which rises twenty-five feet above the ocean's surface.

Whatever actually happened to the *Cape George* in those terrifying seconds, the outcome was that the cutter was now inside the confines of the harbor and was safe.

❊

While we know what the men on the *Cape George* were thinking and feeling, we can only speculate about some of the thoughts and actions of the *Can Do*'s crew. First and foremost, they were trying to keep warm, because without power the *Can Do* had been transformed into a steel freezer. The men would have gone through all the clothes drawers in the captain's and mates' quarters and replaced their wet clothing with as much dry clothing as they could layer on. This was no easy task in the battering seas and would have certainly added more bumps and bruises to the ones they already had sustained.

Most of the time the men were wedged in a sitting position around the table aft of the pilothouse, using their hands and arms to keep their bodies from sliding and banging. They already had put on their life jackets, but they knew that if they did end up in the ocean the life jackets really didn't matter; they'd be dead from exposure in ten minutes. The real reason they put on life jackets was because they thought of their families—their bodies had a better chance of being recovered if they floated. They knew that as much as their families would suffer if they were found washed up on shore, the pain would be even worse if they were never found at all. And from a practical matter, the men were wise enough to know that if life insurance was involved, their families would receive payment a heck of a lot quicker if there was a body and subsequent death certificate. Cold, somber thoughts, to be sure, but the men's minds were free to roam because there were no other tasks that could be done, now that the anchor was set.

The lights were out, so the crew could only see by the bouncing glow of their flashlights. By now they were well beyond exhaustion and almost in a frozen, zombielike stage. Yet sleep was impossible in such rampaging seas, and they needed to continuously use their cramped muscles to brace themselves for each fall of the boat after a wave rolled below. Time slowed to a surreal, painstaking crawl, and their lives were now split in two: life before the Blizzard and life during the Blizzard, with the last six hours making all their prior years almost an insignificant flash. Time was now measured in minutes that felt like drawn-out hours. Get through the next minute, that was the goal. If they allowed themselves to think of dawn, maybe, just maybe, this hurricane of snow would lessen to a point where the Coast Guard could launch a helicopter. If the winds were rocking the helo and the pilot couldn't safely lower the rescue basket to the *Can Do*, maybe the men on the boat could jump into the water and the rescue basket would scoop them up the same way Brian Wallace did in his helo during the *Chester Poling* rescue. It was a long shot, but it seemed like the only way they would escape their prison of water and ice.

Conversation likely ceased between the men, since there was simply nothing more to say—they were all experienced boaters and knew the score. They had already talked over all the scenarios and now there was only a grim determination to hang on a little longer. Each man would have been left with his own thoughts. If one of the crew looked across the table into the eyes of the man opposite him, he might have seen a blank stare or maybe resignation.

Of all the deprivations they were suffering, it's doubtful any approached the agony of simply waiting. But what were they waiting for? Most of the potential outcomes were not something to dwell upon. The waiting experience must have been akin to what a critically ill patient feels when awaiting a last-ditch, dangerous surgery . . . which only 10 percent of patients survive. Some of the men may have concluded that death was certain and even preferred it come sooner rather than later. They didn't want to linger. The storm was simply inexhaustible, and no other gale in their memory was even close.

If their minds were still sharp enough they would have thought longingly of the things that brought them joy: their wives, girlfriends, and children, and they would have realized—as all of us do when we are about to lose something special—just how precious family is. And like many people facing the possibility of death, they may have thought about aspects of their lives they planned on changing, if they somehow came through the storm alive.

Kenny Fuller likely thought of his wife, knowing that if he died it would be especially hard on her because she had lost her first husband to the sea and his body was never found. Fuller would also think of his children and how they'd manage without him. Despite the unbearable anguish these thoughts would bring, it's also possible that reflecting on his children may have given Fuller a steely determination to do whatever he could to survive. Many survivors of similarly bleak situations report that they would have given up if not for the desire to get back and be there for their children. They do whatever they can to live, not so much for the goal of self-preservation but rather to spare their children any pain. Maybe Kenny Fuller swore that if he made it off the *Can Do*, he'd quit his commercial fishing business and never go back on the ocean.

Don Wilkinson would also have thought of his children and maybe felt a sense of pride and gratitude that he had taken the time to have those "family nights" when they would all become immersed in the Monopoly game he so enjoyed. Dave Curley had no dependents, and he might have looked back at the dominoes of misfortune and plain bad luck that had culminated in his being trapped on a boat with no power in the middle of a monster blizzard. And monster would be the only way he could view this thing. It wasn't just a storm; it was a living, breathing beast that wanted in and would stop at nothing to get at the men. It was a roaring lion. First it raked the radar antenna right off the top of the pilothouse. Then it leaped on the bow, swatting out the windshield. And now it seemed ready to pounce on the superstructure and use its jaws to rip the roof off. If Dave thought back on the events that led him to the *Can Do*, he would have first thought back to the marina. It was supposed to be a quick stop just to say hello to the guys—until word came in about the *Global Hope* dragging anchor. The festive mood quickly changed as Frank headed down to the boat and Dave and the others followed, changing their plans in case Frank needed help. Then they listened to the forty-four on the radio, heard how the crew was lost, and knew Frank was going out. Frank told them to get off—told them it was going to be hell out there—but they wouldn't leave their friend.

Charlie of course would have thought of Sharon and how ironic it was that just as he finally found the right person and felt his life complete, it might all be snatched away. Wasn't it just yesterday he had sketched out his dream house and showed it to Sharon? And it was just a couple months earlier he told Sharon it was time to leave the Coast Guard because "I don't want to make you a widow." Of all the men, Charlie was the biggest optimist, and may have thought to himself, *If I got through Vietnam, I'll get through this*. But he also had to consider his premonition. It was that sense that something terrible might happen that likely prompted him to make one last call to Sharon before the *Can Do* set out and tell her he loved her, even though he had said the same thing just twenty minutes earlier.

There seems to be something inside people who work on the sea that gives them an inkling, a gut feeling, of trouble ahead. Time and again we see instances where men and women about to set out to sea have a bad feeling and ignore the warning at their peril. Besides the premonition, Charlie was well aware that going out in any storm is dangerous and there are no guarantees of a safe return. Yet he was not one to calculate risks before taking action if action meant helping another or saving a life. It was just the nature of the way he lived, gutsy and bighearted. Maybe that's why he was writing *The Boat Job:* to give insight, as only he was capable of doing, into the kind of person who would go out on the sea in a storm to help someone in danger. Surely his book's setting—"the granddaddy of all blizzards"—would have made him shake his head that the very things he had written about were coming to pass. On the other hand, his optimistic side would have made him remember that he and Frank had performed heavy weather drills on the *Can Do* and their combined experience was now being tested. Charlie was not the kind of person to back down from a challenge, and this was the ultimate challenge. He knew he was in a twelve-round fight, somewhere near the final round, and that he was losing. But despite the savage beating, he was still standing, and that alone was enough to give him hope. Comebacks happen; miracles happen. Charlie would remember that people said the positive outcome of the *Chester Poling* rescue was a "miracle," and he would have reminded the others of that day, pointing out that there was no reason they couldn't pull it off again.

For Frank, there's no more wrestling the helm, no more working the throttle, and no more straining to see and feel the next incoming wave. Now he's suffering the same excruciating inactivity the others had been dealing with the last six hours, and it's got to be an awful experience for a man who is a natural problem solver, a doer. Getting the job done and working through problems was so essential to his being it's no wonder he named the boat after the Seabee motto. In every other hurdle life had thrown at him he was always able to analyze the problem and then go to work, sometimes for twenty-four hours straight, seemingly oblivious to physical discomfort. So many of Frank's friends, when describing him, used the phrase "there was nothing that Frank couldn't do" or, as his brother liked to say, "If Frank can't do it, nobody can." He had always operated in a proactive way, and now he could only wait and react.

Frank's head was wrapped in blood-soaked bandages, and he might have suffered a concussion from the spinning window motor striking his forehead, giving him a throbbing headache. He and Dave Curley, the electrician, had probably discussed various ideas on how to bring back the power, and Frank and Charlie surely discussed the engine and the merits of whether or not to try to drop another anchor. Like Bucko, it wasn't in Frank's nature to go down without a fight, and he likely was still thinking things through as if in a chess match. Even though he was seemingly out of moves, he could still make mental preparations for steps he would take if they made it to morning. His mind may also have been churning about the events that put the men in this position, wondering what he could have done differently. He probably regretted letting the men other than Bucko come onboard, but as for himself, he knew that given the same situation of two boats in distress, he'd go so long as he had a fair chance of success. He knew Bucko would do the same. They were cut from the same cloth in terms of toughness but very different in personalities: where Bucko was gregarious and at times boisterous, Frank was more reserved and understated. They seemed to balance each other, each feeding off the other's differences. Frank was Charlie's unspoken mentor, passing along his knowledge and sharing common experiences. They were close, not like father and son, nor like brothers, but as friends who had the same passion for the sea, and both had proven they could take the heat when the going got tough. Although Charlie was the logical choice to accompany Frank on such a dangerous trip, Frank may have rued his decision to call him. The phone call to Charlie was made just a few hours earlier, but it must have seemed like a lifetime ago, they had been through so much.

Frank likely analyzed the actions he made during the course of the night and realized that he made the correct adjustments as the storm began to cripple his boat. He would have bitterly thought of how close he was to reaching his objective of Salem Sound before the damn radar went out and forced him to go back, against the seas. No, it was nothing he did wrong; the *Can Do* was simply overmatched by a storm that literally exploded in intensity at the very time he was on the open ocean.

Frank also had a concern the other men didn't have, and that was the knowledge that his family was probably listening to the home marine radio and heard the Mayday and the news that the windshield had blown in on the captain. He wished they had never heard a thing. At least, the family was safe. Audrey and Brian were in the warmth of the house, Maureen with her husband and new baby, and Frank III in far-off Okinawa, distinguishing himself in the marines. And this thought might have led him to reflect on his many blessings. Some fathers never get to see their kids grow up, some husbands never form that special bond with their wife, and some men never find a job they love. Frank had been blessed with all three. He was never a man to complain, and he wasn't about to start now.

Although he had no life insurance, the boat itself was insured. Besides his house, the *Can Do* represented his life savings, and in effect the insurance coverage on the vessel would be the life insurance to get his family through the tough time ahead should he not survive the storm. And he knew his family was strong—Audrey may never be quite the same, but she would make it, if only to be there for her kids and grandchildren. Daughter Maureen was off on her own, and the responsibility associated with motherhood would see her through; there's nothing like the demands of a child to keep you going, to put time between the loss and you. Young Frank was tough in body and mind, and his stint in the marines would only make him more so. In fact, he'd indicated he might even make a career in the marines. Frank had watched his son mature and grow, and much of their time together was right on the *Can Do*, working side by side. In fact, he might have even seen similarities between young Frank and Charlie: both knew how to have fun in this short life, and both seemed just a bit wiser than their years.

Frank's voice was calm on the radio and surely was the same with his crew, not because he didn't feel the anxiety but rather because he'd learned to keep it in check and not let it paralyze his decision-making ability. He was able to carry on, and with each new calamity he still functioned and did "the next right thing." Like the rest of us, he would have felt surges of fear that night, but with men like Frank, fear doesn't necessarily lead to panic or "freezing in the headlights." Author Lawrence Gonzales in *Deep*

Survival offers this insight into men who fight to survive when others give up, and his description is dead on for Frank: "They know safety is an illusion and being obsessed with safety is a sickness. They have a frank relationship with risk, which is the essence of life. They don't need others to take care of them. They are used to caring for themselves and facing the inherent hazards of life. So when something big happens, when they are in deep trouble, it is just more of the same, and they proceed in more or less the same way: They endure."

Frank and crew had survived thus far through a combination of exceptional seamanship, a sturdy vessel, and sheer grit. But now it seemed that in this life-and-death match of wits versus power, Mother Nature was a breath away from checkmate.

| 18 |

DESPERATION

In many respects the predicament of the men on the *Can Do* has similarities to that of mountain climbers who get into trouble and watch their options fail. Expert mountaineers recognize the inherent danger in their sport, which is reflected in one of their mottos: "Getting to the top is optional; getting back is mandatory." The saying emphasizes the need to stay flexible and alter your plans if conditions warrant, which was what Frank did when he made the decision to turn back when the radar went out. Even before he set out, Frank acknowledged he'd take it one step at a time and wasn't married to the plan, telling Paradis, "We'll give it a look . . . we might be right back." Climbers and boaters both know that weather can throw a curve, equipment can fail, and injuries can mean abandoning the objective and retreating to safety. Keeping your options open and not being blindly committed to reaching the goal "no matter what" are essential to those who venture away from civilization. Having a plan of attack is great, but having an open mind is even better.

Turning back, though, doesn't necessarily guarantee survival. It all depends how far into the trip calamity hits: if you're caught too high on a mountain or too far from safe harbor the elements might slow the return trip so much that you're vulnerable to more setbacks. On Mount Everest, the elevation above twenty-five thousand feet is known as the "dead zone," where your body continually weakens even when you are resting. Climbers don't want to spend any more time there than is absolutely necessary, because the longer they stay, the more things can go wrong. For the *Can Do*, the "dead zone" during the Blizzard was anything beyond a half mile or mile outside Gloucester Harbor. Had the radar gone out just a short ways beyond the harbor, Frank could have turned the boat and made a beeline back into the protected waters before the waves pushed him off course. Instead the radar went out when the pilot boat was approximately three or four miles out, and that lengthy return distance—into the teeth of the blasting wind and monstrous waves—increased the stress load not only on the boat but also on the men. Fortunately, the men did not let their emotions rule their logic; they went about their tasks methodically and unhurriedly, trying their best not to make a bad situation worse. When the storm began crippling other parts of the *Can Do*, the men countered by making the correct adjustments, such as stemming the flow of water through the windshield and somehow getting an anchor set when power was lost.

Now, without power the boat was not only pitching up and down against the anchor chain but was also rolling more than ever; sixty degrees one way, then sixty degrees the other, with the pilothouse port and starboard windows alternately hitting the sea. With the men having no ability to maneuver the boat or work the throttle to lesson the impact of the waves, the *Can Do* was totally at the mercy of the seas, and the crew suffered worse than ever. The waves were steep and coming one after the other, with just a short span between each wave in the shallow, confused seas. For the men onboard it felt like they were first going up a steep hill and then when they reached the top there was nothing on the other side and the *Can Do* just fell into the trough or the next wave. This made the conditions worse than being far out on the open ocean where the swells may have been larger, but the distance between each one was longer, allowing the boat to ride up one side and then slide down the other.

Water continued to leak in through the broken window, the main exhaust stack, and probably two small exhaust vents. These inverted U-shaped vents, which allowed hot air to escape from the engine room, were located just aft of the pilothouse. Each time the boat rolled and the deck was submerged water was likely working its way into the vents. And because they were located on the aft deck the men could not seal the vents from the outside, but they may have tried to bang them shut in the engine room. Even that effort, however, wasn't going to totally stop the water accumulating in the boat. Another problem that couldn't be solved was the buildup of ice on the boat's superstructure and deck. Around the deck were hawser holes that acted as scuppers, and they would have been totally clogged by ice, leaving the deck constantly awash and increasing the rate of ice accumulation. With each passing hour the freezing spray continued to coat the pilot boat's superstructure, adding to the extra weight from the water collecting in the hull.

Slowly, the *Can Do* was sinking.

❄

About the only mechanical item still functioning on the *Can Do* was the handheld radio, but at 2:30 a.m. Mel Cole had difficulty hearing Frank. Mel feared he was going to lose all communication with Frank unless they talked more sparingly but also tried to offer a little optimism for what he increasingly felt was a hopeless situation: *"Save your batteries, because you are breaking up a little bit. There's a rig with a multimillion-candlepower light onshore, there's a truck moving in with it, and he's been stuck a couple times. But they're heading down to the general area that they believe you to be [located at] from the very crude bearings we've been able to take. So you might from time to time—if somebody can see aft, and I assume shore is aft—see if you can pick up that light and that will give us some encouragement, Frank."*

"These batteries won't hold for much longer. I'll contact you in thirty minutes."

"Roger, Frank, save your batteries and I'll be here when you come back."

Warren Andrews was listening and also had been receiving updates from Mel. He wanted to make sure everyone involved understood his estimation of Frank's location: *"Beverly Control, this is Salem Control. My last reading when they had their main radios up was one hundred degrees. Now readings are very difficult with all this heavy snow static, but I feel it was a good reading at that time. That would be roughly a line between me and Baker's Island."*

Mel acknowledged Warren's estimation and then waited a few minutes for Frank to come back on. When he did, Mel gave him the latest update: *"Can Do, this is Beverly Base. I have been advised a truck with an extremely powerful light aboard is headed for Magnolia—keep your eyes open for it—Warren suggests you consider digging the auxiliary battery leads from the back of your radio and hook-up to a twelve-volt battery to gain more power."*

"We'd never get to the battery. Action too much out here."

A couple minutes later Mel came back on the air and let Frank know that Robert Wood was still trying to get a radio fix on him from Singing Beach.

Frank responded, *"OK, Mel. Getting pretty cold and weak here—guess the loss of blood caused it. Keep getting wet, too."*

"Frank, why don't you get out of the wheelhouse and go below? I know water is coming in that window. Huddle in with the others and try to warm up. You can't do any good up there in the wheelhouse, and if she does beach, you're better off down below with the others. Tuck your walkie-talkie radio beside you when you lie down, as your batteries are getting low. You were broken on the last transmission and the warmth will revive them."

A minute later Mel gave both Group Boston and Chief Paradis an update on his last transmissions with Frank: *"I just spoke to the Can Do and I advised them to keep together and keep warm. Frank said three of the boys are below in sleeping bags and two are with him, which leads me to think he's counting wrong. He's in the wheelhouse and getting wet as the water comes through the mattress he has stuffed in the window. He's beginning to feel the weakness from the loss of blood that he took earlier in the battle and so I've tried to encourage him to go below with the others. But his batteries were breaking out on him, so I don't know whether he agreed to do it or not. But he did sound receptive to going below with the others; he's really gaining nothing by staying in the wheelhouse."*

Frank's last message indicated his injury was more serious than first supposed by Mel and Paradis. The impact from the shattered glass and the spinning window motor to Frank's head must have caused a deep gash rather than surface cuts. For Frank to even mention his weakness was a clear signal he was hurting far more than he's been letting on. The weakness he felt was probably a result of not only the loss of blood but also exhaustion and the insidious effects of hypothermia. And when Frank, in his usual understated way, said he's getting pretty cold, one can assume that he was really chilled to the bone.

Hypothermia occurs when the body's core temperature falls below normal, and Frank was clearly in the early stage of this silent killer. Although he probably changed into dry clothing just after the windshield was blown out, he continued to get wet and was likely shivering uncontrollably. The last hour had been especially tough because without power there was no heat in *Can Do* and Frank was doggedly standing at the wheel or sitting at the wheelhouse table in freezing temperatures. He likely had his hands, along with the portable radio, tucked under his armpits for what little bit of warmth was there. The armpits are one of the body's hot spots, allowing heat to leave the body quickly because there is little fat or muscle directly under the arms. Another spot is the groin region, because major blood vessels are near the surface. Of course the head and neck are the most critical areas, and Frank would have known to keep them covered.

Frank was likely fighting the urge to give in to the fatigue and cold and just lie down, thinking he needed to be in the wheelhouse in case quick action was required. He probably tried to stretch and move his arms and legs as much as possible to counter the creeping, icy numbness that was spreading through his limbs. Despite his best efforts, however, the cold was wearing him down mentally as well as physically, evidenced when he counted the number of crew incorrectly.

His mind might have dulled, but the cold had not robbed him of his common sense. He was still making sound decisions and explaining them in a logical way, such as when he rationalized that there was way too much motion on the boat for him to rewire the radio to a twelve-volt battery. He surely knew that going below might provide a bit more warmth, but he'd been reluctant to leave the pilothouse because as he was the ship's captain he felt almost an instinctive need to be near the vessel's controls. But without power and at anchor, there was little he could do, and Mel's advice was sound.

The two or three crewmen who had already gone below were also suffering from the cold, and curling up in sleeping bags would have helped to slow the loss of body heat. Lying down, however, would have been extremely uncomfortable with the boat banging on the waves so violently, and the men must have used every spare pillow and cushion to surround themselves and soften the bruising blows. They couldn't sleep of course, but being curled in the fetal position to maximize warmth was better than sitting in the pilothouse. The only advantage the pilothouse offered was that should the boat capsize, it would be easier to escape the sinking vessel from above rather than below.

If the *Can Do* broke free from the anchor line and capsized, the survival odds would probably be less than a hundred to one, but that outside chance must be considered. The remote chances of surviving all depends on whether or not the pilot boat was near the shore; and no one knew exactly where they were. They could be just two hundred yards from shore or Baker's Island or a mile away. The survival scenario might come about in one of two ways: The men could opt to stay below and if the boat got flung up on the shore it's possible they might have escaped drowning or getting their skulls cracked. Charlie Bucko would have chosen this option, because he had always espoused staying with the boat. He was of the opinion that to leave the boat meant almost certain death from hypothermia or drowning. But others might opt to take their chances in the water, viewing the boat as a death trap.

The temperature of the ocean was approximately thirty degrees Fahrenheit, the same temperature as the air. That, however, was where the similarities ended, because freezing water robs the body of heat approximately twenty times faster than the air. This means that after the severe shock of entering the water and the ensuing hyperventilation the body begins to shut down very quickly. The victim initially feels intense pain, followed by muscle tightness. Within three minutes he will loose dexterity, and in approximately five more minutes numbness will occur. The victim will become confused and disoriented while the breathing rate is

diminished. Body fat and the size of the person may slow the release of internal heat, but in New England in February this may
only buy the person an extra few seconds.

When the freezing water lowers the body's temperature down
to eighty-six degrees, which would happen approximately fifteen
minutes after first entering the water, the victim will become unconscious. At this point most people would either quickly drown
or die from the cold in the next few minutes. Some cold-water
drowning victims, however, can actually be revived, even after
being submerged for forty minutes. This is due to the phenomenon called the mammalian diving reflex, which slows the body's
metabolic rate; it is similar to the way whales, seals, and porpoises
are able to stay submerged for extended periods. The reflex shuts
off blood to most parts of the body except the brain, heart, and
lungs, conserving what little oxygen is left. The brain also plays a
role because cold brain tissue requires less oxygen than warm
brain tissue, and for some unknown reason the mammalian diving reflex protects children even longer than adults and they have
greater chances for resuscitation.

If the men on the *Can Do* ended up in the water there were actions they could take to conserve body heat. Most people think
that they must keep moving to keep blood circulating and gener-
ating heat, and activity is the natural inclination of people who
find themselves in freezing water. This is the exact opposite of
what should actually be done. A person in freezing water should
conserve energy (heat) rather than expending it through movement. Minimizing the loss of body heat is critical, and wearing a
personal flotation device is the key way to do this, because the
PFD rather than your own efforts keeps you afloat. The PFD also
helps keep your head out of the water, which is also critical, since
50 percent of the body's heat loss escapes through the head. Victims should also keep their clothes on, because a layer of water
trapped inside clothing will be slightly warmer than the colder

outside water. Buttoning and zipping clothes to make them tighter will also slow the rate of body heat loss. If others are in the water, huddling together as close as possible, chest to chest, also conserves body heat. If alone, holding your knees to your chest, called the HELP position, will slow the loss of heat from the all-important upper torso. Both the huddle and HELP position have been shown to increase survival time by as much as 50 percent.

Of course, in the thirty-foot seas kicked up by the Blizzard, anyone in the water would have a more important struggle on his hands—fighting to get a gulp of air between each battering wave.

| 19 |

DAWN'S DIM LIGHT

At 2:45 a.m. Mel asked Frank if he wanted to try switching from the handheld VHF radio to the CB radio, thinking maybe that would transmit better: *"Frank, do you want to try your CB?"*

"Don't think we'll try to move. Really ripping out here. We're pretty well wedged between the table. Last attempt on [channel] three was no good."

Frank had not taken Mel's advice to go below, because he was still at the table in the pilothouse with another crew member. Maybe Frank thought that if he was going to die on the *Can Do* he wanted to go down near the wheel and not trapped in a sleeping bag. The rolling and pitching of the boat were so severe Frank didn't think it was even worth the effort to try to get to the CB radio. He must have felt as if he were inside a miniature glass snow globe being shaken by a giant hand. For six straight hours the seas had battered Frank and his crew, with the last hour at anchor being the worst. The *Can Do* was thrashing and pulling on the anchor line like a kite in a gale ready to bust loose.

With the *Cape George* docked in Gloucester, the only ship that could possibly come to the *Can Do*'s aid was the *Decisive*. At approximately 2:00 a.m. the cutter likely passed the *Can Do,* but because the ship's radar was malfunctioning it never located the floundering pilot boat. The *Decisive* continued banging its way north, then held position in deep water about a half mile off the northern part of Salem Sound near Magnolia.

During Frank's last radio message, Mel could hear a deep weariness in Frank's voice and Mel decided he had nothing more to say. He told Frank he'd be standing by for whenever Frank wanted to make the next transmission.

A full forty-five minutes passed before Frank came back on the air at 3:30 a.m.: *"We're getting pretty wet up here. Hatch is loose and we're going to try to move aft."*

"OK, Frank, take your time and try to locate some food. You could use the energy. Keep your bodies in contact for warmth and put all the cover over you possible. Don't use your radio unless necessary and keep it between you to warm up the batteries—don't lay on the mike button by accident. Frank, it's only about two hours until dawn and latest weather promises abating seas. Gloucester Coast Guard will get a forty-four-footer under way to your position then."

"OK, Mel. Will hold on. Sure wish we could raise some power. It's really hopping out here, but we're making it."

"OK, Frank. Don't waste your batteries; you were breaking up on that last transmission. Get some rest and I'll be here when you call back."

Mel was praying the men could hang on for another couple hours, but the loose hatch was yet one more ominous sign that the waves were chipping away at the boat's structural integrity. Although he told Frank that the seas would be abating soon, Mel made that up, believing Frank needed some encouraging news to help make it until dawn. "I really thought the worst," says Cole, "but hoped for the best. The seas were just so powerful that night. Even homes a hundred feet away from the beach and up atop granite ledges had their windows blown out. My biggest fear was that the *Can Do*'s anchor line would be chewed right through if it rubbed against a rock."

A half hour then passed, and when no word came from the *Can Do* Mel tried to raise Frank:

"Can Do—*Beverly Base*." No answer.

"Can Do, *this is Beverly Base*." Still no response.

Mel let another agonizing half hour pass and at 4:30 a.m. he tried again:

"Can Do—*Beverly Base*." No answer.

Five minutes later a voice came on the radio, but it was Group Boston and not Frank: *"Beverly Base, this is Group Boston; are you still able to raise the Can Do?"*

"That's a negative—it has been over an hour since my last contact—will keep trying. He had been coming on every half hour and it's been an hour at least now. I have called him on the half hour and maybe more frequently just to let him know we are here. I did encourage him to go below with the rest of the crew and get him out of the pilothouse, which was getting wet due to the window being gone. He may have done it and the walkie-talkie won't reach from below. This is my supposition at this time."

"Just so I understand, how big of a boat is the Can Do?"

Warren answered for Mel, *"Coast Guard Group Boston, Salem Control. The pilot boat Can Do is forty-eight feet [actual size is fifty feet] and a steel hull."*

Paradis then came on the radio asking Mel if he knew of any experienced divers. Dawn was just an hour and a half away and the station commander wanted to get the forty-one and forty-four out looking for the *Can Do*, but first he must be assured the boats were seaworthy after the pounding they'd taken. Ironically, Paradis called Mel because the diver he would have normally called was Frank Quirk. Mel called Jim Cahill of New England Divers, and within minutes one of the company's employees, Gus Faulstick, was on the phone with Mel discussing divers and boat locations. Mel's next calls were to the Manchester and Beverly fire departments. He explained the situation regarding the *Can Do* and asked for a listing of telephone numbers of people who lived directly on the coast. Mel then contacted dozens of coastal residents and asked them to be on the lookout for the *Can Do*. Meanwhile Mel continued to try to raise the *Can Do* on the radio at half-hour intervals.

❁

At 6:30 a.m. a trace of dim gray light filtered through the driving snow and the men on board the *Decisive* hoped that with the slightly improved visibility they could conduct a more thorough search for the *Can Do*. Instead, the *Decisive*'s radio crackled to life and Boston RCC immediately instructed the cutter's captain to search a wide area outside Gloucester Harbor: a radio Mayday had just been received. It turned out there had been another boat, the *Taormina B,* lost in the storm.

The *Taormina B* was an eighty-one-foot dragger and the six men aboard had just gotten their radio working after surviving a hellish night in the monstrous seas. *Decisive* machinery technician Rich Fitcher recalls that the *Taormina B* had lost every one of their navigational aids and had been searching for the entrance to Gloucester Harbor all night but really had no idea where they were. The *Decisive* quickly located the lost vessel and guided them to the entrance of Gloucester Harbor. Fellow *Decisive* crew member Jim Quinn recalls that even though there was now a bit of visibility there was still plenty of danger. Quinn was down in the engine room as the *Decisive* was guiding in the *Taormina B* when suddenly the engines went full astern. "We backed down as fast as we could," says Quinn, "and I ran up to the bridge and learned

that the breakwater had been right in front of us and we didn't
see it until the last minute. Even though it was daytime, the radar
was still malfunctioning, and there was so much snow and sea
foam in the air we couldn't see much better than at night."

Once the *Taormina B* was safely in port, the *Decisive* headed
slowly back down toward Salem Sound, searching for the *Can Do*
along the way. The intensity of the Blizzard was just as bad as the
previous night, with breaking, confused seas still topping thirty
feet. With intermittent radar the 210-foot cutter made sweeps of
the coastal area with no results. When it reached the outskirts of
Salem Sound the cutter still could not risk venturing inside and
stayed out in deep water. No one knew if either the *Can Do* or
the *Global Hope* was afloat.

❊

Back at the Quirk house in Peabody, Brian Quirk was trying to
convince his neighbor Don Lavato to try to drive to Station
Gloucester. There was now a travel ban in effect for all of Massachusetts, but Lavato was a policeman and after listening to
Brian's pleas decided to give it a shot. Lavato's car was a big,
heavy Lincoln Continental, which did an admirable job of driving through deserted snow-clogged streets. "There were a few
drifts in excess of six feet," recalls Lavato, "so all I could do was
punch through them. We couldn't do this too fast because there
might be a car under a drift. I think all my years driving a police
cruiser paid off that day, because somehow we made it to
Gloucester; then the car died."

They walked the final half mile to the station, weaving their
way around rocks and debris hurled up on Rogers Street. Outside
the station they saw Coasties placing sandbags around the building, hoping their efforts would prevent the next high tide from
inundating the ground floor. Lavato and Brian entered the station and Paradis sat them down and explained what was being

done and how there was still no news on the fate of the *Can Do*. Lavato recalls that Brian was smart enough to know things looked bleak after so much time without communication.

It was now midmorning, and there had been no word from the *Can Do* for over six hours. The Coast Guard men at the station all knew Brian Quirk, and they took him to the mess hall and tried to get his mind off the *Can Do*. Brian, however, wanted to know what they thought had happened to his dad. Ralph Stevens, the young seaman who had been on the forty-one when it tried to go to the aid of the *Global Hope,* remembers it was an awkward situation. "Brian was a nice kid," recalls Ralph, "and most everyone knew him because he was always with his dad on the *Can Do*. We tried to say encouraging words to Brian that morning. Guys would come up to him and say things like 'maybe the *Can Do* is hard aground onshore or washed up on some beach and your dad's wondering when we are going to find him.' We came up with all sorts of possibilities of how we were going to find the guys alive, even though in our hearts we had pretty much lost hope."

Some of the theories offered were long shots to be sure but possibilities nevertheless. One Coastie said the men might have crawled above the high water on one of the islands and taken shelter in the cavelike crevices formed below rocky outcrops. Another said the *Can Do* might have crashed into shoreline rocks and be upside down with the men alive but trapped inside. It was also possible the pilot boat was still at anchor, but the radio was dead.

Brian described the *Can Do*'s life raft, offering that as another possibility of salvation. The life raft was a large rubber inflatable model that could be inflated quickly by pulling a cord attached to an air canister. Enclosed by a modular-shaped canopy, it could hold eight people and offered far more protection than an open life raft. If the men were able to get inside it, they would have been tumbling over and over in the sea but perhaps be blown to shore. The problem, however, would be first getting inside the raft. With 90-mile-per-hour winds it would be all but impossible to launch the raft and somehow manage to get inside before it was blown away. Even if the men could somehow tie themselves to the raft and then inflate it in the water, they still would face the daunting challenge of having to crawl inside the raft with thirty- and forty-foot waves breaking on them. That scenario might be doable in calmer seas or in warmer weather, but not in the middle of a blizzard where just five minutes in the water meant a loss of dexterity and strength. The Coast Guard men probably all knew this, but nobody was going to tell Brian. They also knew that Frank was probably of a similar mind-set to Charlie Bucko, figur- ing his best chances were to stay with the boat as long as it was still afloat. Utilizing the life raft would only be an option if the men had a minute or two to act before the *Can Do* went down, and if the anchor line broke there would be no time at all.

Leaving a boat in distress too early has meant the needless death of many a sailor. In World War II crew members leaped off torpedoed boats only to drown while the boats remained afloat. One such incident happened on the torpedoed tanker *Harry B. Sinclair*. The ship appeared to be sinking and men jumped over- board and died in the sea, which was flaming with gasoline. It was a needless and tragic loss of life, because the tanker itself re- mained afloat for another week. Another ship, the *Francis Pipes*, floundered off Nova Scotia during the war and quickly broke in two. Some men took to the lifeboats while others opted to stay on the crippled sections of the ship. The men on the ship were rescued three days later while those in the lifeboats were never seen again.

One of the more senseless early abandonment accounts oc- curred not in wartime but in 1964 when the SS *Smith Voyager* was crossing the Atlantic with a cargo of wheat.

The freighter encountered heavy seas on December 20 and its

cargo shifted, causing the vessel to list heavily to starboard. Fearing the *Voyager* would capsize at any moment, the crew panicked and immediately launched the vessel's lifeboat. Thirty-eight crew members set out in the lifeboat while the captain, third mate, and two seamen stayed on board the ship. Breaking waves crashed over the lifeboat's bow and soon filled it with icy water. Help arrived three hours later in the form of the *Mathilde Bolten*, a German merchant ship, whose crew lowered cargo nets, ladders, and lines over the side to the freezing survivors in the pitching lifeboat. In the mad scramble to leave the lifeboat four men were either crushed or drowned when they were caught between the surging lifeboat and the side of the *Mathilde Bolten*. There were no casualties, however, back on the *Voyager*, whose crew all came through in fine shape after being rescued the next day by the Coast Guard cutter *Rockaway*.

The *Voyager*, which the men initially thought would sink in seconds, remarkably stayed afloat for seven more days. The families of the men on the *Can Do* were hoping the crippled pilot boat could also beat the odds.

PART III

THE SEARCH

Although Warren Andrews had been on the radio for approximately thirty-six straight hours, at noon on Tuesday he was still helping coordinate the search for the *Can Do*. He knew that his last radio fix on the pilot boat placed it somewhere near Baker's Island, and he stubbornly held to the belief that the boat might be either wrecked on the island's granite shore or still holding at anchor near the island. Without aircraft to search the island, Warren contacted the Baker's Island lighthouse keeper, asking him to try to walk the perimeter of the island. The lighthouse keeper did so, with no sighting of the *Can Do*. A half hour later Warren asked him to try again. The lighthouse keeper responded, *"Warren, in the next couple of minutes I'll get bundled up and take another look around. Negative sightings so far. I'll get back to you in an hour. I'll make another sweep of the east side of the island from the lighthouse to the southern end of the island."*

The *Decisive* also moved in closer to Baker's Island but still was not able to enter the sound. The cutter's skipper gave Group Boston an update: *"Be advised weather conditions are still atrocious."*

"Roger, we will pass that to the air station. What is your present position right now?"

"We have less than two hundred yards visibility in snow and the wind is blowing fifty-five gusting to sixty-five and I've got to wait probably for this to clear a little bit to get in there. Will stay off the shore until the weather abates and then look for flare sightings and also conduct a shoreline radar search."

"Roger, the Can Do *should give off an excellent radar presentation, being it's an all-steel construction."*

"Roger, do you have a clue on the Gooseberries? Is it up around Magnolia?"

"It is the section just south of Baker's Island."

"Roger, we will conduct a radar search of that area and then if it stops snowing and blowing we should have a good chance of seeing if there are flares along the beach at night and we will keep the air station informed."

In the meantime Boston RCC was feeding data into a new but very basic computer search program in hopes that it could narrow the search area for the *Can Do.* The pilot boat's last known position, along with wind speed and elapsed time, was entered in the computer. The computer then indicated that an area south of Baker's Island would be the likely spot the *Can Do* would have been pushed to if it had broken away from its anchor. Because the computer program was rudimentary, the indicated area was quite large and the men had to use their own judgment on where to focus, ultimately settling on a ten-mile stretch of water from Baker's Island to Nahant. However, some men felt the *Can Do* had actually made it to the vicinity of Gloucester when they dropped anchor and so they could not rule out the region along Magnolia shore. The *Decisive* would continue the search, but it was hoped that aircraft would soon assist and cover a much wider area in just a fraction of the time.

Although no helicopters were ordered out in such hazardous conditions, pilot Brian Wallace, who rescued some of the men off the *Chester Poling,* wanted to give it a try. "I asked my three-man crew," says Wallace, "if they wanted to risk going up to look for the *Can Do,* and each one said yes. All we knew was that the pilot boat lost its engines during the night and we figured it was a long shot anyone onboard was still alive. But we decided to go and we took off from Air Station Cape Cod (at Otis Air Force Base). Our helicopter was an HH-3F, weighing twenty-two thousand pounds, and we had about three and a half hours of fuel. The wind was blowing sixty knots and it was snowing like mad. We flew especially high at about fifteen hundred feet. We hadn't gone very far—somewhere near Provincetown—when the crew noticed ice was building up on the nose dome."

Wallace could barely see out the windshield because of the icing, and he had to make a tough decision. He weighed the risks and realized that the situation he was in was different from that of the *Chester Poling* rescue. With the *Poling,* he knew there were still people alive on the tanker, whereas now he doubted the men on the *Can Do* had survived the night: "If we had confirmation that someone on the pilot boat was alive, I probably would have risked it and pushed on. The only possible way we might have made it would be to have gotten rid of some of the ice by flying really low over the ocean so that the salt spray would hit the helicopter, and maybe some of the ice might have melted. But we knew if that didn't work we would have gone down, and if we went down that would be that—we'd be dead; there would be zero chance of survival. So we turned back and made it to base safely."

About midafternoon Warren called the *Decisive* to check on their progress: *"Have you had any luck contacting the pilot boat* Can Do?"

"We are two and a half miles south of Gloucester and we did a

radar search just south of Kettle Island and Great Egg Rock with neg-
ative results. We will stand by in this area until the weather abates.
We'll keep you advised. Would appreciate a call if you hear anything
further. Visibility is two hundred yards and still heavy snow."

Warren, exhausted to the point of collapsing, must have wondered if it would ever stop snowing. By now the fate of Frank
was looking more and more like the disappearances that were
frighteningly common to ships caught in North Atlantic storms.
Even with the improved communications equipment of the latter
half of the twentieth century, boats disappeared without a trace.
Sometimes boats vanished when the weather was fine and the
surmised causes ranged from rogue waves catching a vessel beam-
on to onboard fires and collisions with other vessels. When one
thinks about the sheer expanse of the Atlantic Ocean, it's quite remarkable that two vessels can intersect in a small patch of water at
the exact same moment. Small fishing vessels are sometimes over-
run by giant freighters, tankers, and barges, where the operators
of the larger vessels never even know they have plowed right over
the smaller boat. There are other times when the captain of a
freighter or tanker is quite aware he has hit something but de-
cides not to investigate in the interest of keeping the ship on
schedule. No one really knows how often this happens, but every
now and then the Coast Guard matches streaks of paint on a
larger vessel's hull to that of a missing boat.

The one thing disappearances do have in common is that they
are sudden and traumatic, where there is simply no time to radio
out a Mayday. One typical disappearance occurred just two years
before the Blizzard, when a Panamanian oil tanker, the *Grand
Zenith,* sank without a trace northeast of Cape Cod. The Coast
Guard conducted a nine-day search by air and sea and never
found the vessel or any oil. Thirty-eight crew members died.
Even with the advent of EPIRB's boats still disappeared, such as
the SS *Poet* in October of 1980. The *Poet* was a general cargo

vessel transporting grain across the Atlantic from America to Egypt when it vanished in early November. The Coast Guard commenced a ten-day air and surface search covering 296,000 square miles. No trace of the crewmen, the vessel, or debris was ever found, and the ship's EPIRB never activated. The Coast Guard inquiry offered many scenarios as to why the ship was lost, but the one they determined most credible was the theory that "a loss of hull integrity occurred, and the ingress of water could have gone undetected by the crew long enough to lead to the sudden loss of the ship by plunging, capsizing or foundering." The report went on to say that damage to the hull might have resulted from grain shifting during heavy seas. The failure of the EPIRB was even more perplexing, and the Coast Guard offered several theories regarding why it didn't activate, including damage to the system and the possibility that no aircraft were in the vicinity when it was activated (in 1980 EPIRB technology still relied on aircraft within one hundred miles to pick up the distress signal). The report also suggested the EPIRB might have failed due to improper storage, comparing the *Poet*'s situation with that of the *Chester Poling*: "The EPIRB [may have been] stowed in the pilothouse or another location versus its float-free container. This is believed to be a fairly common practice in spite of the regulations. It was contributory factor in the failure to transmit of the EPIRB on the *Chester A. Poling* when that vessel sank."

Disappearances of vessels usually occur far out in the Atlantic, but the *Can Do*'s last known location was just a mile or two from shore. While the Coast Guard men of Station Gloucester were losing hope the pilot boat's crew would be found alive, they still thought the vessel would be quickly discovered rather than joining the long list of vessels and crews that were swallowed by the Atlantic never to be seen again.

❀

Finally, just after nightfall on Tuesday, the driving snow and blasting winds began to slacken. Somehow Warren was still functioning, and he received a report from the Baker's Island lighthouse keeper that visibility was improving but he still could not see the lights from the mainland or any sign of the *Global Hope*. This report was followed by one from a land-based mobile CB operator on the Beverly shore: *"I can see all around Beverly. Is this tanker supposed to have any lights on it? I can see the lights all the way across at Peaches Point in Marblehead and—"*

Warren interrupted, *"I've just had a landline call from RCC Boston and they request visibility and ceiling."*

"If you're talking about getting a helo up here, he's got a mile of visibility or better. And he has a two-hundred-to-three-hundred-foot ceiling to play with anyway."

"We hit pay dirt; I just had a call from a pilot over in Marblehead who has been listening on his scanner. He's an airline pilot, and he says he can see the utmost light on the chimney at New England power, and we know that is five hundred feet high. I'll pass this to RCC immediately."

About the same time visibility began clearing, a chilling discovery was made by the Marblehead harbormaster, John Wolfgram. A boat fender with the name *Can Do* written on it washed up in Marblehead. Wolfgram relayed the news to Station Gloucester. Paradis had sent young Brian Quirk upstairs to the rack to get some rest, but Don Lavato was with the chief when the news came in. Although it didn't conclusively prove that the *Can Do* had sunk, the boat fender was a dire sign. An hour later another call came in and this one said a foam life ring buoy with the words *Can Do* had also been found.

"At that time," recalls Lavato, "Brian had woken up and came downstairs. Paradis then sat him down and said, 'You know what I'm going to tell you, don't you?'"

Brian struggled to hold back the tears and said, "Yes." Paradis then explained that in all likelihood, finding the debris from the *Can Do* meant the boat had capsized and the men aboard were dead. Lavato says Brian handled the situation as well as could be expected. "And Paradis," says Lavato, "did his best also. He didn't pass this unpleasant task on to somebody else; he did it face-to-face."

Mike Paradis had gone thirty-six hours without sleeping and had spent the prior night making life-and-death decisions as the station commander. He had almost lost his own boat crew on the forty-four, and now he felt that the men aboard the *Can Do* were drowned. He had kept his stress and anxiety largely in check, and he still had more difficult decisions to make with regard to sending boats out to look for the *Can Do*. Perhaps the only time he let his emotions get the best of him was earlier that morning when he went to the Cape Ann Marina. There he located Gard Estes and Louis Linquata, looked them in the eye, and said, "I did not order those men to go out." Paradis didn't wait for Gard or Louis to respond; he simply turned around and went back to the station. Both Gard and Louis were somewhat taken aback, because neither of them had blamed Paradis for anything that had transpired.

Tuesday was also an especially difficult day for Frank's daughter, Maureen, and his wife, Audrey. The police had given Maureen, her husband, and their baby daughter a ride to Audrey's house that morning, and they spent the day monitoring the marine radio and conversing with Chief Paradis. Local news media contacted the Quirks for updates, adding to their stress. The *Daily Peabody Times* had a front-page article titled "Rescue Try Hurts City Man." The paper reported "a Gloucester Pilot Boat was in trouble off the North Shore this morning in mountainous seas and blizzard conditions." It went on to say that "Quirk was apparently injured when a wave rushed over the craft." The

Gloucester Daily Times was more pessimistic in their coverage, titling an article "Can Do Feared Lost" and reporting that "the Coast Guard held out faint hope late this morning for skipper Frank Quirk and crew." The story described how the *Can Do* battled thirty- to forty-foot seas and lost power somewhere off the Magnolia coast before disappearing: "The vessel was taking on water and there was no accurate approximation of its position. Attempts to sight the vessel from shore this morning were hindered by driving snow that limited visibility to less than 100 yards, said Coast Guard spokesman John Bablitch. Estimates of the crew's chance of survival varied widely with Bablitch saying there was still hope while knowledgeable observers on the waterfront doubted the powerless vessel could endure."

Despite the bleak picture painted by the newspaper and the finding of the *Can Do*'s fender, Maureen Quirk held on to her faith that her father had found a way to survive. "We waited at the house all day Tuesday," says Maureen, "and it seemed like time had dragged to a crawl. It snowed hard all day, and there was still no word from the *Can Do*. Even when they found the fender and life ring I didn't give up hope—I thought somehow Dad would be found alive."

| 21 |

THE *GLOBAL HOPE*

Maureen's hope that maybe Frank was alive was not as far-fetched as it sounds. Throughout history, against all odds a few shipwrecked souls have survived incredibly harsh conditions and then stunned loved ones when they ultimately returned from the sea. From Shackleton and his men in Antarctica to modern-day sailors adrift on the high seas in life rafts, some remarkable mariners have demonstrated their tenacity for enduring hardship. One of the most incredible examples of survival is that of Ephraim Howe of New Haven, Connecticut, whose small ketch was caught in a terrible storm off the Massachusetts coast in October of 1676.

Howe's trouble began on the second leg of his voyage, when he and his two sons and two other sailors set out from Boston bound for home. On October 10 a terrific storm swept down on the crew when they were off Cape Cod. Lashing himself to the helm, Howe managed to keep the boat afloat while the winds and waves battered the vessel, pushing it far out to sea. The ketch's rudder broke and the men were constantly wet and suffering from hypothermia, which soon claimed both of Howe's sons. On November 21 the vessel crashed into a desolate island near Cape Sable off the southern tip of Nova Scotia. The three surviving crew members managed to salvage a few useful items from the vessel, such as canvas, a musket, a cask of gunpowder. All the food onboard had long since been eaten, but they did rescue a barrel of wine and a half barrel of molasses.

The musket proved to be the most useful item, because with it they were occasionally able to bring down a crow or a seagull. This was their only food. Over the course of the winter two of the men died, leaving Howe to struggle on alone. Amazingly he survived the winter and into the spring before a passing fishing vessel spotted him and rescued him. He had survived over forty days adrift in the freezing North Atlantic, and seven more months on a windswept, rocky, barren island. One can imagine his wife's shock when Howe eventually made it back to New Haven after being presumed dead for several months.

Every few years since the days of Ephraim Howe, a shipwrecked mariner miraculously survived a terrible gale even when fellow crewmen fell victim to the seas or winter's cold. The same might have been possible for one or more of the men on the *Can Do*. Until bodies were actually found, families naturally clung to a degree of hope, knowing that while the odds were against them, surviving the Blizzard was a possibility. Although the *Can Do* had not been spotted, the pilot boat might have sunk near an island or the shore and the men might have been only in the water for a matter of minutes before being flung up on the rocks. If uninjured, maybe, just maybe, they could crawl beyond the surf and out of the wind and survive for a few hours.

That was what everyone hoped, and now, during the early evening of Tuesday, February 7, the *Decisive* was, at long last, able to enter Salem Sound. Their radar was back in business, and while they could not locate the *Can Do,* they did, however, spot something much larger. Approximately halfway into the sound at Coney Island Ledge sat the *Global Hope,* hard aground and still intact. The *Decisive*'s searchlight illuminated the six-hundred-foot hulk of steel, and men could be seen waving frantically on the deck. But the seas were still heavy and the wind had plenty of punch left, gusting to 60 miles per hour. Since the men on the tanker were in no apparent danger, the skipper of the *Decisive* wisely decided not to try for an immediate evacuation. The *Global Hope*'s crew would be safer on their crippled ship rather than attempting to disembark on a rope ladder dangling above the *Decisive*'s bobbing rescue boat.

An hour later the first helicopter successfully launched from Air Station Cape Cod and went directly to the *Global Hope.* The winds buffeted the chopper about and the pilot struggled to keep the chopper hovering above the tanker while a crew member kept their searchlight on the ship. Then they lowered a microphone, and for the first time since the original call for help the previous day the Coast Guard could communicate with the *Global Hope.* The tanker's captain reported that the men were safe but cold and that the ship had lost all power when water flooded the engine room. The Coast Guard responded that they should sit tight and in the morning conditions should be moderate enough for the *Decisive* to evacuate them with their rescue boat.

Next the helicopter pilot began searching for the *Can Do,* first combing the inner shoals of Salem Sound while he continually tried to raise the missing pilot boat on the radio:

"Pilot boat Can Do, *this is Coast Guard Rescue Copter one-four-seven-three. If you can read us we will be searching the general area and you should be able to see our lights. If you have any kind of flares set them off. We will be searching in the area. If you can transmit, come up on sixteen."*

Warren radioed the helicopter: *"Coast Guard Copter one-four-seven-three, this is Salem Control; last evening the pilot boat advised me he was approaching Baker's Island when his radar was blown away. He came about and he was heading back to Gloucester. The Can Do was a fifty-foot steel hull with five men onboard. They have a ten-man life raft and have portable marine radios."*

Warren's choice of words is telling when he uses the past tense to describe Frank's boat, saying, "the *Can Do was* a fifty-foot steel hull." He knew that with no word from the *Can Do* in over eighteen hours the outlook was bleak, and finding the boat's fender only reinforced that view. Still, he wasn't going to abandon his radio until he literally dropped from exhaustion.

The pilot let Warren know he agreed with the suggestion to focus on Baker's Island: *"All right, we'll start at Baker's and look every island over. We've got the Nightsun on and we'll look at everything east. You said he did have a portable, so I think what we'll do is monitor sixteen in case he can hear us or if he's very weak we can hear him overhead."*

While slowly flying over Baker's Island the pilot felt a ray of hope when he spotted footprints in the snow and wondered if they could be from one of the shipwrecked men on the *Can Do*. He immediately contacted the *Decisive*, whose skipper in turn radioed Warren: *"This is the cutter Decisive, our helo is over Baker's Island, and they request to know if anyone is living at Baker's Island at the present time."*

"This is Salem Control. There is a caretaker at Baker's Island; he can be contacted on sixteen FM."

"Salem Control, cutter Decisive. Roger, nothing further. This is the Decisive, out."

When the pilot received this information he contacted the caretaker directly: *"Baker's Island, this is the helicopter. Do you live in the light or where are you living?"*

"Negative on the light. We're, ah, in the large building right near the base of the pier; we're up top, over."

"Did we just go by you?"

"That is affirmative, almost came in my window."

"Aha, I thought I saw somebody in the bathtub! Ha. We're just looking for anybody in the Can Do *and thought you would know about all those footprints."*

Despite the pilot's attempt to break the tension with humor, being airborne at night in 60-mile-per-hour winds and lingering snow was no pleasure ride, especially when flying just a few feet above the island and ocean. The footprints seen by the pilot were from the lighthouse keeper.

As the chopper pulled away from the lighthouse the keeper quickly asked if there was any word about the fate of the *Can Do*.

The pilot responded, *"Nah, nothing definite; there's some wreckage down by Nahant that could possibly be from the* Can Do.*"*

While the helicopter pilot was searching the waters around Baker's and Great Misery Island, a second helicopter took off from Air Station Cape Cod. On board was Barry Chambers, the commander of the Atlantic Strike Team based out of Elizabeth City, North Carolina. Chambers was accompanied by three other members of his team, and it was their mission to find out if oil was leaking from the *Global Hope* and, if so, to figure out a way to minimize the flow and damage.

Chambers and his men were veterans, having battled oil spills up and down the East Coast, including an unsuccessful effort to save the *Argo Merchant* and slow its leaking oil. On that mission the Atlantic Strike Team toiled on board the stricken tanker hour after hour before the men were airlifted off just minutes before the vessel's hull began buckling and then broke apart like it was made from glass rather than tons of steel. Chambers knew that the *Global Hope* was not in jeopardy of sinking or breaking apart, but no one knew the status of its cargo of oil.

Before taking off, the strike team had boarded the helicopter with a minimal amount of gear that included diving equipment, an ADAPTs pump, and radios. "When we took off flying conditions were marginal," recalls Chambers, "and we were buffeted about by fifty- to seventy-knot winds and snow was still falling. I knew we were going to be dropped to a tanker in trouble, but that's about all the information I could get in advance. Not much was known by anyone because there had only been one sortie flown, which located the tanker about the time we took off. I hadn't even asked where we were going; I just knew it was somewhere off the Massachusetts coast. I think the reason my superiors wanted me out there so quickly was to get some answers as to what the hell was going on."

When Chambers reached the *Global Hope* the pilot did his best to maintain position above the tanker's deck while Chambers donned a harness known as a "horse collar," which attached around his upper body and beneath his arms. The harness was then clipped onto a wire rope, and Chambers stepped out of the copter and into the black void, to be lowered down. He preferred the horse collar to the rescue basket because he was able to maneuver better; a couple times in the past Chambers was inadvertently lowered into a ship's rigging on the masts and the horse collar allowed him to free himself quickly.

"I don't think any of the crew on the *Global Hope*," says Chambers, "even knew we were being dropped down. Nobody met us, so I sent my guys to scout out the ship and I made my way down to the officers' dining area and that's where we found the whole crew. I was angry at these people that they had panicked, particularly the captain. The tanker was high and dry up on a shoal and in no danger of breaking up. I talked to the captain very briefly and didn't cover my disgust. He had cried wolf and he was still saying his crew needed rescuing."

Using flashlights, Chambers and his men negotiated their way farther into the belly of the tanker and found the engine room flooded, with oil on the top of the seawater. They then checked various cargo tanks to see how much oil was in the hold and to determine if they were flooded: "We eyeballed the level of the liquid in the tank, and if it was the same as the outside ocean level that gave us a good indication there was a problem—which there was." Then the men took soundings around the vessel to determine the depth of water around the ship and calculate the ship's angle.

Chamber recalls that the tanker was a typical Greek vessel for that era, quite similar to the *Argo Merchant:* "Greek and Panamanian vessels were typically run with minimal upkeep; they would keep running them until they just couldn't go anymore, usually until the boilers broke. Many tankers are sunk intentionally, most often off the East African coast. Sometimes they run the ships right up on the beach and walk away. There are dozens and dozens of tankers that have just disappeared."

Chambers was aware that the *Can Do* was missing and was quite upset because he had gotten to know Frank the prior year, when Chambers was doing work on the *Chester Poling* wreck. His team's job was to cut three-foot-wide strips off the stern section of the hull at a point where it had not been damaged. It was an especially difficult job because the men were diving in about ninety feet of water. Every day they'd cut a little more, and when they had long strips they would be brought to the surface by a winch. Each piece would be brought to the Gloucester Coast Guard Station, and when the entire section was cut it was trucked up to Pease Air Force Base, where the National Transportation Safety Board examined it to determine why the structural failure happened.

"Frank would come out on the *Can Do,*" says Chambers, "to where we were working and watch what we were doing. He was very interested in how we did our work and interested in what we were learning about the *Chester Poling.* We would shoot the shit, and sometimes at the end of the day have a drink at the Cape Ann Marina where I was staying. He was very personable and straightforward. Good company."

When the job on the *Chester Poling* was just about over, Chambers "borrowed" the ship's bell and brought it back to Elizabeth City Air Station and hung it up in the Chief's Club. The bell was a large one, about eighteen inches in diameter and twenty-four inches tall. Chambers also borrowed the bell of the *Argo Merchant*—"that one is on my back porch."

"The night I got dropped down to the *Global Hope*, I couldn't help blame the captain for whatever had happened to Frank. All the captain had to do when he was first taking on water was to take soundings and he would have known he was sitting hard aground and his vessel wasn't going to sink. It wasn't like the tanker was out on the open ocean. The crew and officers didn't care; once I got onboard they just wanted off. None of those guys had any attachment to the ship—it was as if they had checked out a rental car and now they were done with it."

| 22 |

DEVASTATION

Sunrise on Wednesday morning revealed an incredible landscape to residents of eastern New England. Gone were familiar landmarks, replaced by a scene of stark white. There was an absence of color, and just about every tree, bush, road, and home was enshrouded in snow. People could not get out their doors, because the storm doors, which opened outward, were firmly sealed shut by snow that reached waist-high. The lucky ones had young teenagers who could climb out a window, flounder toward the door, and then scoop away the snow around the doorway so that parents could then step outside. Others went into their garage and opened the garage door, only to discover that snow had drifted to the roof, sealing them inside. Those who could do so began the multihour task of shoveling a short path toward the street. If one had an eye for natural beauty he or she would surely have been awestruck at the way the snow blanketed over the straight lines of man-made objects, replacing sharp edges with smooth white curves. Drifts, looking like cresting waves, turned flat lawns into miniature mountain ranges, and the old familiar neighborhoods were virtually unrecognizable.

This was the scene most people woke up to, except those who lived along the coast, where the landscape looked more like a war zone. It was as if the sea had gone mad and left its normal domain to assault anything in its rampaging path. Over the course of the last two days the sea claimed several portions of the shore by carrying off huge chunks of land. Not since the Great Hurricane of 1938 had the coast been altered to such a magnitude. Through a combination of sheer power in the relentless pounding of waves, coupled with the more subtle but equally devastating erosion that followed, the Atlantic reshaped the coastline. Even where seawalls had been built to prevent this very devastation, the waves dismantled, in a matter of hours, what it had taken many years to make and dragged the cement and granite seawall blocks back out to sea.

In Gloucester and Rockport coastal roadways looked like the surface of the moon, where massive sections of asphalt had been ripped away and the remaining sections were under three feet of fist-sized cobbles and beach ball–sized boulders. Here and there, a lobster boat lay on its side, blocking the few sections of street that were free of debris. On one street, crabs, starfish, and lobsters were mixed in with the rubble, snow, and seaweed. Almost every home had damage ranging from a few missing shingles, to six feet of water in the basement, to more serious structural damage where entire walls were smashed to smithereens. The Olson house at Rockport's Pigeon Cove Harbor was split in half, while the Williams house was yanked from its foundation and flung into Rockport's Old Harbor, where it joined several upside-down cars.

Many more homes were destroyed just to the south of Boston in Scituate, Marshfield, Hull, and Kingston. Some had their second stories blown off, while others lost their first floor only to have the upper stories come crashing down. Homes were pushed off their foundations and back into marshes, while others were carried piecemeal into the sea. Many of the survivors of those homes had only seconds to escape before the seas came crashing into their living rooms. The United Press International reported that "Scituate's Shoreline Isn't There Anymore." The article went on to quote a National Guard major assisting in evacuations: "It's like someone came along and dropped a bomb." He was asked about the Scituate Shore Acres area. "It isn't there anymore." The causeway on Eagle Beach? "It isn't there either." Massachusetts governor Dukakis viewed downtown Scituate from a helicopter and said it looked like "scrap lumber."

One of the helicopter pilots who flew dignitaries over the coast was Dan Voner, a captain in the Massachusetts Army National Guard. "It was an unbelievable scene," says Voner, "so many houses were wiped out, taken right off their foundations. Often the only items intact were a bathtub and toilet, still standing erect, but the rest of the house was gone. The only reason the tubs and toilets remained was because they were connected to piping that went underground. In Revere all we could see was water; it looked like the whole town was buried."

Dan Voner and the other National Guard pilots had the skies to themselves because no planes were flying on Wednesday. Voner took up a general who wanted to survey the damage, and when they were over Quincy the general spotted some Guardsmen working down below, so he said, "Let's go down and thank them." Searching for a landing spot, Voner chose an intersection in the city, and the general hopped out and told the men they were doing a good job, and then off they flew to the Red Cross Center. At that time the Red Cross was located near Fenway Park, and Voner made quite a few flights there, bringing blood, medical supplies, and even cots. One of the eeriest sights he saw was Route 128 where "the abandoned cars were just snow-covered bumps all over the highway."

The storm's fury lashed out as far south as New York and New Jersey. On Wednesday, February 8, the United Press International released an article with the heading "Drifts Blocking NYC Canyons." The report went on to say that the worst snowstorm to hit New York City since 1947 had paralyzed the city, stranding thousands of motorists and causing ten deaths in the metropolitan area. New York and New Jersey each received about eighteen inches of snow and strong, damaging winds, but both states recovered rather quickly, and by Wednesday many of the main highways were open.

Massachusetts and Rhode Island, however, were a different story with thirty to forty inches of snow, and both states remained crippled not only on Wednesday but also well into the weekend. Thousands of cars were abandoned on highways throughout both states, but Route 128, the beltway around greater Boston, was in the worst shape, with three thousand cars and five hundred trucks stranded. A particularly bad stretch was the southbound lane from Needham to Canton, where cars were stacked up bumper to bumper in all three lanes. Cell phones had not yet been invented, so the only way for the police and National Guard to know if people were trapped inside was to check each and every automobile. Sometimes the only way to discern where the car's passenger side door might be located was to spot the car's antenna sticking out from the mound of snow entombing it. Police rapped on the window and brushed away snow to peer inside. When a passenger was found, the police would escort him or her to a volunteer on a snowmobile or across the median strip to a waiting National Guard truck. In a couple of sad instances police peered inside the car only to see a frozen body or bodies. One such tragedy occurred near Route 1 in Norwood where two women, trapped in their car, ran the car's engine to stay warm. They were careful to crack the window open a bit to let fresh air into the car, but it was not enough. The exhaust pipe was clogged with snow, and as the women talked and waited for the storm to end carbon monoxide built up in the car, killing them in its stealthy, silent way.

The police, fire department, and National Guard had their hands full rescuing stranded motorists, but they also had the grim task of searching for the missing. One of the most heart-wrenching events of the blizzard involved the search for ten-year-old Peter Gosselin, who had gone out to shovel snow and never returned. Peter lived in the small town of Uxbridge, Massachusetts, in the south-central part of the state, and on Tuesday afternoon he and his brother went out to shovel the walkway of their grandparents, who lived a short distance away. The boys then returned to their own neighborhood on Mary Jane Avenue but became separated while playing. When Peter's brother went inside their home without Peter, the family first checked their immediate neighborhood and then expanded their hunt to the grandparents' street with no results. The family then called the police, who immediately launched a full-blown search.

Originally it was thought that Peter could have been hit by a snowplow, and police and volunteers probed snowbanks with long sticks, the way rescuers do after an avalanche. Another possibility was foul play, and the police checked the owners of all the vehicles seen in the area. Police soon discounted the abduction theory because the streets where Peter was last seen were inaccessible to outsiders. The hunt continued into Wednesday and Thursday, when 110 searchers continued the stick-probing and also began shoveling areas where he might have fallen. Front-end loaders were brought to the scene and began moving snowbanks, but there was still no sign of Peter. The entire town was on the lookout for the missing boy, keeping their eyes peeled for one of his mittens or his red and blue hat.

Searchers continued their grim work for several days, expanding their investigation into nearby woods using snowshoes and snowmobiles. Specially trained dogs were brought to the scene in hopes they could pick up Peter's scent. The boy's parents held out hope that he might be found alive and put his picture in area newspapers, hoping someone might recognize their son. The days dragged on and people kept searching.

Approximately three weeks after Peter's disappearance the local postman noticed a mitten in the snow of the Gosselins' yard, next to the front doorsteps where an eight-foot pile of snow had melted down to three feet. When he went to pick up the mitten he saw a boot. Fearing the worst, the letter carrier rushed to the house next door and called the police. Police Chief John Emerick arrived at the Gosselins' home and quickly located the boy's body, almost on the bare ground under the snow pile. Peter's head was up against the side of the cement steps and his legs were higher than his torso, leading police to believe that he had fallen from a bank of snow next to the house and struck his head.

⁂

Governor Michael Dukakis declared a state of emergency and President Jimmy Carter did the same, sending 130 military aircraft loaded with trucks, front-end loaders, ambulances, compressors, and generators to Massachusetts and Rhode Island. A thousand army troops from Louisiana, Texas, Georgia, Kentucky, and North Carolina were also sent to aid in snow removal and they arrived on Wednesday night. Dukakis was a calming voice on TV and radio during the storm, keeping citizens informed of what was happening and detailing progress made in rescues and snow removal. (Most newspapers couldn't be delivered; the Tuesday edition of the *Boston Globe* never made it to the public—the first time that had happened in 106 years.) He instituted a driving ban so that the plows could do their work, explaining, "I know some of you have been getting kind of stir-crazy or are coming down with cabin fever after staying indoors for so many days. I hope you will just remember that we have some people in this state that barely escaped with their lives, who are sitting homeless and in very, very desperate straits. I guess the only thing I can suggest is that you go out and take a walk or shovel some more snow, but please leave those cars in the driveways." Dukakis was lucky in that the night the Blizzard first struck he happened to be at the WBZ studios on the David Brudnoy show. After the show Dukakis remained at the studio and went over to the TV side of the studio and used that medium quite effectively to keep an anxious public informed of what was happening and where to go if shelter was needed. Many people hadn't seen loved ones since the storm trapped them in their vehicles, and Dukakis let folks know that almost everyone had been rescued and taken to various shelters.

While most of the public's attention was on the clogged roadways and stranded motorists, Coast Guard stations up and down the New England coast had their hands full using small boats to rescue people from flooded homes. Frank Reed was a first-year Coastie at Station Point Allerton in Hull, Massachusetts, who was put to work on a fourteen-foot Boston Whaler. "A couple of us," says Reed, "ran the Whaler through flooded neighborhoods, maneuvering it up to the front doors of houses which were half-underwater. We brought the people back to the station. Petty Officer Al Torren and I, along with other Coasties, then began cooking for the evacuees. One of the dishes we served was lobster which had been washed up live and frozen on the beach."

At Station Scituate the crew of a forty-four footer had a close call when they were dispatched to render assistance to a fishing vessel aground. The forty-four lost its port engine near the town pier in heavy seas. The crew could not return to the station, so they tried to set the bow and stern anchors in an effort to secure the boat. A huge wave then lifted the boat and hurled it onto a nearby seawall, where the vessel struck the rear wall of the Harbor View Restaurant. Luckily, all crew members were able to escape without injuries.

Similar situations were playing out in New Hampshire and even as far north as Jonesport, Maine, where Carl Lawson, a skipper of an eighty-two-foot Coast Guard patrol boat, tried to guide his vessel to protected water. Lawson attempted to drop an anchor in the lee of Beals Island, but the anchor wouldn't hold. Rather than risk injury to his crew, he ordered the anchor line cut, which turned out to be the right call, because they were in danger of going aground. The radar was still working and the patrol boat was able to navigate the narrow Mossebec Reach. "Our anemometer broke," says Lawton, "when it registered wind gusts of one hundred miles per hour, but we were able to ride out the storm. We were lucky; two other station rescue boats went aground that night. The thing I'll always remember about the storm was how suddenly it hit. One hour the winds were ten miles per hour and the next thing we knew they had jumped to sixty."

In New Hampshire, the hardest-hit area was at Hampton Beach, where several homes were destroyed and hundreds of residents had to be rescued by boat. Just across the border in Newburyport, Massachusetts, the one road connecting Plum Island with the mainland was blocked by ice floes, and residents were trapped in their homes as the ocean battered its way inside through broken windows and doors. Power and heat went out on Monday and had not returned, so those who were lucky enough to still have homes huddled by their fireplaces. On Tuesday, the National Guard began a three-hour effort to cross the two-mile access road to the island. Guardsman Norm Crocker led the way in a giant Caterpillar tractor that rammed the ice floes off the roadway. Crocker was quoted as saying, "I couldn't believe what I was seeing; it looked like the north pole." When he and the crews following behind in large trucks reached Plum Island the residents were lined up on the streets with blankets and suitcases, anxious to get off the island before the next high tide hit. Guardsmen became just as frightened as the residents when they saw a wave—more monstrous than anything they could imagine—crash over homes and sweep down on the roadway they were on.

The scene was much the same in Salem and Marblehead as it was in the other coastal communities, only there some residents complained that the snow was streaked with oil. The oil was courtesy of the *Global Hope*. The gash that allowed water to fill the engine room had also extended to one of the cargo tanks, and the tanker had been slowly leaking oil since Monday evening. And now, on Wednesday morning, without snow falling, the massive *Global Hope* itself was clearly visible, just a half mile off the Marblehead and Salem shore.

There was no sign, however, of the *Can Do*.

23

DISCOVERIES

On Wednesday morning the seas were still huge, only now they were rolling swells rather than breaking waves, making them much easier to navigate. With the first hint of dawn's pale light, the *Cape George* and Station Gloucester's two forty-one-foot utility boats set out from Gloucester Harbor to look for the *Can Do*. The boats headed south toward Baker's Island.

Before the cutter left, Boatswain's Mate Dennis Hoffer made sure to call his family to let them know he was OK. There were rumors flying that the *Cape George* had gone down in the Blizzard. Hoffer also let his family know he was heading back out on the *Cape George,* but conditions were much improved. Outside of Gloucester Harbor there were enormous rollers, but they weren't breaking, which made all the difference in the world; instead of pounding over the waves the *Cape George* rode up and over. The ocean was filled with debris: wood, trees, even part of a home's roof, but no sign of the *Can Do*. Hoffer recalls that when they searched around Baker's Island he saw the *Global Hope* in the distance with the *Decisive* alongside it and a helicopter above.

Cape George executive petty officer Myron Verville remembers that prior to conducting the search for the *Can Do* the men on the cutter had spent part of Tuesday using baseball bats to knock thousands of pounds of ice off the ship. Group Boston had sent engineers to Gloucester, and they had repaired the cutter's electronics. As the cutter headed toward Salem it made radar sweeps but never found the *Can Do*. "Every man on the *Cape George*," says Verville, "knew Charlie and Frank, and we were determined to help in some way. Frank was the Coast Guard's best friend. He was one of us."

On board one of the forty-one-foot utility boats was Bill Cavanaugh, and he remembers riding the huge groundswells all the way down to Salem Sound: "I remember seeing the *Decisive* enter Salem Sound and I was glad I wasn't on it. They were rolling at unbelievable angles. I'm sure the guys on the *Decisive* were looking back at us and thinking, *Thank God we're not in that little boat.*" The other forty-one-footer was piloted by Bob McIlvride: "We were down near Marblehead and the swells were still ten to fifteen feet, but our boat was handling well. There was no sign of the *Can Do,* and I kept thinking about what might have happened to them. I had heard about how the windshield crashed in on Frank, and my thought was that it was a log that did it rather than a huge wave. I thought about different scenarios of what might have happened after their last communication, but I wasn't optimistic we'd find anyone alive."

Inside Salem Sound the seas had abated and the *Decisive* moved closer to the *Global Hope*. Crew members from the cutter then lowered a twenty-foot motor surfboat to the ocean and made the short run to the tanker, where *Global Hope* crew members immediately began climbing down a hanging ladder thrown over the side of the ship. The surfboat then ferried the men back to the cutter. *Decisive* crew member Rich Fitcher says that once the *Global Hope*'s crew came onboard they quickly got them down into the heated mess deck. "Only one man could speak English," says Fitcher, "so he was the translator and spokesman. I remember how cold those men were and how they stayed cold for a long time. I guess that big chunk of steel didn't exactly retain any warmth." Fellow *Decisive* crew member Jim Quinn adds, "When those men came aboard they were the most grateful guys you've ever seen. They thanked us over and over because they'd never experienced a storm like that. Later, when we got into port I watched the nightly newscast and Walter Cronkite was talking about all the Blizzard casualties. I remember thinking I could have been one of them." *Decisive* crew member Jim Sawyer had a similar thought: "I remember thinking we went through all this just because this tanker was taking on a little water in its engine room. It was in no jeopardy of sinking, and we all risked our lives because the captain of the *Global Hope* panicked."

❈

At the very time the crew of the *Global Hope* was being ferried to the warmth of the *Decisive* the fate of the *Can Do* became known. Warren Andrews, worn-out and haggard, was back on his radio and a call came in from one of his friends at the Boston Yacht Club.

"Good morning, Warren. I just wondered if you got the message the Marblehead PD wanted you to call?"

"Ah, Boston Yacht Club, this is Salem Control, roger, roger. Thank you very much for that, sir. I'll get to them right away. It's just with all these receivers going and telephones I probably didn't hear his call."

Warren called the Marblehead police and heard the words he'd been dreading: Frank was dead. The sea had just given back his body.

The Marblehead police had received a call from the police officers in Nahant that a body, identified by a driver's license as Frank

Quirk, had been found on Nahant's Short Beach, approximately eight nautical miles south of Baker's Island. Frank was dressed in street clothes, frozen stiff, and clinging to a life preserver. On his body was a service revolver, as Frank was a special on-call police officer. A second body, later identified as that of Don Wilkinson, was also found just a hundred yards away. The police put both victims on two sleds and started pulling them toward the station. Frank's body fell off the sled and rolled like a snowball back toward the sea. The police officers retrieved it and resumed their sad trek. Once at the station the bodies were held in the garage until a Coast Guard helicopter was sent to fly them back to Station Gloucester.

Ironically, Bob McIlvride had just returned to the station and assisted in taking the bodies off the helicopter. "That's when it all sank in," says McIlvride. "Prior to that I probably took it for granted that when we went out on rescues everything would work out. Maybe the *Chester Poling* had something to do with it. Even though I wasn't involved, I was at the station when that occurred and I remember how pumped up everyone was about that rescue. We were all gung ho, that's why we joined, and the *Chester Poling* reinforced that we could go out in terrible conditions and handle them. But after carrying the body bags out of the helo, it hit me that there are other outcomes."

Seaman Ralph Stevens was in his room on the third floor of Station Gloucester when he heard the helicopter land. He looked out his window and saw Paradis, Brad Willey, and a couple other men walk to the helicopter and unload the bodies. Stevens says that scene "was absolutely heartbreaking to watch."

Paradis then called the Quirk family and told them the bitter truth. Maureen answered the phone and Paradis broke the news as best he could, telling her that her dad's body had been found washed up in Nahant. Maureen, who had held out hope despite the long odds, was stunned. Her brother Brian and mother Audrey were at home with her, but rather than tell them immediately, she knew she'd need help. She ran next door to neighbor Marilyn Lavato and told her what had happened, saying she needed her at the house. "Marilyn was close to Mom and I wanted her there when we broke the news. It was awful. Both Brian and Mom were inconsolable."

The devastating news was just as bad for Frank III, who was halfway across the world, stationed as a marine in Okinawa. "I was marching my troops when the captain called me in," says Frank. "At the time I was a lance corporal and I was up for a promotion to corporal, so I thought that's why he wanted to see me. When I saw the chaplain in his office I knew this wasn't a promotion. They told me 'your father had an accident and his body was found. There was also an unidentified body found and there are still people missing.' I ran out of the office and found a phone. It was hard to get through because so many lines were down in New England, but after a couple hours I reached Maureen. The first thing I said was, 'Is Brian alive?' Brian and Dad were inseparable and he was always on the boat with Dad. I had no idea how bad the storm was and I thought Brian might have been aboard.

"The guys in my platoon got all my stuff packed up for me and I flew from Okinawa to mainland Japan. Then I flew to San Francisco but had trouble getting to the East Coast because airports were a mess from the snow. Finally I got to New York. There were no flights to Boston, so I tried the trains, but they were all filled. Eventually the Red Cross helped me and got me a pass for a train. I was exhausted mentally and physically but still could not believe a storm sank the *Can Do*."

After three days of travel and delay, young Frank arrived in Boston and was absolutely shocked by all the snow, getting his first indication that this particular storm was one of a kind. "There was snow everywhere, huge mounds like I've never seen before. Boston looked like a war had been fought there, with National Guard trucks trying to clear clogged streets. Don

Lavarto used his police identification to drive, and he came down to Boston and picked me up and brought me to Peabody. The whole thing was surreal."

※

Shortly after the helicopter brought Frank's body to Station Gloucester it was driven to a local funeral home, where Frank's brother went to make the final identification. Frank's face had a huge gash in it and part of an ear was sliced off. These injuries were probably caused when the windshield broke rather than from his being washed onshore, because Wilkinson's head had no major cuts. While Frank had downplayed his injuries on the radio to Mel Cole, they were in fact serious, and that explains why he mentioned he was getting tired from loss of blood.

On Wednesday afternoon, about the time the bodies of Frank Quirk and Don Wilkinson were being driven to the funeral home, more grim discoveries were made. The bodies of Kenny Fuller and Dave Curley were found washed up in Marblehead, on Devereaux Beach and Goldthwaite Beach, respectively. Tattered pieces of the *Can Do*'s life raft and a box of flares were also found. Only Charlie Bucko and the *Can Do* itself were still missing.

※

We can only speculate about the last minutes of the four men's lives, but one thing for certain is that after a night of their eluding death the sea got the upper hand, like a predator relentlessly pursuing its prey. During the height of the storm, waves assaulted and yanked the boat, ceaselessly trying to part the *Can Do* from its anchor. The predatory sea had stalked the boat, trapped it, and in those last minutes finished the job before the light of day could offer any hope of help.

More than likely, the line holding the anchor slowly weakened where it rubbed against rocks, and when it broke the *Can Do* was doomed. The boat might have capsized immediately or it might have been swept along with the seas before eventually crashing into a ledge or being toppled by the thundering waves. If the latter scenario happened, the men had a minute or two to stay with the boat and judge the depth of the seas by the wave action. It's possible that when they knew they were in shallow water each person made his own decision on if and when to jump off.

The fact that four bodies were found outside the boat indicates they may have had a few seconds of precious time to scramble out on the deck and jump ship. Mel Cole's last conversation with the men mentioned how some of them were down below in sleeping bags trying to ward off hypothermia. If the boat had capsized in an instant, they likely would have been trapped and their bodies would still have been in the hull of the *Can Do*.

Death likely did not come immediately, but neither was it a drawn-out affair. Survivors of similar situations report that when they first hit the frigid ocean they suffered severe shock and intense pain, some describing it as like being stabbed by a thousand knives, while others say that a searing pain shot through their skull. Almost all say that for a moment they could not catch their breath due to the cold's attack on the heart and breathing muscles. In some people the shock is so severe it's fatal, owing to the loss of consciousness and subsequent drowning. If the crew of the *Can Do* survived the initial plunge they then would have had to battle the raging seas slamming them around as if in a washing machine. The waves would have crashed over them, and they would have struggled just to get air. Even when they had a second to bob to the surface in the wave's trough it would be difficult to breathe because of the sea's churning froth. They would have gulped in seawater and foam with each bite of air.

Even if they wanted it to end quickly, it would have been virtually impossible to overrule the body's instinct to survive. The brain simply will not allow one to purposely breathe in water;

it will command the body to fight to the last second, like a re-treating army that may give up ground but never surrender. The men would do everything they could to keep their head above water. And in those two or three moments before hypothermia slowed their thought process, they must have wondered where the rest of the crew was. After a night of buoying one another's spirits, they now had to face death in the blackness, utterly alone in an uncaring sea. Just one minute in the water would seem an eternity to the men trapped in their icy world.

Thankfully, the fight didn't go on for long, because as each wave swept over their heads it was speeding the hypothermic process, carrying away vital body heat. As the body core tempera-ture dropped, it got more difficult to move arms and legs and conscious thought became confused, perhaps blending past and present. The initial pain upon entering the water would recede, and some of the men may have even felt they were in a comfort-able, pleasurable state. Instead of feeling intense cold they may have felt a soothing warmth—an illusion just before death claimed them. As less and less oxygen flowed to the brain and the men's in-ternal electrical impulses slowed to a crawl, they no longer even knew they were in the water.

Within ten or fifteen minutes unconsciousness mercifully took over, and their heads dropped forward into the water. Actual death was by drowning, but it was the ocean's frigid fingers that set them up for the asphyxiation.

❋

Despite knowing what likely happened, there were still so many unanswered questions. Did the men have time for a last farewell? Did they get the life raft inflated? Did they try to stay together in the water? Did they ever discuss using Frank's gun if the anchor line broke and they knew death would follow? And most impor-tant, where were Charlie Bucko and the *Can Do*?

24

THE WEEK AFTER

While the families of Wilkinson, Fuller, Curley, and Quirk were grieving and in shock, Charlie Bucko's fiancée, Sharon, alternated between the depths of despair and glimmers of hope. Logic told her the love of her life was gone, but because Charlie had not been found she could not—would not—close the door on a miracle. Maybe, she thought, he had somehow made it to a secluded section of shoreline, injured but still alive. Or maybe the *Can Do* was now high and dry on some secluded, overlooked rocks and Charlie was alive but trapped inside.

Sharon had not slept in over forty-eight hours. During Monday night and early Tuesday morning she listened to the radio scanner, sick with worry. The reception was poor and she could only pick up bits and pieces of what was going on, but at least she knew Charlie was alive. Then when communications ceased she went through the same agonizing wait as the other family members, praying that the men would be found. She somehow got through Tuesday, cursing the snow and wind that still blasted down on her Gloucester apartment. Tuesday night she was back listening to the scanner, this time trying to follow the progress of the helicopter pilot as he searched the dark seas for any sign of the *Can Do*. And on Wednesday morning she sank even lower, learning that the bodies of the other crew members had been found.

Sharon was just nineteen years old and the thought of Charlie being dead was more than she could bear. Just two days earlier she and Charlie were planning their May wedding, and now she was terrified that all was lost. She remembers that Wednesday morning like it happened an hour ago. At dawn she called Gloucester Station and Mike Paradis said, "It doesn't look good," and then asked Sharon to call back a little later. When she called the second time, Paradis said, 'I'll be right over.'" He arrived at Sharon's door just twenty minutes later, pale and wrung out from exhaustion.

Paradis took two steps into Sharon's apartment, stopped, looked her in the eye, and said, "They ran into trouble. Frank's and Don Wilkinson's bodies have been found. We don't know what happened, but resign yourself that Charlie is not coming back, there's just no hope for him."

Sharon lost it, screaming, "Get the boats out there and find him!" Then she pounded on Paradis's chest and shouted, "I know Charlie's alive—he's probably washed up on some island, just waiting to be rescued. You've got to find him!"

Explaining that he was doing everything in his power to find Charlie, Paradis told Sharon he would keep her updated. After an awkward silence, the station commander left, not wishing to lie and give Sharon false hope.

Sharon sat alone in the apartment, shaking from the emotional pain that left her feeling ice-cold. For comfort she had Charlie's dog, Radar, a German shepherd he had bought because it was abused. Sharon thought about the name Radar and the irony that it was the radar failing in the storm that first caused problems on the *Can Do*. Sharon knew she needed someone to lean on, and although she and her father were not particularly close she called him and said, "I need you." Her father came right over and they waited together in what Sharon describes as the most awful hours of her young life.

It wasn't any better for Charlie's parents, who lived in New London, Connecticut. "We found out something was wrong," says Eleanor Bucko, "when we called Charlie's apartment on Tuesday to see how he was making out during the storm. We had no idea he'd be out at sea, because he had left the Coast Guard. Sharon told us he went out on the *Can Do* and that the boat was missing. I was stunned. We wanted to drive to Gloucester immediately, but because of all the snow it was impossible. Then on Wednesday we learned they found the other bodies, and we just decided to wait." Eleanor held out hope, as did Charlie's younger sister Joan. "When they told us he was missing it was just incomprehensible," recalls Joan. "I thought that since he made it through Vietnam and had even been shot twice, he could somehow make it through this." Charlie's father, Frank, however, felt differently. He had seen the power of the sea while serving in the navy and knew that only a miracle could have kept Charlie alive through the storm. And so the family prayed for a miracle.

❋

Barry Chambers and his Atlantic Strike Team had endured a cold Tuesday night aboard the *Global Hope* and welcomed the sunshine on Wednesday morning. They had many long hours of work ahead of them, but at least they wouldn't be battling the snow and winds. That morning a helicopter delivered a sixteen-foot Zodiac rubber boat with an outboard motor, and Chambers ran that into Salem. It was the first time Chambers could see just how much snow had fallen. "I couldn't believe it," recalls Chambers. "It looked like something out of a fairy tale set in Switzerland. There was snow up to the roofs of many buildings. From where I beached the Zodiac I had to crawl and claw my way through the snow into town. There was a state of emergency declared and the National Guard had commandeered a McDonald's restaurant to serve as our temporary command post. A few additional members of my crew had arrived from New Jersey and we got down to business, discussing setting up booms and pumping procedures."

Chambers still wasn't sure exactly how much oil was on board the tanker, but early estimates were approximately 80,000 to 150,000 gallons. He knew there was a potential for a significant oil spill, particularly if weather conditions deteriorated, causing new cracks in the tanker's hull. He ordered larger capacity pumps and open water barrier booms, which were flown from around the country to Air Station Cape Cod. Because the highways were a snow-clogged mess, the equipment was rushed to Salem via the Coast Guard cutter *White Sage*. More equipment was brought down from Maine aboard the cutter *SPAR*. When the booms arrived Chambers had them placed around the stern of the vessel to contain escaping oil, while inside the ship his attention was focused on the engine room. It was filled with a mix of oil and water, and Chambers installed a pump that siphoned off liquid and deposited it into the tanker's wing tanks, which were thought to be unharmed. A day later, however, personnel found that these tanks had been breached and the polluted water was leaking.

Chambers was fairly certain the main crack in the hull was where the rudderpost entered the vessel, but he now knew there was a second crack and he suspected there were more. On Friday, divers confirmed there was a four-foot gash at the rudderpost, but they also saw that the hull had multiple cracks throughout its length and the rear end of the keel had been ripped off the hull, rupturing some of the fuel tanks.

During those first three days Chambers and his men worked almost nonstop, with very little sleep. Having been flown onto the *Argo Merchant* a year earlier, Chambers knew he had to get as much accomplished as possible while the weather held. He found that the *Global Hope* was not well maintained, and his written report said "she appeared to have been worked hard, with a bare minimum spent on upkeep." The description sounded like that of a mistreated old horse, still moving but neglected.

The ship's captain was still on board the tanker, but since he was no longer needed he left the vessel on Friday and got a hotel room in Salem, where he wisely kept a low profile.

Over the coming days, the estimate of oil on board the tanker jumped to 270,000 gallons and later was revised upward again to 340,000 gallons. A mobile command post was set up in Beverly, where Coast Guard captain Lynn Hein, commanding officer of the Marine Safety Office in Boston, began overseeing all operations. In Coast Guard terms he was the On Scene Coordinator (OSC), and because he was federally appointed, he had the clout needed to sort through the mess caused by the *Global Hope*. One of Hein's first acts was to inform the Coast Guard's commandant that the *Global Hope*'s owner was failing to take adequate action to stop the pollution. He then requested and received full authority under federal law to make all decisions concerning removal of pollutants regardless of what the tanker's owner or captain suggested. Hein had three primary goals: to safely remove the thousands of gallons of oil still on board, to get the tanker out of Salem Sound, and to coordinate the cleanup. None of these objectives would be easy to reach.

Barry Chambers and the Atlantic Strike Team had been successful pumping out approximately half the oil on the tanker into a barge, but some of the heavier-grade fuel could not be moved because it had to be heated first. By Sunday, February 12, the Coast Guard estimated that 10,000 gallons of heavy oil had washed ashore and another 30,000 washed out to sea. (Subsequent studies revealed these estimates were far less than the actual amount of 60,000 gallons released. Much of that oil escaped on the night of the storm, but the amount was understated because snow had covered it up along the shore.) Oil-fouled birds were dying in the vicinity of Salem, and the thick black goo had settled on the north-facing coastline of Marblehead. Some homes' roofs and windows were covered with oil, carried there by the Blizzard's wind. Even as far away as Wellfleet, on Cape Cod, oil globules washed ashore.

On Monday, February 13, efforts to free the tanker by salvage companies proved futile. The tugs wrenched the tanker around to a new position, but its stern was still firmly in place on the rocks. The *Boston Globe* reported that sources in the shipping communities said that if the salvage should prove too costly, it was possible the insurance underwriters would pay off the ship's owners, Trent Shipping of New York, and the tanker might be abandoned where it was, as had been done in the past in the Delaware River approach to refineries. Although this worry never panned out, it had the residents of the north shore up in arms—they certainly didn't want the battered and rusted *Global Hope,* with all it represented, as a permanent memorial in Salem Sound.

❉

Barry Chambers had a rough week on board the tanker. His body's resistance had been weakened by the long hours toiling on the cold metal ship, and he came down with a nasty case of the flu that he couldn't shake. Chambers and his men had done all they could to stop the flow of oil, and it was about time to pack up and turn the operation over to a private salvage company. Before he left, however, he met Gard Estes at the Cape Ann Marina, and the two men discussed the *Can Do.* The pilot boat and Charlie Bucko had still not been found, and the Coast Guard had called off the search. The *Decisive* had just steamed out of Salem Sound en route to the waters off Cape Cod, where the cutter was already involved in another search and rescue, this time for a sixty-three-foot scallop boat that had not been heard from in two days.

Estes and Chambers talked about potential locations where the *Can Do* might have sunk. Chambers had a pretty good track record of finding lost vessels: after the 1975 sinking of the SS *Edmund Fitzgerald* on Lake Superior, Chambers helped pinpoint the wreck. (The last words from the captain of the *Edmund Fitzgerald* had a familiar ring—he had lost his radar and he radioed that "these are the one of the worst seas I've ever been in," and, "We are holding our own.") Now Chambers worked with Gard using charts, wind speeds, and sea conditions in conjunction with listening to Frank's words on the audio tape, trying to determine the *Can Do*'s location. Chambers soon came to the conclusion that the vessel might be found south of Baker's Island, close to shore near Marblehead Neck. Mel Cole had come to a similar conclusion when he wrote to the Coast Guard Marine Safety Office: "*We are of the opinion the Can Do was actually not making continuous forward progress and for a fact was being driven southwest into the Gooseberry shoals south of Baker's Island after his [Frank's] pilothouse window was broken. He said repeatedly I'm just joggin along here trying to locate the Harbor (meaning Gloucester) and in 100 feet of water. Very suddenly he went from 100 feet to the report where they had apparently struck something like rock.*" Mel's letter closed with this final thought: "*It is a sad day when all the equipment each of us had at our disposal could not overcome the fury of this storm and save their lives. We still have a long way to go.*"

The Coast Guard had searched south of Baker's Island, but perhaps they missed a clue. Frank's friends would give it another look, just as Frank had done when he went back out to the *Chester Poling* for one last attempt to recover the body of the drowned seaman.

25

WRECKED BOAT,
WRECKED LIVES

Monday, February 13, was a day of mourning for the families and friends of the four men whose bodies had been found. Funerals were held in various locations on the North Shore and people came out in droves to pay their final respects.

Kenny Fuller's wife had lost her first husband at sea twelve years earlier, after they had been married just three months. His body was never found and she went weeks hoping he might still turn up alive. Now she was burying her second husband and it was small consolation that this time a body had been recovered. She did, however, tell a newspaper reporter that this time "at least I know [what happened]." Kenny Fuller left behind five young children, a son and four daughters. He was buried at Calvary Cemetery in Gloucester. His good friend and fellow crew member Dave Curley was buried just a short distance away in Gloucester's Beechwood Cemetery. Don Wilkinson's remains were laid to rest in Rockport at Beech Grove Cemetery. His son Donald, seventeen at the time, remembers the funeral service was packed even though everyone attending had to get a special pass just to be allowed to drive. Young Donald recalls that his father's sudden death was especially hard on his dad's second wife: "She was absolutely devastated, and I'm not sure she got over it. She died just two years later from a brain aneurysm."

In Peabody, the police reported that "thousands of mourners flocked to attend Captain Frank Quirk's wake," with lines stretching far down Church Street near the funeral home. At the next day's funeral service on Monday there was such a crush of people that most could not fit inside the church and instead stood hunched and shivering outside in the snow. Gard Estes recalls that he had to hire buses to bring people from Gloucester to Peabody. They included commercial fishermen, recreational boaters, marina employees, cops, firemen, Coast Guard personnel, and all the people who were on the receiving end of Frank's offers to help. It seemed everyone who owned a boat or lived near the waterfront knew Frank. And those who didn't know him felt like they did simply because they had seen him on a daily basis, year after year, in Gloucester Harbor, coming and going aboard the *Can Do*. After the church service the buses and the cars with the special passes started a long procession to St. Mary's Cemetery in Salem, where Frank was laid to rest. Over his grave his family had two markers erected. One lay flat over the burial plot with the inscription reading: *Frank E. Quirk Jr., UTC US Navy, Korea, September 16, 1928–February 8, 1978.* A larger granite marker stood next to the site, and this one simply had the word *Quirk* underneath an engraving of the *Can Do* slicing through calm waters.

❋

As the funeral services were being conducted, Sharon and the Bucko family were left in a hellish limbo, now resigning them-

selves to the widespread belief that Charlie was dead. Most everyone who knew Charlie was aware of his mantra that the best
chance of survival meant sticking with the boat, and they felt certain his body was trapped inside the *Can Do*. But with no signs of
the boat there would be no body. On that sad Monday, Charlie's
parents could not bear waiting in New London any longer. Mrs.
Bucko had a feeling Charlie would be found within the next day
or two. "The whole prior week had been a nightmare, as if we
were in a slow-motion, tragic movie, and now I knew Charlie was
going to be found. I told my husband, 'They're going to find
Charlie and we should drive up to Gloucester.' I think it was a
mother's intuition." When they arrived in Gloucester they spent
some time with Sharon and packed up a few of Charlie's belong-
ings. Then they went to the Coast Guard station, but there was
no news. Next, they stopped in a pub to get a drink and while
they were there a group came in who had just been to a service for
one of the other men. The Buckos told them who they were, but
nobody knew what to say. The group just stopped talking, and
the Buckos could tell how uncomfortable the group was, so they
left and returned to their hotel.

On Wednesday, February 15, friends of Frank's launched an
aerial search to try to find the missing boat. Retired Delta Airlines
pilot Robert Ward rented a small plane at the Beverly Airport,
and he and Coast Guard coxswain John Burlingham began making slow runs up and down the coast, concentrating in an area
southwest of Baker's Island, the region suggested by Barry
Chambers. Looking down into the seas, they thought they spotted the black hull of the *Can Do* in about twenty feet of water between Marblehead Neck and Tinkers Island. The location was
approximately three nautical miles southwest of Baker's Island.
Ward and Burlingham made several passes in the plane and became convinced what they saw was in fact the *Can Do*, sitting upright on the ocean floor leaning to its port side.

On Thursday four members of the Essex County Sheriff's Department Search and Diving Team donned their gear and boarded the Beverly harbormaster's small boat for the run down to Tinkers Island. The team consisted of dive master Richard Peverada and divers Steve Archer, John Riley, and Norman "Dugie" Russell. Russell had worked with Frank on several search and rescues, so this was a difficult dive for him to make. "It was the first time I was diving to a vessel where I knew the boat and the captain," says Russell.

Large swells were rolling in from a distant storm and it was a bitter cold day. Russell was in a dry suit, but the other three men were in wet suits and they would feel the effects of the cold sea and air as the day progressed. When they arrived at the location of the *Can Do* they could not see it from their boat because of poor visibility in the water. Russell, Archer, and Riley went down first to find the exact location and make sure it was the *Can Do*. Visibility was about three or four feet. They found the boat in about twenty-five feet of water sitting upright. Russell swam to the stern and saw the ghostly outline of the words *Can Do* on the stern, and "immediately got a chill up my spine, and it wasn't from the cold water." The superstructure and most of the deck had been ripped from the boat, and there were jagged pieces of metal protruding everywhere. The bow was buckled in, twisted toward the port side. A full seven or eight feet of the bow was crushed and pushed back like a pleated skirt. Russell thought it looked as if the boat had surfed down a giant wave right into a rock: "The stainless-steel railing around the boat was banged to hell and everything that wasn't bolted down had been torn away. There were dents all along the hull. It appeared as if the boat had been tumbling over and over on the rocks. Nothing remained of the beautiful mahogany furnished quarters below."

The divers then groped along the topside of the hull and came to the dark opening of the engine room. As the sea tossed them from side to side, they held on to the hull as best they could to prevent themselves from being impaled on the jagged metal. Upon entering the engine room John Riley reached for something to hold on to and he realized he had grabbed Charlie's foot. Charlie was floating lifeless in the water, dressed in a black wet suit and a jacket, with his arms outstretched. The men tried to extract Charlie from the engine room, but a ladder and cables prevented them from doing so. To Russell it seemed as if the predatory sea did not want to relinquish Charlie and it would make life miserable for anyone who tried.

Russell and his crew did not have any tools to cut the cables, so they got back on their boat and returned to Beverly and secured bolt cutters and a hacksaw. Archer and Riley were frozen to the bone because they were in wet suits, but Russell was only slightly chilled, because he was in a dry suit. When they returned to the *Can Do*, Archer and Russell went down again. Russell started cutting the ladder with a hacksaw while Archer used bolt cutters on the cables. Because of the swells, Russell was cutting with one hand and holding on to the ladder with the other. At one point he felt a stabbing pain in his neck, and although he didn't know it he had just slipped a disc. The men finally got Charlie's body up on the boat and then motored back to Beverly. By this time Archer was on the verge of hypothermia and Russell's neck was causing him severe pain.

Russell's problems were only just beginning. The next day he couldn't get out of bed, and he ended up in the hospital undergoing surgery to repair his injured vertebrae. While he was recuperating he learned that things would get worse: because the dive team consisted of volunteers, the county commissioners refused him insurance and would not pay for his surgery or for the months of work he was going to miss as a court officer at the Salem Superior Courthouse. Russell went through an awful period. He ended up on welfare and his bank was going to foreclose on his house.

If not for his fellow court officers chipping in to pay for his mortgage, he would have been homeless.

✻

Finding the wreck confirmed the suspicion that the *Can Do*'s anchor line broke, leaving the vessel at the mercy of the roaring waves. Charlie was down in the engine room, trying to restart the pilot boat's power, when the anchor line gave way. Now, instead of having its bow into the seas, the *Can Do* was likely spun around 180 degrees by the wave that broke the anchor line. The next wave, or one soon thereafter, drove the boat, bow down, at a speed of 20 to 30 miles per hour, into solid rock. Once it slammed into the granite bottom, the boat would have pitchpoled, with its stern lifting over the bow and crashing down, leaving the *Can Do* capsized. By this time the men, except Charlie, had either jumped overboard or been swept out of the pilothouse. Charlie, mercifully, may have been killed instantly by the force of the impact, when his head slammed into the engine or the hull. If he somehow avoided this fate, his consciousness would have lasted no more than a couple of minutes. He'd suddenly be upside down and the seas would have poured in through the engine room's only exit. In shoal water the boat would have continued rolling, being pushed violently by each breaking wave, and Charlie would have become totally disoriented. Even if an air pocket remained in the engine room it would not have mattered, because Charlie literally would have been tumbling with the boat, unable to fight his way out of the cramped and flooded engine room. Whatever air he was holding in his lungs would have been replaced with seawater when he could no longer hold his breath, and his fight would be over.

Although the boat was found by Tinkers Island, that may not have been the location where it first capsized. There was enough buoyancy in the vessel and the waves were so powerful it easily could have been pushed in the direction the waves were going, which was to the southwest. If that was the case, the boat would have originally capsized somewhere to the northeast where there was shoal water. Drawing a line on a nautical chart from where the boat was found back up to the northeast toward Baker's Island, it's logical to conclude that the *Can Do* was at anchor at the ledges and islands known as the Gooseberries or perhaps just off Cat Island. Mel Cole, Warren Andrews, Barry Chambers, and Frank's son Frank III all arrived at this conclusion when the bodies were first found, and the location of the wreckage did not dissuade them.

※

Mr. and Mrs. Bucko were still in Gloucester when they heard reports that Bob Ward had spotted the overturned *Can Do* from the air. Eleanor knew her intuition was right and that Charlie would be found inside the boat, but the wait in Gloucester had become unbearable. She and her husband decided to head home and let the local funeral parlor arrange for the body to be sent to New London. When Eleanor arrived at home the phone rang and it was Mike Paradis, saying, "Why did you leave? You've got to come back and identify the body." Eleanor told him there was no way they were going back.

The Buckos made a wise decision—the last thing they needed was to view Charlie's body after it had been in the ocean for a week and a half. It was tough enough for them when the funeral director called. "When the funeral home had Charlie's body," says Eleanor, "they called me. The man asked if we would mind if they removed the lining from the casket—he said Charlie's body had swollen up too big to fit inside. I was stunned. All I could think of was the book Charlie was working on about the men who died at sea. He wrote about what happened when their bodies were found. I remember there was a section of the book that said before the funeral one of the bodies had swelled up from being in the water and could not fit into a normal-size casket."

Sharon also learned Charlie's body had been found from Mike Paradis. "He did the tough thing," says Sharon, "and came to me in person. He simply said, 'They found Charlie's body.' I just started beating on his chest and screaming. It was just too much. I look back now and I think about Mr. Paradis. That poor man, he was so good to us. He was suffering just like I was."

| 26 |

"CROSSING THE BAR"

The funeral for Charlie was held in New London, and Sharon drove down with Brad Willey and his wife for the final good-bye. It was attended by family, boyhood friends, fellow Vietnam veterans, and Coast Guard companions. The Color Honor Guard of the U.S. Marines also gathered at the funeral home and stayed throughout the service. Two of Charlie's newer friends, Doug Parsons and Ben Cavagraro, from the Gloucester Marine Railway Company, also joined the service and with great emotion described Charlie's last day with them. They mentioned dropping Charlie off at his apartment with the snow swirling down and how happy they all had been, never suspecting what lay in store.

Charlie's father, Frank, requested the reverend read a poem by Alfred Tennyson, titled "Crossing the Bar":

> *Sunset and evening star,*
> *And one clear call for me!*

And may there be no moaning of the bar,
When I put out to sea,

But such a tide as moving seems asleep,
Too full for sound and foam,
When that which drew from out the boundless deep
Turns again home.

Twilight and evening bell,
And after that the dark!
And may there be no sadness of farewell,
When I embark;

For tho' from out our bourne of Time and Place
The flood may bear me far,
I hope to see my Pilot face to face
When I have crossed the bar.

When the service ended, those in attendance went to New London's Cedar Grove Cemetery to pay their respects at the burial site. Charlie's body was lowered into the ground, and later a simple headstone with an engraving of the Gloucester Mariner at the ship's wheel was placed above the burial site. The inscription read:

CHARLES F. BUCKO
1948–1978
"They that go down to the sea in ships"
Blizzard of 1978

Afterward, back at the Bucko home, Charlie's commanding officer at Point Allerton, Pete Lafontaine, had a quiet moment with Frank Bucko. "Charlie's father and I were up in Charlie's room sitting on his bed," recalls Lafontaine. "Mr. Bucko was very proud of his son, and we talked about the things he had accomplished in the Coast Guard. Charlie was an unusual young man— if there was a shot at helping anybody in trouble he would do it. It was as simple as that."

Frank Bucko was familiar with sacrifice. While in the navy during World War II he was wounded in Sicily, and that same year he lost his brother, Charles (whom Charlie was named after), when his ship was sunk during combat. A couple weeks after Charlie's funeral Frank Bucko was asked by a local newspaper reporter if he thought his son feared for his own life before embarking on the rescue. "He just did the job. I don't think he had concern for his own safety. He wasn't that type of person." The paper went on to address whether the men on the *Can Do* were foolhardy to attempt a rescue, and Frank Bucko responded, "Hindsight is easy, but there's a type of person—and there's very few of them around— that when everybody else is backing away, they're going forward."

※

For Sharon, the funeral was just the beginning of her despair. To dull the pain she started drinking, sometimes to oblivion. Some of the worst pain inflicted on her was the result of other people's insensitivity. A couple of people told her, "Move on; after all, you weren't married."

But she couldn't move on and in fact started making solitary three-hour drives from Gloucester to New London just to sit by Charlie's grave and feel close to him. Another way in which she stayed close to her soul mate was by keeping a journal. Her entries in the journal were really letters to Charlie, and in those written words it's easy to understand how she entered the abyss and couldn't pull herself out:

It feels as if my whole world is crashing in around me. Did anyone really know how much I loved you? People tell me to move on, and it's really hard to hear these so-called words of advice. Times aren't getting easier, only harder. Everybody keeps saying it will get easier. When will that happen? The days are so long and lonely without you. I'm sure that if you knew the pain I would go through you may have had second thoughts about leaving that night.

Sharon tried to help patch the heartache by planning a memorial service for Charlie in Gloucester so all his Coast Guard friends could easily attend. In her journal she wrote about the struggle to arrange the service several weeks after Charlie's death. She first asked the priest who was going to conduct her wedding to perform the memorial service at the Fisherman's Memorial in Gloucester. He declined because it was out of his district. Sharon then turned to a priest in Gloucester, but he, too, declined, saying she was not a member of his church. Sharon doggedly went from church to church and she wasn't successful until she contacted a Baptist minister who took pity on her and actually took the time to talk about the pain she was enduring. Sharon put a notice in the paper announcing the date, and on the day of the service the boulevard was packed with Charlie's friends.

Sharon's instincts for survival from her depression were the correct ones in terms of seeking closure and leaning on family and friends, but they weren't enough. A few weeks after the service she made another journal entry, this one just as pained as the others:

It is now what should have been our wedding day. I now work many hours, including Saturdays and Sundays, just to keep busy. I hoped that I would get over your death, but I just can't. I still scream at God, asking Him why he allowed this to happen. Why did he take you away from me? Why is he making me go through this alone? Will I ever know the reason?

I loved you so much. At times I can't bear the thought of going on without you. And I can't bear the thought of removing my engagement ring, even though everybody thinks I should. If you're up there in heaven, please look down upon me and help me through these times. I don't know how I'm going to make it without you.

Sharon's battle with grief and alcohol was just as courageous as Charlie's fight for survival on the *Can Do*. That summer she knew she needed to stop drinking, and she began taking steps. First she stopped drinking alone and then she started staying away from certain people who seemed to trigger more drinking. Then she quit altogether when she realized the alcohol wouldn't really dull the pain, intuitively understanding that only time would. She learned that the grief might ease, but the feeling of loss would never go.

There was one night, not long after Charlie died, that Sharon thought he tried to comfort and reassure her. "I remember one evening I woke up out of a sound sleep with him calling me. He was sitting on the edge of the bed next to me. He told me it would get better, that he was OK, and that I'd see him again. Then he was gone. He had said what he had to say and he just disappeared. I never even got to touch him."

Sharon says the other strange thing she experienced was when she tried to reread Charlie's manuscript, *The Boat Job:* "It was as if he was writing about what happened the night he died on the *Can Do*. There were just so many parallels: a winter storm, the windshield on a boat being blown out, and a body found later in the capsized boat. How did he know these things? He never told me he had a premonition, but something was certainly going on."

Gard Estes also had an unnerving experience. "A couple months after the men died I was in my apartment all alone when I looked up and there they were: Frank, Charlie, Dave, Don, and Kenny. Frank walked up to me and put his hand on my shoulder

and said, 'Gardy, I've got to tell you something.' Just then somebody knocked on the apartment door and the men vanished. This
was not a dream. I was wide awake. Other people have had something similar happen, but they asked me not to give their names."

※

By the end of February life was returning to normal for most
people on the north shore, but the *Global Hope* still stood hard
aground in Salem Sound, reminding everyone of the sad events
that had transpired. Of the 340,000 gallons of oil on the ship,
60,000 had leaked into the ocean and another 260,000 were
safely pumped out of the ship and into a barge. The remaining
20,000 gallons of oil were still in the tanker, clinging to the sides
of the vessel's cargo tanks. Because the last of the oil could not be
removed, it was decided that the only way to totally eliminate the
threat of more leaking oil was to patch and refloat the vessel, then
haul it from the scene. There was discussion of towing it out to
sea and sinking it, but the threat to the rich fisheries of nearby
Georges Bank was deemed too great. Eventually a plan was for-
mulated to install temporary patches on the *Global Hope*, then
tow it to the Bethlehem Steel Shipyard in East Boston, where
more permanent repairs could be made. Later the tanker would
be towed to a port in Texas where it would be sold for scrap.

On March 8, after 2.4 million federal dollars had been spent
on cleanup efforts, several tugs attached their hawsers to the
Global Hope and yanked it off Coney Island Ledge. The tanker
floated free and the tugs successfully towed it to the East Boston
shipyard. There permanent patches were installed, and in May
a large tug began towing the vessel on its final journey to
Brownsville, Texas. Yet there was one last event for this cursed
ship, when the ocean tried to finish what it started. A Coast
Guard Situation Report said: "The *Global Hope* is sinking slowly

in the vicinity of Key West, Florida. Engine room flooded. Vessel down by stern with list to port and port side main deck awash." The last available situation report in the Coast Guard archives mentions a tug towed the floundering vessel to deeper water. It is unknown whether it sank or was scrapped, but the doomed ship never again plied the seas.

※

With the removal of the *Global Hope* from the North Shore, marine commerce resumed its usual pace. Tankers continued to enter Salem Sound, and fishing vessels left the friendly confines of Gloucester Harbor to harvest the sea's bounty. Snow and bitter cold were replaced by springtime's easterly breezes, followed by the long hot days of summer when recreational boaters swelled the ranks of oceangoing traffic. In September one of Frank Quirk's friends, Skipper Cosmos Marcantonio, set out on his eighty-six-foot fishing vessel the *Captain Cosmo*, to drag the ocean's depths for bottom-dwelling fish. Marcantonio, age thirty-six, and five crew members steamed from Gloucester to the Georges Bank, lying one hundred miles east of Cape Cod, Massachusetts. The *Captain Cosmo* fished Georges Bank's outer (eastern) side for several days before getting ready to return to port on Friday, September 8. A sudden gale sprang up, and Captain Marcantonio had to ride it out, radioing another vessel that his position was 180 miles east of Cape Cod. He described the seas as rough, with fifteen-foot waves, but indicated no trouble. On Saturday, the day the *Captain Cosmo* was due back in port, the seas were still bad, but Marcantonio was a good skipper and no one in Gloucester was alarmed when the day came and went without the vessel returning. However, when another day passed with no word from the *Captain Cosmo* the Coast Guard launched a massive air and sea search. Airplanes and a helicopter from Cape Cod Air Station and

Elizabeth City, New Jersey, were joined by the cutters *Cape Horn* and *Dallas* in a search that was to cover eighteen thousand square miles of ocean. Four days passed with no sign of the boat or its crew. The September 14 edition of the *Gloucester Daily Times* led with a headline reading *"Search Widened for Captain Cosmo,"* and the article went on to explain that reconnaissance planes from Florida and Iceland had joined six other aircraft in the continuing hunt. The story also gave the first indication that the conditions on Georges Bank the prior Saturday were much worse than previously thought: *"One crabber fishing near Corsair Canyon below Georges Bank took 36 hours to steam home to Fall River, Massachusetts, after being smashed around by the rough seas and two huge violent waves that knocked windows out of the pilothouse and damaged the vessel's steel hull and fishing equipment."*

On Monday, September 18, the search was winding down when new hope arrived in the form of a tiny mark found on a photo taken from a surveillance plane. The *Gloucester Daily Times* reported that "the mark, showing what could be a disabled vessel, was discovered late last week when film was developed following an Air Force U2's flight in search of the vessel on Thursday." Despite the encouraging development, fishermen in Gloucester were not optimistic, theorizing that after a week of failing to find any trace of the vessel or crew the boat must have met with a quick demise at the hand of a giant wave that drove it down.

The Coast Guard continued to search all day Monday and Tuesday, but at dusk on Tuesday the search finally came to a halt. The vessel had not been heard from in eleven days. Fishermen at Gloucester's waterfront bars resigned themselves to the fact that the boat was lost, but what they couldn't understand was how it could vanish without a trace. Surely some piece of gear or part of the boat would have floated free of the sinking vessel. Captain Marcantonio's wife agreed, saying, "This is not the Bermuda

Triangle here; boats don't just disappear." But nothing was ever found.

Just as the *Gloucester Daily Times* ended its coverage of the missing *Captain Cosmo,* the paper reported a different boat, the *Alligator,* was overdue. The *Alligator* was a fifty-two-foot fishing vessel with a crew of three, and it had failed to return as scheduled from what was to be a two-day trip to Seal Island, Nova Scotia. It was confirmed that the boat reached Nova Scotia, where it took on a load of swordfish, and then headed back toward Gloucester. On board was captain Carlo Sinagra, brother James Sinagra, and crewman Glen Guittarr. Again the Coast Guard launched an intensive air and water search, hunting from Seal Island to Gloucester Harbor. For four days no trace of the boat was found, but on October 2 the cutter *Duane,* searching 110 miles east of Gloucester, spotted an empty life raft from the *Alligator.* A day later hope grew again when a sunken hull was spotted off Montauk Point, Long Island. Rumors swirled that the wreck was either the *Alligator* or the *Captain Cosmo,* but the next day divers dived to the boat and determined it was neither and instead was a seventy-five-foot offshore lobster boat, *Lobsta I,* which had been missing from Galilee, Rhode Island, since September 23. The search went on for the *Alligator* and eventually covered more than sixty-five thousand square miles of ocean from Cape Cod north and east to Nova Scotia and up into the Bay of Fundy. When nothing more was found the search was halted on October 4.

The loss of nine men aboard the *Alligator* and *Captain Cosmo* added to the gloom on the Gloucester waterfront, coming on the heels of the *Can Do* tragedy. Even without the loss of Frank's pilot boat, 1978 was a true killer year, with more Gloucester fisherman dying than in any year since 1951. And in the years since 1978, including 1991, when the *Andrea Gail* sank, there has not been a year as devastating. On a countrywide basis 1978 also had the distinction of having the highest amount of Coast Guard search and rescue cases since accurate records were kept beginning in 1964.

In so many ways 1978, with the Blizzard it produced, was a murderous year. Besides the loss of the five men aboard the *Can Do,* the Blizzard took ninety-four other lives, and it wasn't done yet.

BRIAN AND FAREWELL

In the months immediately following the Blizzard the men who were on board the *Can Do* were posthumously awarded Gloucester's highest honor: the Mariner's Medal, given for courageous action at sea. This was the second Mariner's Medal for Charlie Bucko, who had received an earlier one for his role in saving the men of the *Chester Poling,* and the third for Frank, succeeding the ones he received for the Michael Almeida rescue and the *Chester Poling* rescue. The five men also received the Carnegie Hero Medal awarded to civilians who "voluntarily risk their life to an extraordinary degree while saving or attempting to save the life of another person."

The medals and ceremonies held in honor of the men were appreciated by the families but also took their toll on the fragile psyches of grieving loved ones. This was especially true for fifteen-year-old Brian Quirk, who felt an obligation to attend the many observances for his dad, even though he was reeling from the sudden loss. In this vulnerable period Brian probably needed to be around other teenagers doing anything other than pondering the tragedy. Instead he found himself at ceremonies, sitting stiffly with his mother and siblings, accepting honors on behalf of his father, such as when the City of Salem presented the families of the deceased with a seal of the city. At the conclusion of that particular observance, Brian and other family members patiently stood for a photograph to commemorate the occasion. In the photo, published in the *Salem Evening News,* each family holds the city seal they were given and their somber faces are etched with sadness while their eyes stare blankly at the camera. Brian is in the middle of the group, his long brown hair partially covering the pain in his eyes. His jaw is clenched and his head bowed, and in his expression there is something different from the sadness reflected in the others. Brian's look is one of anger, as if he's ready to spring at the camera and hurl it to the ground.

Brian was also present when the mayor of Gloucester awarded the Mariner's Medal, pointing out that Frank was the only person ever to have received the medal three times. After the ceremony Brian tolerated the small talk of city officials who reminded him how proud he must be of his dad. Brian awkwardly stood around and shared in a buffet while the dignitaries reflected on the men who were lost. There were other awards made by well-meaning citizens, but for a fifteen-year-old boy, who had spent many of his waking moments by his father's side at sea, the process of listening to men in suits and ties talk about his father only increased his anguish. He had not yet come to accept that his father was really dead and half-expected the *Can Do* to motor past Dogbar Breakwater, into Gloucester Harbor, pass Ten Pound Island, and pull up to the familiar slip off Rogers Street.

When the awards ended, the legal troubles began. Some families of the men on the *Can Do* sued the Quirk estate for wrongful death claims, learning through lawyers that the *Can Do* was insured for liability through a rider the Quirks had on their home owners policy. Depositions were taken, but the plaintiff's lawyers knew they would have a tough time convincing a jury there was any negligence, because no one had forced the men to go with Frank that night. In fact, Michael Gelinas, the last person to see the men alive, testified in his deposition that Frank told everyone to get off the boat (except Bucko, who wasn't there yet) as he was preparing to leave. Eventually the litigation was settled out of court for a small amount to be split among the surviving widows.

Rumors also circulated that the men on the *Can Do* were drinking. But again Michael Gelinas testified that while he could not remember what the other men were doing, he saw Frank at the radio with a Coke in his hand. And Charlie Bucko wasn't even on the boat for more than a few minutes before it set out. He had worked up to 4:30 p.m., then went back to his apartment and had dinner with Sharon. Frank called him during dinner and he went straight to the *Can Do,* and they left shortly after his arrival. When the rumors of drinking reached Mel Cole he helped put a stop to them through a newspaper and magazine interview. Mel was listening in on Frank's and Charlie's communications all night and was the last person to talk with the men on the boat and emphatically stated that they were remarkably calm and clearheaded given what they were going through. "Frank was unflappable," said Mel, "even during the worst of it." The tapes back up this assertion.

But the rumors nevertheless hurt Audrey deeply, and she wondered why anyone would want to drag her husband down after he'd given so much. Frank III was sufficiently worried about his mother to give up his career in the marines so that he could be with his mother in Peabody. First young Frank had Peabody mayor Nick Mavroules and Senator Edward Kennedy write on his behalf to the marine brass and request a transfer to the New

England Region. Frank III then followed that up with a letter of his own, writing to the commandant of the Marine Corps: "My mother is unable to cope with this situation by herself. She has always relied on me for support in the absence of my father who has spent a lot of time working as pilot boat captain. I also have a brother, 15 years old, who I also think needs my assistance to guide him in growing up."

Frank soon received his transfer back to New England and used his free time to be with his family. He and Brian were helped by Maureen and her husband, who bought the house directly across the street from the Quirk home, and the family gathered around Audrey and helped her get back on her feet. Frank recalls that when his father was alive he took care of so many responsibilities that Audrey have never even balanced a checkbook. Although family friends offered to help in any way they could, Audrey had to get through this alone and week by week got stronger. After a few months she went out and got a job cleaning apartment buildings and took great satisfaction in her work. "Without Dad's income," says Frank III, "it was rough for a while. He only had a small life insurance policy, and although there was insurance on the *Can Do,* the boat was heavily mortgaged. Mom adapted to her new situation as best she could, but she never fell in love with another man, and I don't even think she went on a date, even though she was just forty-eight when Dad died." This came as no surprise to those who were close to Audrey: she often said, "Frank was the best—I was lucky to have been married to him."

Young Frank told his mother he was ready to ask for a discharge, but Audrey wouldn't hear of it. Frank stayed in the marines for another year and a half until his hitch was up, then moved back into the family home with his mother and Brian.

Frank recalls that they left his father's office just the way it was before he died. "My dad," says Frank III, "loved anything to do with the sea. He seemed to have every nautical manual ever written and he loved to read about all manner of men who made their living on the ocean. His office at home was really something to see with all the books, radios, and equipment. On the outside door he even had the original wheel from the *Can Do* when he first bought it. Before he owned it, it was named the *Grampus,* after a type of killer whale."

While Frank III drew a measure of comfort from his father's office, Brian might have seen it as a constant reminder of the way in which his father died. Michael Gelinas was close to Brian before the accident and described him as "full of fun." Gelinas recalls that Brian had a small Boston Whaler they would often take out in Gloucester Harbor and that he took longer trips with the Quirk family on the *Can Do*. After the *Can Do* sank, Gelinas said the fun seemed to go out of Brian and he became withdrawn. "I remember," says Gelinas, "I visited Brian after I hadn't seen him in a while and all he could talk about was how his dad died. It was as if he still couldn't believe it. I asked him if he had got his driver's license, and he said in a couple weeks, but it seemed he didn't even care. I knew he was really hurting not to be excited about that."

Other people, including Brian's brother and sister, also knew he was hurting, but trying to talk with him about it didn't seem to help. Besides, it was hard to tell just what Brian was thinking, and like most teenagers, he wasn't articulating his feelings. But inside he was filled with rage and grief. And although he didn't tell anyone, he was drowning just like his father, only slower.

In a sense, when Frank died, Brian lost his father, a best friend, and a way of life. Brian had loved his time with his father, and because he was mechanically inclined, he had learned everything he could about the boat. While other kids were spending their weekends playing football and baseball, Brian was out on the ocean. He even participated in a grim search for a drowning victim. A sixteen-year-old boy had just gotten his diver's license and was diving off his father's boat when he disappeared. The Coast Guard asked Frank to help search for the body, so he and young Frank suited up in their diving equipment and held on to the tow bars of the Salem harbormaster's Boston Whaler and slowly searched the bottom of the harbor. Brian was on the Whaler, and while the harbormaster slowly drove the boat, Brian used a grappling hook to find the body. The dead boy was wearing socks inside his flippers rather than diving booties, and the hook snagged a sock and Brian pulled him up. It was a depressing experience, recalls Frank III, but the three Quirks knew that finding the body meant a lot to the boy's family.

Most of Brian's outings on the *Can Do,* however, were joyous affairs. Since the *Can Do* was a kind of "floating hotel," Frank often let his sons bring friends for sleepovers. "Sometimes we'd go diving," Frank III reminisces, "and other times just take a long ride or have a barbecue on an island. We would have friends come with us, because we could find room for fifteen people to sleep on the boat, and our friends loved it."

Such a big part of Brian's day-to-day activities was tied to the *Can Do* that when the boat was gone part of him went with it. He tried to replace the void in some measure by renaming his Boston Whaler the *Can Do* and painting it the same color. Cruising around Gloucester Harbor, Brian became something of a loner, rarely taking friends with him on his outings. Often he dressed in fatigues and a black T-shirt like Frank wore. Trying to emulate his father, however, wasn't a good idea. Family friend and Coast Guard chief Brad Willey thinks that Brian put his father on a pedestal and tried too hard to be like him, which would be an impossible task for just about anyone.

It's probable that Brian's spending time alone on his boat in the very places where he and father had good times only served to make him feel more forlorn and bitter. And there was another factor adding to his grief—he blamed himself for not being on the *Can Do* to save his father.

"Brian had this notion," says Frank III, "that he should have been on the boat with Dad as he usually was. He felt that had he been there he might have done something that would have saved Dad's life. I'd tell him, 'The storm killed Dad and had you been on the boat you would have died, too,' but he didn't seem to listen. When I moved back home I tried to take Brian under my wing. When he graduated from high school I got him a job with me maintaining apartment complexes. He was a very smart kid, and could fix anything. I knew he was having tough periods, but it was difficult to distinguish depression from the usual up and down moods of a teenager."

The one person who might have eased Brian's pain was Charlie's fiancée, Sharon. She had been in the same emotional state, feeling hopeless and isolated, but because she was a few years older she was better equipped to pull herself out of the despair. When she stopped drinking she was on a slow road to recovery and might have helped Brian negotiate through his dark tunnel of grief. But with Charlie and Frank gone, Sharon and the Quirks saw little of each other, especially since Sharon was in Gloucester and the Quirks were in Peabody.

Maybe by working with his brother at the apartments Brian might have slowly put the past behind and channeled his energies into future endeavors. But in 1981 something happened that made Brian relive the painful past all over again: the *Can Do* was raised from the ocean's floor.

＊

When Audrey collected the insurance money on the boat and settled the legal claims, she lost salvage rights to the *Can Do*. At the time, that didn't seem important, especially since all that was left of the pilot boat was the rusting steel hull, dented and crumpled in twenty-five feet of water off Tinkers Island. But a small marine contracting company acquired the rights and thought the steel hull was worth retrieving and repairing. The owner knew Frank and thought he would have wanted the boat off the ocean floor and working again. Brian Quirk, however, felt very differently, and his rage boiled to the surface.

Before the *Can Do* could be lifted from the water the marine contractor first used an underwater vacuum to remove the tons of sand that had settled inside the boat. Then a fifty-ton crane, mounted on a barge, slowly brought the hull to the surface. The hull was then laid crosswise on the barge and brought to Tinkers Island, where it was left onshore overnight. Temporary patches were placed onto some of the more gaping holes, and on Saturday, August 14, 1981, the *Can Do* was towed to Salem Harbor, its original destination the night of the Blizzard.

"We watched," said Frank III, "along with lots of other people, as the *Can Do* was towed under the Beverly-Salem Bridge and up the North River. Brian was really upset. He kept saying they never should have touched the boat. He talked about sneaking back at night and cutting it loose. I didn't like seeing the boat raised, either, but there was nothing we could do. I tried to tell Brian that the real *Can Do* was gone forever, and that was just a hunk of metal. Maybe I wasn't very convincing."

Other people close to Frank had similar reactions of anger and frustration. John Quirk, Brian's uncle, recalls that he was listening to the radio when the announcer said, "Today they're towing the remains of the *Can Do;* it just went by the Jubilee Yacht Club, where members gave it a salute."

"I jumped up," says John, "and shouted, 'What the hell is going on!' I was furious. At the time I didn't know Audrey had signed away the salvage rights. I didn't want anyone touching the boat, and thought it should have stayed where it was. I went racing down to the Beverly-Salem Bridge. Some of Frank's friends were already there and there could have been trouble. Then we found out that Audrey signed away the salvage rights, so all we could do is just watch it go by."

Dugie Russell, who dived down to the *Can Do* to retrieve Charlie's body, also watched the towing of the pilot boat. He recalls that the fishermen in Gloucester were upset and never thought the boat should have been raised, out of respect for Frank, and certainly didn't want it coming up to Gloucester, because it might bring bad luck. The fishermen put the word out that they never wanted to see the boat in Gloucester Harbor.

Once the *Can Do* was out of sight and repairs began, most people forgot about the episode. But not Brian. When he mentioned cutting its lines again a couple days later, brother Frank said, "Look, Mom needed that insurance money and that's why she gave up the rights. There's nothing we can do about it."

That last sentence from young Frank showed that although it was painful, he had accepted the loss of his father, simply because it was beyond his control. There was no one person to blame, no one piece of equipment to fault, and nothing to direct his anger at. How do you get revenge on a storm?

Brian, however, didn't have the maturity to view it that way. The tragedy happened when he was fifteen, and he simply didn't have the life experiences necessary to help him cope. Before the accident he had a happy, carefree, and exciting life, and then in one terrible night it was all gone. Now, seeing the rusted hull of his father's boat in someone else's control was more than he could bear. It was like watching the family home being carted off by a total stranger. He could not understand that the *Can Do* and all it represented was a manifestation of Frank and when Frank died the real *Can Do* went with him. No, for Brian it was like watching a ghost emerge from the water, and it haunted him.

❋

A little over a year and half after the *Can Do* was raised Brian made a decision about what to do with his life. Late one evening over Memorial Day weekend he called a few friends and talked a little about the things they had done together. Then he went down into the basement of his father's home and ended his young life with his father's handgun.

Just as Maureen had to break the news to her mother about the death of Frank when his body washed ashore, now she had to tell Audrey about Brian. "I'm the one who found him," recalls Maureen sadly. "It was Memorial Day weekend, and Brian had just turned twenty. The night he killed himself Mom and I were at a movie. The next morning I came over with my friend Debbie to do some laundry. As I was going down the basement stairs I saw what I thought was red paint all over the floor. Then I saw Brian lying there. I screamed to my girlfriend to get my husband. I thought maybe Brian was just unconscious and nothing more, because he still had his hat on. I figured maybe he'd been drinking or maybe he fell and hit his head. But when my husband got there he saw the gun and kept me away."

There was no suicide note, but one wasn't really needed. Everyone who knew Brian traced his troubles back to the night the *Can Do* went down.

Neighbor Don Lavato was the last person to see Brian alive. Ever since Don drove Brian to Station Gloucester during the Blizzard he had stayed close to him. "Several times," says Lavato, "I talked to Brian about what happened, explaining there was nothing anybody could have done. I told him terrible things do happen, but we just have to carry on. But Brian never really recovered; he seemed just plain lost."

❋

Just as Sharon continued to wear the engagement ring Charlie gave her, Gard Estes, Louis Linquata, and Warren Andrews found ways to make sure no one forgot about Frank. Gard and Louis did so anonymously, placing a wreath of flowers at the Fisherman's Memorial every February 6 with a note that read: *To the men on board the Can Do*. Gard also believes he received a last message from Frank. Gard and a plumber were at the marina doing work that required them to turn off all the power. Once the power was out they saw that a lone lightbulb was still shining. They walked over and unscrewed the bulb and realized it was one of Frank's because it was from a specially ordered batch of bulbs that had the *Can Do* stamped on them. Gard wonders if the mysteriously shining lightbulb was Frank's way of letting him know he really hadn't gone anywhere.

Warren Andrews took a different approach in remembering Frank. Warren didn't want the last audio tape about Frank to be his friend's last words from the final transmissions from the *Can Do,* and instead Warren created a tape about Frank's life. He presented Audrey with the tape, and she labeled the tape with the words: *My husband, Frank Quirk*.

On the tape Warren's voice is rich and deep, full of warmth and good humor. It's clear he loved Frank like a brother. The tape must have taken days to make, because it's clear Warren put his heart and soul into it, first organizing his thoughts before recording, then adding touches of background organ music, similar to that used by a church choir. A first-time listener might call some of Warren's phrases old-fashioned, but he was just being Warren, and his message was sincere. He began his recording by saying, "A fellow recently asked me how well I knew Captain Frank Quirk of the pilot boat *Can Do*. I asked him if he had about twenty-four hours. Seeing he didn't, I said, 'OK, pull up a chair and I'll try to cap it all up in about twenty-five minutes.'" Warren then warms to the task, sounding like a retired sea captain rather than a blind shipping control radioman. He describes the many happy days he spent with Frank on board the *Can Do* as well as

Frank's visits to Warren's communications room, about which Warren comments, "People would kid Frank when he'd come up to see me and say, 'Going to see your chaplain, hey?'"

Most of the recording is about various rescues Frank was involved in and the way he'd go out of his way to help fishermen and boaters who needed a hand. Warren chuckles on the tape, recalling the many calls he made to Audrey, telling her, "Frank will be late coming home tonight"—the same message given before the *Can Do*'s final voyage. But the best part of the tape is Warren relating one of the high points of his life: the time he got to drive the Coast Guard forty-one-footer. "When the Coast Guard got the new four-one-three-five-three, Frank knew how anxious I was to get aboard the new craft and check it out. The CO, Frank, and I got aboard with the coxswain. Once we cleared the mouth of Gloucester Harbor the coxswain slid out of the seat and Frank said, 'OK, Mr. Andrews, you claimed you know Coast Guard boats; get up here and show us.' Well, I climbed into that seat with Frank on my left and the CO on my right giving me steerage instructions. I grabbed that wheel and those throttles and had the time of my life for the next forty-five minutes. That was Frank, always doing something for somebody else."

Warren later commented that God must have needed a good captain, so he took the very best. Then, in a soft voice, Warren said a final farewell to his friend; "Well, God bless you, buddy, and keep a strain on that towline."

Epilogue

And because I have known this outer and secret world, and been able to live as I have lived, reverence and gratitude greater and deeper than ever possessed me.

—HENRY BESTON

Far better it is to dare mighty things, to win glorious triumphs, even though checkered by failure, than to take rank with those poor spirits who neither enjoy much nor suffer much, because they live in the gray twilight that knows not victory nor defeat.

—THEODORE ROOSEVELT

WARREN ANDREWS

Warren passed away in the early 1990s. In an interview a few years after the Blizzard he said, "If only we knew what was happening to the *Global Hope*, all this could have been averted. But the fact is we didn't know, and there were thirty-two men on-board whose lives could have been in danger."

Warren's son Ken related the following about his dad: "The Coast Guard had so much respect for my father, and they knew how close he and Frank were, so they gave him the life vest Frank was clutching when he was found. That life vest was like the Holy Grail to my father; it meant the world to him."

JOHN BURLINGHAM

John is retired from the Coast Guard and lives on Boston's north shore. "The *Can Do* was a great sea boat; it was low and was a deep boat, drawing six feet of water. It had proven itself in many storms and heavy seas. The seas during the Blizzard were just unbelievable, and even if it was daytime I'm not sure things would have been different, because it was a total whiteout."

BILL CAVANAUGH

Bill is currently in the Coast Guard Auxillary and is the director of technology for the Chester Academy in New Hampshire: "Going out to the *Chester Poling* in those seas made me consider my obituary, and I remember at eighteen there wasn't much they could put in it. Prior to the *Chester Poling* and Blizzard of '78 I used to think nothing could happen to me—those experiences sure made me think otherwise."

BARRY CHAMBERS

Barry retired from the Coast Guard's Atlantic Strike Team in 1979. He then went into marine salvage and environmental services. At one point he scrapped navy ships in Brownsville, Texas, the intended destination of the wrecked *Global Hope*. His memory of the *Global Hope* is one of anger: "That captain cried wolf and it set in motion the events of that night."

MEL COLE

Mel Cole is retired and still living in the same home atop Indian Hill in Beverly. "That night I tried to keep the men's spirits up; that's why I said the storm would be abating when I knew it probably wouldn't. What you offer another person is hope. Your comments bring extra adrenaline, where maybe if the boat can hold together he can make it. It was important just to maintain contact.

"People ask me if I'm haunted by what happened that night, and I'm not. But I do think about it from time to time, especially when I'm out on my sailboat. When we sail by the Gooseberries I think how close Frank was to shore and even closer to Baker's Island. But that night it didn't matter. When you go by the Gooseberries on a calm day it's hard to picture the night of the Blizzard because the islands are such a peaceful spot, where we have often stopped to picnic and swim."

VERN DEPIETRO

Vern has retired from the Coast Guard and lives in Oregon. "After we got the *Cape George* into the safety of Gloucester Harbor, I had radio duty and I listened to what was going on with the *Can Do*. I knew when they lost power they were in real trouble and the chances of them making it were slim. Even if the *Can Do* was driven to shore, the coast north of Boston is all rocky and the men would not have survived. Maybe if there were sandy beaches like in areas of the West Coast they might have, but even then I doubt it—the seas were just incredible. I've thought back about how the *Can Do* went out that night, and I think most of us would have done the same thing. There are a few images burned into my mind over the years. One is Frank skippering the *Can Do* out one morning while we were tied at the pier at Station Gloucester. It was a nice morning, and I had the radio watch. As *Can Do* made her way out of the harbor, I gave Frank a wave and he waved back. An old salt acknowledging a young sailor."

BOB DONOVAN

Bob now lives near Gloucester and is a commercial fisherman, usually going for tuna and lobster about ten to fifteen miles offshore. He has never experienced seas like the night of the blizzard on board the *Cape George*.

GARD ESTES

"Frank did so many things for all of us, it's impossible to describe him except to say he was special. It was very difficult losing those five men; I was good friends with them. For years I've had a wooden sign Frank made which had a carving of the *Can Do* and a tanker on it. I kept it up in my attic, because I couldn't handle looking at it every day." But on the twenty-fifth anniversary of the Blizzard I hung the sign in my garage, where I can see it every day. Now I look at it and smile." For Gard, it seems Frank was lost just yesterday. "I can still see the black hull of the *Can Do* coming up the Annisquam River and Frank at the wheel."

Gard still lives in Gloucester. He and Louis Linquata never forgot the men who searched for the *Can Do* and those on the boat. In fact, this writer first became aware of Gard's friendship with Frank when he came across a notice in the *Gloucester Times* on the twenty-fifth anniversary of the Blizzard. It read:

In Memory of the Pilot Boat Can Do and its crew, Captain Frank Quirk, Donald Wilkinson, Charles Bucko, Kenneth Fuller, David Curley.

Special thanks go out to the U.S. Coast Guard and all personnel of the 41353, 44317, 95 Cutter Cape George, 210 Cutter Decisive, Helicopter Pilots, Strike Force Team. Your efforts will always be remembered.

"We Gave It Our Best Shot"

Gard Estes, Louie Linquata.

RICH FITCHER

Rich Fitcher has retired from the Coast Guard and now lives and works on Cape Cod: "The Blizzard changed my outlook on life due to the near-death danger we experienced. I cherish every day as not many others do. To this day I can recall the fifty-five-plus-degree rolls we took on the *Decisive*. Our faith in the CO and bridge crew was unquestioned as we engineers kept things going down below. Teamwork got us through the storm, and the men on that ship had an unmatched camaraderie that can't be fully explained in words.

HERB FULTON

Herb Fulton is no longer a fireman and is a general contractor: "That night [of the accident in Scituate] is something I'll never forget. It was rough afterwards. Back then there was no counseling offered to firemen, no special treatment for post-traumatic stress. The first two years after Amy's death were very difficult for me. The cloud finally lifted after Hanover fire chief Wendall Blanchard talked to me for several hours about what happened that night. And after the accident Sally sent me a nice letter, thanking me for trying when others didn't. We have been friends ever since."

MICHAEL GELINAS

Michael Gelinas now lives in New London: "Frank had a huge influence in my life. It was because of him that I went into the navy. I remember how patient Frank was teaching Brian and me about the sea. When he showed us how to do something, we learned it inside and out. All I can say about Frank is that people don't fully know just what we lost when he died."

From the car dealership where Mark currently works he can look out and see the headstone of Charlie Bucko's grave in New London.

JOHN HALTER

John Halter left the Coast Guard shortly after his experience with the *Chester Poling*: "I moved back to Minneapolis and was in my first year at the University of Minnesota when I picked up the paper one morning at breakfast. A front-page story told of a terrible blizzard in New England that had claimed the crew of a pilot boat called the *Can Do*. I learned later that Charlie was among the missing. CWO James McDevitt sent me the story of how they found him. Charlie Bucko was a pretty special person in my life. I shuddered watching the movie *Perfect Storm*, knowing that Charlie's death was not unlike those aboard the *Andrea Gail*. But that's not how I want to remember Charlie; I'd rather think of the last time we were together when he was putting the moves on my sister who had come to New England to visit. He was charming and funny and of course my sister fell madly in love with him—he was that kind of guy."

John has worked on the Mississippi River for the past twenty-five years and is currently writing a book about the river and his experiences.

DENNIS HOFFER

Dennis Hoffer served in the Coast Guard for twenty-one years and is now a corrections officer in Massachusetts: "Even before the Blizzard I admired Frank. I can remember being on the *Cape George* one winter when we were tied up in Gloucester. The inner harbor was all iced in and Frank came by in the *Can Do* and broke all the ice behind the cutter so we could back up without any problem. A few years later when I bought my first boat I named it the *Can Do*. That's how much I thought of those guys."

BOB KROM

After surviving both the Blizzard and the later pitchpoling of the forty-four you would think Bob would have had enough of the sea and forty-fours. But after serving four years in the Coast Guard he spent two years as a commercial fisherman before becoming a Massachusetts State Police officer in the Marine Division: "I love my job; I'm out on the ocean and the patrol boat I use was one the state police bought from the Coast Guard—it's a forty-four."

SALLY LANZIKOS

Sally Lanzikos has suffered with the pain of losing Amy. She looks back on the night knowing in hindsight that had she and Amy stayed in the house they would have survived the storm. She remembers Mr. Hart and how he released his grip on her so that she would live. She thinks of her time in the ambulance and wishes the fireman had brought Amy to her and placed her by her side.

Amy was buried the Friday after the Blizzard. Immediately after the accident some friends with children drifted away from Sally, perhaps feeling uncomfortable that their children were fine while Sally was alone. Others withdrew because they didn't know what to say. Sally then moved nineteen times in a short period, hoping a new place would ease the heartache. It did not. But over time she realized that children were her salvation. First she was a child-care worker at the Perkins School for the Blind and later she became a preschool teacher, working with children the same age as Amy for nine years. She also remarried but never had any more children. Recently she has retired from teaching and is an artist: "You never think you're going to bury your children. Love them and hug them every day. I have no regrets with Amy—we said, 'We love you,' every day."

DON LAVATO

"Having helped Frank on many piloting jobs, I know how cautious and careful Frank was, and he never would have done anything to put people in jeopardy. He might risk his own life but never anyone else's. That night he just didn't know how bad it was and thought he could turn around if he needed to. If there was ever an emergency, Frank was the guy you would want to be by your side—he was always calm and he could size things up immediately."

LOUIS LINQUATA

"I don't think our friends on the *Can Do* would consider themselves heroes. They went out for all the right reasons." Louis still lives in Gloucester and visits his friend Gard Estes regularly.

JIM LOEW

Jim Loew recalls the *Chester Poling* rescue as a defining moment in his career: "To have participated so directly in saving two lives is a reward that cannot be compared. I'll never forget the sight of the *Chester Poling* as she came into sight and we got closer . . . seeing a large ship actually broken in half was incredible. The bow and the stern were sticking out of the water, the ship's screw (propeller) was exposed above water, and waves were crashing over the where the ship had broken, making the life raft inaccessible. With the *Poling* swinging unpredictably and the propeller bearing down on us, this was a very difficult rescue. The one fortunate factor was that the winds were out of the southeast rather than the northeast. It was rare to have a big storm in New England in January with winds predominantly from the southeast and rain rather than snow. If it had been just a couple degrees colder the helo could not have launched at all and our crew would have had to battle icing on our weather decks."

Jim compares the *Chester Poling* and Blizzard of '78 incidents with an overarching theme of the value held by Frank and others in assisting fellow mariners in trouble.

After serving twenty-five years in the Coast Guard, rising to the rank of captain, Jim retired in 1998. He is now the director of the Florence-Lauderdale County Port Authority in Alabama.

ROGER MATHURIN

Roger Mathurin spent four years on active duty in the Coast Guard and then became a reserve. He is currently a marine operation supervisor in the Army Corps of Engineers at the Cape Cod Canal.

Mathurin recalls being on the *Decisive* several years after the Blizzard and noticed that up in the bridge was a small plaque that said the worst conditions the *Decisive* ever encountered were during the Blizzard of 1978.

BOB MCILVRIDE

Bob is currently a software technical writer living in Canada. After the Blizzard he soon transferred to a Coast Guard ice cutter, seeing duty from Alaska to Antarctica. He decided to leave the Coast Guard after four years of service: "The Coast Guard was beginning to do more law enforcement and less search and rescue and I was uncomfortable with the new rules. I got my fill of adventure on the high seas, and there were other things I wanted to see and do in life." He then traveled the globe, working in such distant countries as Thailand and Chile, while continuing to advance his training and knowledge of Transcendental Meditation and earning his masters' degree in technical writing.

"The experience of the Blizzard sobered me, but it also helped reinforce my belief that if you have faith in yourself and God you can move ahead even when the way is not always clear. Losing Frank Quirk was a huge loss to the Gloucester community—he was so well respected."

EDMUND MIKE PARADIS

Commander Paradis retired shortly after the Blizzard and moved to Maine. He passed away in 2000.

JIM QUINN

Jim served just over five years of active duty with the Coast Guard and is currently a detective with the Worcester Police Department. "After serving over two years aboard the *Decisive*, mostly in the North Atlantic, I had a newfound respect for the ocean and for those who make a living on it. The Blizzard of '78 reinforced the importance of teamwork to the entire crew. Without it, we wouldn't have been able to survive the storm and carry out our mission."

AUDREY QUIRK

Audrey Quirk never remarried. She passed away in 1999.

NORMAN "DUGIE" RUSSELL

Dugie has semiretired from his position as a court officer, and he no longer scuba dives: "Diving down to the *Can Do* was difficult, because I knew the boat when it was beautiful. At least we were able to get the job done so that the Bucko family could give Charlie a proper burial."

GENE SHAW

"Those guys on the *Can Do* were true sailors—people were in trouble and they went to help. Unfortunately that night they needed help themselves, and there was nothing any of us could do."

RALPH STEVENS

Ralph Stevens served four years in the Coast Guard. Today he works for the Commonwealth of Massachusetts Shellfish Purification Plant at Plum Island. He remembers how the initial plea from the *Global Hope* spurred everyone into action, without enough thought beforehand. "When something like that happens people operate on adrenaline rather than taking a step back and analyzing the situation. I understand how in some circumstances there is no time to waste, but in the case of a six-hundred-foot tanker it wasn't going anywhere in that harbor. We should have taken a step back, and before putting the boats out on the rescue the officers should have paused and looked at the big picture, and let common sense dictate action. Besides going out during the Blizzard on the forty-one, I was on the same boat when we rushed to the *Chester Poling*—I'm lucky we made it back from that one. If it wasn't for John Burlingham's skill handling the boat we would have capsized. Both times the forty-one should have never been sent out.

"Losing those guys on the *Can Do* was awful. It was heartbreaking then, and it's still heartbreaking now."

BRIAN TULLY

Brian retired from the Coast Guard in 2003 after twenty-four years of service. He is now working for a local police department in Florida: "The blizzard made me aware of the fact that even us in the Coast Guard could end up going from rescuers to rescuees if events turn against us, natural or otherwise. So many of the Coast Guard fleet from the 1970s, decades old then, are still in use now, like the *Decisive*. Finally a high-cost program named "Deep Water" will replace our aging boats. But I loved being on the *Decisive* . . . those were great days."

MYRON VERVILLE

After Myron's harrowing night on the *Cape George* he stayed on in the Coast Guard, attaining the rank of warrant officer, and retired after twenty-nine years of service. He now resides in Petoskey, Michigan: "My overriding memory of that night is how well we performed as a team. It also taught me that at any given moment you must be ready to meet your maker."

SHARON WATTS

Sharon is now happily married and has children. She has never forgotten Charlie Bucko: "Even though I'm married now with three children I still wear the diamond Charlie gave me. My husband understands. He is a wonderful, strong man. I feel very fortunate to have found someone so special after Charlie.

"While helping with the research for this book I was going through an old box from my days with Charlie and in it I found a sketch he drew of the design for the house we hoped to build. It was dated February 5, 1978."

CAN DO MEMORIAL

Ten years after the *Can Do* tragedy, family and friends gathered at the Cape Ann Marina and held a dedication ceremony where a granite plaque was unveiled commemorating the lives and deaths of Captain Frank Quirk, Charlie Bucko, David Curley, Kenny Fuller, Jr., and Don Wilkinson.

| Author's Note |

In our world of big names, curiously our true heroes tend to be anonymous. In this life of illusion and quasi-illusion, the person of solid virtues who can be admired for something more substantial than his "well-knownness" often proves to be the unsung hero.

—DANIEL BOORSTIN, WRITER AND HISTORIAN

One of the most exciting aspects of a book project is at the very beginning, long before you type your first word. I'll never forget the moment when I learned that the *Can Do* was much more than another casualty of the Blizzard and maybe, just maybe, there was a book to be written.

I first stumbled on the story during a difficult period in my life, the summer of 2002. My mother was dying of cancer and I had flown down to my parents' home in Florida to help my dad, who was caring for both my mother and my sister, who had been seriously injured in an auto accident twenty-six years earlier. At night, to take my mind off the stressful situation, I often wrote a short bit of text for *The Blizzard of '78,* a book of photography I had contracted to do with *On Cape Publications.* I had copies of the *Boston Globe* from the week of the Blizzard and noted that Tuesday's edition (February 7) mentioned that "a 682-foot tanker was reported aground about one mile off Salem Sound. The Coast Guard in Boston said it lost contact with the tanker, with 34 crewmen aboard . . ." In Wednesday's edition I came across the first reference to the *Can Do*: "a pilot boat that had run to the foundering tanker's rescue had not been heard from since Monday night, when it lost its navigational equipment in towering waves." Thursday's edition seemed to wrap up the event in a short article that said the crewmen of the pilot boat had died and bodies had been recovered.

Those three editions might have been the end of my interest, but a few months later, before giving a lecture at the public library in Norton, Massachusetts, I was looking through some archival material and came upon a special edition of the *Boston Globe* put out shortly after the storm. This issue included a more detailed story, and my pulse quickened when I read some excerpts of Frank Quirk's radio transmissions the night of the Blizzard. I was amazed: how often do we get to find out what it was like on a boat where all hands were lost? I read the article three times, riveted to Quirk's every word, wondering if more had been recorded.

There was only one thing to do—try to find his family. To my surprise there was a Frank Quirk listed in Peabody, Massachusetts; and I knew it must be the skipper's son. How would he react, I wondered, to a telephone call from a total stranger? Would he tell me the whole episode was too painful and that he didn't want to relive it?

I called Frank and explained that I was an author and I was intrigued by what little I'd read about the *Can Do* and wondered if anyone had written down more of what his father said on the radio that night. Frank was gracious and invited me up to Peabody so we could talk more. Then, before he hung up, he shocked me by saying, "You haven't heard anything yet; there's a whole tape of my father on the *Can Do* that night." He closed our conversation by surprising me even further, saying, "I've been waiting twenty-five years for your call. I always thought this story needed to be told in its entirety."

In the five days between my phone call and my scheduled meeting I thought of nothing else but the *Can Do* and read everything I could get my hands on about the boat and its captain. When I arrived at

Frank's apartment in Peabody, he met me at the door and introduced me to his sister, Maureen. The three of us talked about writing, their father, and the night the *Can Do* went down. I knew there was a book here, and as I turned my tape recorder on I knew my journey had begun.

Over the next two weeks I realized that without Maureen and Frank there would be no book. Not only did they send me off with a box of information, including the cassette tape of their father's communications on February 6 and 7, but also Frank knew the *Can Do* inside and out, from his days of working alongside his father. Even better, he was kind enough to patiently answer my many questions and hunt down missing information. I came to rely on him not only for his technical knowledge about the *Can Do*, seamanship, and the waters between Gloucester and Salem but also because over time Frank became a source of energy. I got in the habit of calling him every two or three weeks to share information, and after each call I felt rejuvenated, eager to return to my writing and research. As my knowledge of the saga of the *Can Do* grew, I realized Frank was the only other person who knew as much as I did about what happened and together we were finding and fitting together the pieces of this amazing puzzle. Frank had the same strength of character that his father possessed. Warren Andrews had a saying about Captain Quirk that would have fit young Frank equally well: "He's the guy you want by your side when the going gets tough."

✻

I structured my research so that it chronologically followed the events of that fateful night. Some of my earliest phone calls were to the men who saw the crew of the *Can Do* just before they set out on the ill-fated mission. I located Bill Lee, Mark Gelinas, Gard Estes, and Louis Linquata. Gard had the same passion I did for the endeavor, and we had many long phone calls and two visits. I'm sure our conversations caused Gard a few sleepless nights, because he confided that losing five close friends at once was more painful than people could imagine.

I also tracked down John Burlingham and understood that the *Chester Poling* episode was essential to the story. Not only did Frank and Charlie participate in that rescue, but it's also likely it influenced their thinking before setting out the night of the Blizzard. (The fact that the crewmen on the *Chester Poling* were just moments away from certain death might have led the men on the *Can Do* to think the crew of the *Global Hope* was in similar peril.) In addition, several Coast Guard men, such as Bill Cavanaugh, were involved in both of the two events and could add insight into the similarities and differences.

Instrumental in understanding the events surrounding the *Chester Poling* rescue were the thoughts of Jim Loew, commanding officer of the *Cape George*, which was the first cutter to reach the sinking tanker. After I worked with Jim Loew on the *Chester Poling* chapter, I realized his attention to detail and his knowledge of all facets of the Coast Guard were superb and I asked him to proofread all my chapters. Jim added wonderful insights, and as with Frank III, I drew energy and perseverance from his enthusiasm. Jim also knew many of the Coast Guard men involved the night of the Blizzard and gave me the names of several people to contact, all of whom enriched the story. (Incidentally, the captain of the *Chester Poling* didn't forget the way Frank risked his own life trying to get to the ship. A week after Frank died, a letter to the editor appeared in the *Gloucester Daily Times* from Captain Burgess that said: "Quirk came to our rescue without thought to himself or the danger involved.")

Not everyone, however, wanted to relive that sad night. Some people found it too emotionally draining, and more than one person asked me, "How did you find me and why are you writing this, now, after twenty-five years?" A couple people simply ended the conversation by saying, "It's just too overwhelming to talk about." I respected their feelings and moved on. In one case, however, the same person who couldn't talk later called me back and said that since I called they could think of nothing else and they had decided to help. Later still this person called and said the process of recalling this episode was actually cathartic and they were glad the story was coming out. Many others said reliving that night had the same effect—it was painful, but in the end they were glad they did it.

Early in my research I utilized a Coast Guard Web site called Fred's Place, and through the reunion hall posting board I was able to find three of the four men on Station Gloucester's forty-four-foot patrol boat that set out to find the *Global Hope*. Tom Desrosiers, Roger Mathurin, and Bob Krom all took the time to walk me through their hazardous mission, greatly enhancing what information was already on the tape of their communications. I even had the good fortune to go out into Boston Harbor with Bob Krom on his state police vessel, which was a forty-four-foot patrol boat formerly used by the Coast Guard. What better way to understand what Bob and his crewmates endured than to listen to his recollections while standing next to him in the pilothouse as we motored through the harbor?

Locating key people such as Bob was like finding buried treasure. But there were some people who, despite my best detection efforts, seemed to have disappeared off the face of the earth. Such was the case with Bob McIlvride, the skipper of the forty-four. I'd listened to his voice on the tape countless times, and he began to take on a mythic importance, probably because he was central to the story yet could not be found. His fellow Coasties all said they hadn't heard from him in almost twenty-five years, and no one could remember which part of the country he was from or where he had settled. I contacted the Coast Guard retirement department, but try as they might, they, too, came up empty-handed.

The search for Bob McIlvride consumed me, and he became like the lost Holy Grail, and I was reluctant to give up the hunt. The flaw in my quest was that I had limited it to the United States and it wasn't until I entered the name McIlvride in an ancestry Web site that I saw a note posted from an R. McIlvride in Canada. I immediately sent an e-mail, saying: "Are you the Bob McIlvride who was in the Coast Guard during the Blizzard of 1978?" I won't soon forget the next day when I opened my e-mail and there was a note from a Robert McIlvride that said: "Now that's an interesting question. Yes, I am, how did you know?" I pumped my fist in celebration and then pounded back this quick response: "I've been listening to you on tape over and over and have been searching for you for months—send me your phone number!!" And that began a series of phone calls and e-mails that clarified so many ambiguous areas I'd been trying to nail down. Bob had a razor-sharp memory, and he went out of his way to help me. I remember asking Bob if he knew the *Can Do* was on its way to assist him, and he said he did, adding, "It was comforting to know those men were trying to help us."

I knew I wanted to weave in the terrible tragedy of Amy Lanzikos's drowning in Scituate, because it occurred simultaneously to my central story and to leave it out would be an omission of the storm's wider destructiveness and the pain it caused. One can imagine the difficulty a mother would have discussing the night her daughter died, but Sally Lanzikos showed real courage in talking with me, deciding that Amy's story needed to be told. This was the first interview I've conducted where *I* had to stop the interview and take a break because I was too choked up to think straight. I will never forget my meeting with Sally.

The same holds true for former fireman Herb Fulton, who wanted to make sure the Scituate episode was told correctly and with compassion. Herb's wife, Ellen, also helped fill in the missing pieces, and through a conversation with her I began to investigate some of the eerie similarities between the Blizzard of 1978 and another blizzard, in 1898, the Portland Gale, named after the steamer *Portland,* which sank. Like the Blizzard of 1978, the Portland Gale exploded with an incredible sudden fury, and the pilot boat *Columbia,* with five crewmen on board, was caught in its grip off the Scituate coast. The captain managed to drop two anchors in an attempt to keep the boat from being smashed on coastal rocks, and the anchors held through the night. Sometime during the early-morning hours, however, the anchor chains broke and the boat capsized before being

driven ashore. Searchers found the body of one man down in the
hold, and the other four were found washed up on the beach, exactly
like the victims of the *Can Do* capsizing.

❋

Locating the men from the *Cape George* and *Decisive* was easier than
most of my other hunts, and I had fascinating conversations with
Vern DePietro, Brian Tully, Myron Verville, Gene Shaw, Bob Donovan, Rich Fitcher, Dennis Hoffer, Jim Quinn, and Jim Sawyer. They
did not hold back, nor did they try to sound like heroes, but instead
described how they relied on one another to battle the storm and
keep fear from taking over. Our conversations had a latent effect as
well. Often, a day after we talked, some of these men would call me
with additional information as recollections bubbled to the surface
and say they felt like they had been back aboard their cutter as it was
being slammed by giant waves. All these former Coasties went the
extra mile to help me, and I couldn't help but wish that I had joined
the Coast Guard when I was a young man. These were just the kind
of people I'd like to be working with.

I had actually written a rough draft of the first few chapters before I realized what a colorful and unique character Charlie Bucko
was. It seemed anyone who knew him "lit up" with warmth and humor while recalling Charlie's exploits and friendship. I remember
scrolling through some year-old entries on the Fred's Place Web site
and saw one that started with the words "God Bless Charlie Bucko."
That is how I found John Halter, and he was typical of Charlie's
friends: they just could not forget this man with the ready smile and
warm heart. Tracking Sharon down was a bit more difficult. I had the
good fortune of talking with Charlie's mother, Eleanor, and sisters
Joan and Janice, who supplied me with all sorts of useful information and anecdotes to better paint the picture of Charlie. They told
me Sharon's last name, but I could find no one by that name on the
North Shore and thought she might have gotten married and given
up her maiden name. But I figured it couldn't hurt to make some

calls to anyone I could find with the same last name, and I got lucky and located her brother, who put me in touch with Sharon.

Sharon was a key contributor to this book. She told me it still felt like it was just yesterday that the Blizzard struck and, though she had moved on with her life, losing Charlie was seared into her soul. She also added to the story by sharing the detailed journal she wrote in the days immediately following the tragedy, and her written words were so moving, tears fell the first time I read them. But not all of our correspondence and discussions were sad. One of the most satisfying moments in my research was when Sharon, Gard, Frank, and I all met for lunch in a Gloucester sub shop (which had a mural of the *Can Do* on the wall). None of those three special people had seen one another in almost twenty-five years, and prior to that lunch I had never met Gard or Sharon in person. We were all nervous for the first ten or fifteen minutes, but by the end of that lunch both new and old friendships were formed. I couldn't help but think how much easier the months after the tragedy might have been for all of them if only they had stayed close.

After I tracked down Sharon she called Janice Bucko to reconnect, and after that conversation Janice called me: "It was a wonderful talk I had with Sharon, but something odd happened while we were talking. My husband was moving some filing cabinets around and he found a slip of paper behind one of the cabinets. He handed it to me as soon my call with Sharon ended. It was a poem from Charlie. What are the odds that during my first conversation with Sharon in almost twenty-five years we find one of Charlie's poems?" The odds were long, I thought, but maybe it was just Charlie letting us know he's doing fine. Charlie had impulsively scribbled the poem on a brown paper bag and sent it to his sister in celebration of her birthday and of the birth of her son Colin in June 1977. "To Janice" it said,

Spring has sprung, summer has come,
and your life as a mother has just begun.

So watch the seasons with your babe,
and understand the beautiful reasons nature has made.
Rumble the drum and raise the fife,
my sister Janice is giving life!!!
Happy Birthday, Love, Charlie.

✳

Finding family members of the other three men who died on the *Can Do* was difficult and I was never able to locate members of the Fuller or Curley families, but Gard Estes and Bill Lee stepped in to recall the personalities of these two men. And hearing Dave Curley's voice on the tape he sent to young Frank when he was in the marines was almost like talking to him, and it helped greatly. I did find Don Wilkinson's son, Don Jr., and he shared memories of his dad with me, which helped greatly.

Mel Cole turned out to be a real gem of a guy. I spent an afternoon with him at his home in Beverly and left with all sorts of key information. Mel not only had a crystal clear memory, but he also had kept meticulous notes chronicling exactly what Frank said and when he said it. This was critical because Frank's voice on the tape during the *Can Do*'s last hour was largely inaudible. Mel was also a sailor, and together we pored over his nautical charts of greater Salem Sound and I could almost picture what was happening to the *Can Do* as it battled those monstrous waves churning out of the northeast.

Helicopter pilot Brian Wallace was as difficult to find as Bob McIlvride, even though he lives only an hour's drive away from my home. Wallace goes by the first name of Brian, even though his actual name is James Brian Wallace. Consequently my hunt took several weeks, but when I did locate him it was worth the wait, especially because he was flying his helo, risking his life, during both the *Chester Poling* rescue and the search for the *Can Do*.

Barry Chambers was easier to find, because he was so well known in Coast Guard circles. He was featured in an excellent book about the *Argo Merchant* disaster, titled *Hard Aground,* so I felt like I already knew him when we talked on the phone. Chambers had a great sense of humor and didn't pull any punches with his opinions. When I first called him I had no idea he knew Frank Quirk, but after he informed me of his friendship I couldn't help but see the irony in how the two men's paths crossed with the *Chester Poling* and then later with the *Global Hope*.

I interviewed or was assisted by over a hundred people for this book, and while I can't name them all, I do want to acknowledge the following key contributors who helped me with my "obsession": Pete Lafontaine, William Webster, Dean Jones, Ron Conklin, Bowen Spievac, Elmer Borsos, Dan McLean, Jim McDevitt, Richard Pettingell, Brad Willey, Larry Zaker, Marty Risard, Doug Parsons, Peter McDougal, Ken Andrews, Don Lavato, Joe Carro, Ellen Keefe, Robert Thompson, Kristin DiRoma, Keith Nelson, Bob Gesking, Wes Dittes, and Ralph Stevens.

Early in the project I was fortunate to have three people critique my work: my buddy Jon Cogswell, brother Mark Tougias, and agent, Ed Knappman. All of them put some serious time into reading my first draft, and all made insightful suggestions. The encouragement from former governor Michael Dukakis and authors Nathaniel Philbrick and Spike Walker is also greatly appreciated. Editor Marc Resnick gained my appreciation for understanding that the story of the *Can Do* was "not another *Perfect Storm,*" as one publisher told me, and later impressed me by the subtle improvements he made to the book while not changing my writing style. Few editors can do that. At home, my wife, Mary Ellen, daughter, Kristin, and son, Brian, listened to me talk about the *Can Do* day and night and watched as a room in the house became my *Can Do* room. It was crammed with hundreds of files, and the walls were partially covered with chapter outlines and photos related to the event. The only way I could tackle this project was to fully immerse myself, and my family offered encouragement rather than resistance.

✳

"Dugie" Russell was one of the last people I interviewed, since his involvement in the story was his dive to the sunken *Can Do*. Besides his retrieval of Charlie's body, Dugie had taken some outstanding photos of the *Can Do* after it was raised. In one photo a man is on a ladder holding on to the side of the *Can Do* as he looks at the crumpled bow. At the bottom of the photo Dugie had written: "That's my friend Edward Mees. He later died at sea." I couldn't help but think how once the *Can Do* went down it became cursed, and I asked Dugie about the circumstances surrounding Edward Mees's death. Dugie explained that Mees had gone out fishing in a fourteen-foot aluminum boat just off the shore of Nahant (this was where Frank's body was found). It was an extremely calm and warm day, but somehow Mees must have fallen out of the boat, because the vessel was recovered adrift a little to the north of where Mees launched. An article in the *Salem Sunday Post* titled "Man Vanishes off Local Coast" reported that "an examination of the boat revealed the gas line to an external engine was broken off . . . hanging over the side of the boat into the water. Police theorize Mees either broke off the line as he fell off the boat or tried to grab it and get back on board." No trace of Edward Mees was ever found.

There were many strange coincidences involved with either the *Can Do* or the men onboard. Charlie Bucko's manuscript, which basically described his own death, was especially chilling. I remember meeting Charlie's father, Frank, and I mentioned how his son's book outline showed a surprising literary maturity for a first book by someone so young. Mr. Bucko agreed, saying, "I think ultimately, had Charlie lived, he would have made his living as a writer. He had a real talent."

I agreed; from what I could glean from Charlie's writings, he would have gone far. But it was emotionally wrenching for me to read a fellow writer's efforts, be impressed by his writing, but know that his manuscript would never be completed or published. But then again, I honestly believe Charlie, along with his pal Frank, helped me write this book, and no one can tell me otherwise. Too many strange synchronicities happened during my writing and research for me not to believe those men had a hand in this project. And if there's an afterlife and I meet the five men of the *Can Do*, I'll use one of Frank's sayings and explain to them that, for better or worse, "I gave it my best shot."

About the Author

MICHAEL J. TOUGIAS is a *New York Times* bestselling author and coauthor of thirty books for adults and eight books for middle readers. He is best known for his nonfiction narratives of survival and rescue stories. These include *The Finest Hours, Ten Hours Until Dawn, So Close to Home, A Storm Too Soon, Overboard!, Rescue of the* Bounty, *Fatal Forecast,* and *Extreme Survival: Lessons from Those Who Have Triumphed Against All Odds.*

The Finest Hours has been made into a Disney movie starring Chris Pine and Casey Affleck. *Ten Hours Until Dawn* was selected by the American Library Association as "One of the Best Books of the Year." Tougias also cowrote *King Philip's War* and wrote a novel set during that war, *Until I Have No Country. The Wall Street Journal* and NPR featured Tougias's book about the Cuban Missile Crisis, *Above & Beyond.*

He has also written several humorous nature books, including his memoir *There's a Porcupine in My Outhouse: The Vermont Misadventures of a Mountain Man Wannabe,* which won the Independent Publisher's Best Nature Book of the Year Award. His latest two books are *No Will Set You Free* (an inspirational self-help book) and *The Waters Between Us: A Boy, a Father, Outdoor Misadventures, and the Healing Power of Nature.*

Tougias's rescue books have been adapted for eight- to thirteen-year-olds and are part of his True Rescue series and True Survival series.

Tougias speaks to groups across the country and has a slide lecture for each of his books. He also speaks to business groups on his inspirational lecture sharing what he has learned from survivors and rescuers about overcoming adversity and making decisions under pressure. Tougias splits his time between homes in Florida and Massachusetts, where he is an avid fisherman, vegetable gardener, swimmer, and bicyclist. Visit his website at www.michaeltougias.com.